REAL
GOOD
FOOD

NIGEL SLATER

FOURTH ESTATE · LONDON

First published in Great Britain in 1995 by
Fourth Estate Limited
6 Salem Road
London, W2 4BU

A catalogue record for this book is available from the British Library.

ISBN 1–85702–370–6

Typeset by Type Technique, London W1
Printed in Great Britain by Butler & Tanner Ltd, London & Frome

REAL GOOD FOOD

NIGEL SLATER

Mum, Have a very Happy christmas + enjoy Nige! lots of love Hols xxx

Have a ha ... ike the chapter on 'Leftovers'.) Matt xxx

For an amazing babe,
the beautiful boys,
and to T, with love

CONTENTS

ACKNOWLEDGEMENTS

It is not easy to get a collection of newspaper columns to work as a book in its own right. That this collection does is due to Christopher Potter and everyone at Fourth Estate; and I should like to thank them for so graciously accommodating my suggestions, demands and inefficiencies. My thanks are due to Michael Pilgrim and his team at *Observer Life* for his continued support, and to Lindsay Baker and Jane Thomas who somehow manage to extract a weekly column out of the most disorganised cook ever to put his ideas into print; to my agent Araminta Whitley at Peters, Fraser and Dunlop for tightening the nuts and bolts of my life so successfully, and to Matthew Fort of the *Guardian*; to all of the authors who have kindly agreed to their recipes being included in this volume; to Kevin Summers for taking such beautiful, startling and original photographs of my cooking each week, and to Tim Rooke for taking time off from photographing the rich and famous to photograph the not so rich and famous. And thanks to 'them' again.

INTRODUCTION

Since 1993 I have written a weekly column in the *Observer*. I have enthused, grumbled and, according to my bulging mailbag, delighted and infuriated, about everything from salsa to sausages, beans to barbecues and focaccia to faggots. This book is a collection of those columns and their recipes – a good two hundred – the majority of which are new, although a few have previously appeared in *Real Fast Food* and *The 30-Minute Cook*.

The best part about writing a weekly cookery column is the immediacy with which your ideas appear in print. Your wonderful new way with a courgette is in front of your readers before you have time to say zucchini. Or more to the point before the home-grown ones are out of season. The amazing idea you had on Monday morning is being cooked all over the country the following Sunday. (The downside, of course, is that there are sometimes thousands of people up and down the country all cursing you at the same time.) Your better ideas end up spotted with food in someone's kitchen drawer, your not so clever ones lining the cat's litter tray. That's why I didn't want my photograph to appear – but it did.

I am flattered by Fourth Estate's idea to publish my recipes and ruminations in a more permanent form. At least it may stem the continual demands to supply back-copies of recipes – 'The end of the page got stuck to the bottom of the saucepan and I am not sure what to do next,' was one of many cries for help. Now you know why I am not in the phone book.

The recipes are not all new or particularly innovative. This is more a hotch-potch of ideas, both new ones and also some that have been forgotten, become unfashionable or have been simply overlooked. It is a mixture of forgotten classics and new ways with familiar ingredients. I am not going to be the one to suggest you eat kangaroo au gratin when what you really want is reminding just how nice Lancashire hotpot can be.

Each recipe has been tested at home, in a domestic kitchen. But they have not been tested to death, so you will find a few rough edges here and there. I always suggest that any recipe should be used as a springboard for your own ideas, adding bits and pieces or leaving things out as you go, rather than seen as a chemical formula to be followed to the letter. I might take this opportunity, though, to thank all the readers who have written such encouraging and appreciative letters, sharing recipes, information and tips with me. Particularly encouraging when you remember that *Observer* readers have become familiar, for twenty years, with the beautiful words and joyous recipes of Jane Grigson. This book is for them.

REAL GOOD FOOD

NIGEL SLATER

ASPARAGUS

Grilled Asparagus with Leeks and Parmesan

Salty, savoury Parmesan cheese is a fine partner for asparagus, bringing out the flavour of the vegetable. Use a vegetable peeler to shave off large, thin wafers of the cheese.

6 thin leeks, trimmed and washed
12 asparagus spears
olive oil
Parmesan cheese

Get a ridged griddle really hot; if you do not have one, heat an overhead grill. Brush the leeks with olive oil, then place them on the griddle or in a grill pan and slide them under the grill. Cook for 1 or 2 minutes, then turn. Add the asparagus, brushed with oil, lower the heat and cook, turning occasionally till tender.

Check that the asparagus and leeks are cooked right through, then lift out and place on warm plates. Sprinkle with salt and long, thin shavings of Parmesan.
Serves 2

Part of the fun of asparagus is waiting for it to come into season. Despite the magnificent efforts of our supermarket chains to give us year round imported spears, I am not one to be tempted by a 365-day asparagus season. While I will happily pick up a punnet of Spanish strawberries to cheer up a February fruit salad, asparagus with melted butter before mid-May is like watching Wimbledon at Christmas.

Call me old-fashioned, but I want fresh, perky asparagus that has never even seen the inside of an aeroplane. A few hours on the M5 in the back of a truck is more than enough travelling for my supper. The whole point here is freshness, which is far more important than the variety. A rummage through the market when the time is right will reveal English sprue, those thin spears bought loose by the handful from a wooden crate. They have a fine flavour and, though used mostly for soup, I treat them with the reverence usually reserved for long, thick specimens. Boiled for three minutes and dipped into melted butter, they are a real treat for no more than 50p or so.

At a smarter venue I had the choice of three different types: straight, tight-budded mauve and green spears from a Suffolk farm, cheap green bent ones from Spain, and huge, expensive bundles of ivory and lavender stems from the Loire valley. Charming though the latter were, their flavour was not a patch on the English spears. But it was nice to have the choice. Freshness is not difficult to detect in such a vegetable. The buds at the head should be

Asparagus with Bacon

450g/1lb asparagus
30g/1oz unsalted butter
75g/3oz diced unsmoked bacon
3 tablespoons grated Parmesan cheese

Simmer the asparagus in boiling water till tender. Drain carefully and lay the spears in a shallow, ovenproof dish. Heat the oven to 200°C/400°F/Gas Mark 6. Melt the butter in a shallow pan and fry the diced bacon in it till the fat is golden. Tip the bacon and its cooking butter and juices over the asparagus, then sprinkle with the grated Parmesan. Bake for 10 minutes till the cheese has melted.
Serves 2

Roast Asparagus with Mint

Finding that mint has any sort of affinity with asparagus was a bit of a surprise. The discovery came about after I had used the cooking water from new potatoes to cook asparagus in. It makes a pleasant change from cheese and cream.

450g/1lb asparagus
2 tablespoons light, mild olive oil
1 tablespoon lemon juice
2 tablespoons finely chopped mint leaves

Place the spears on a large sheet of kitchen foil. Drizzle over the oil and lemon juice and scatter with the chopped mint. Season with salt and a little freshly ground pepper. Bring the edges of the foil up and seal loosely. Bake for 15 minutes at 180°C/350°F/Gas Mark 4 or until the spears are tender. Very thin spears will take less, perhaps only 10 minutes or so. Serve warm.
Serves 2

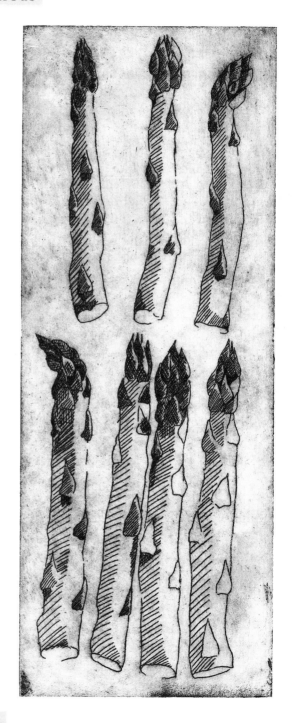

closed tight – they open with age; the stalks should snap crisply and noticeably bleed juice even if the stalk ends are dry. The ends should smell lightly of soil rather than be neatly trimmed and spotlessly green. The stalks should look as if they left the ground not long ago. And once you have bought, then cook and eat them the same day.

There is a lot of twaddle talked about cooking asparagus. I have read over and over again the detailed intructions on how to tie the spears and cook them in boiling water leaving their tips uncovered to cook in the steam. The suggestion that new potatoes should be used to support the stems while they cook is positively daft, though I suppose it might save tuppence worth of gas. Fact: asparagus cooks well in a large saucepan of energetically bubbling water, just as you would cook peas or broccoli. Forget all this tying up and making foil hats for the tips to steam in – someone is having you on.

Fine though these esteemed stalks are when eaten alone or with a drizzle of mild, lightly fruity olive oil, there are a few other foods you could list as friends: eggs (try chopped cooked spears folded into an omelette or fat green spears dipped into a fried egg), Parmesan or Caerphilly cheese, shaved or crumbled over, and butter. Asparagus loves soft, barely melted, unsalted butter. Mint, cooked in the asparagus water, has its fans, as does the matching of the grilled spears with members of the onion family, either as grilled spring onions, baby leeks or finely chopped shallots stirred into melted butter. But little else will do this particular vegetable any favours.

Of course, it is worth remembering that these long, extraordinarily rude spears are considered by some, including the herbalist Nicholas Culpeper, to be an aphrodisiac. I am not sure I believe in such things, but would certainly agree that sitting opposite someone devouring a plate of asparagus in the traditional way, it can be easy for one's mind to wander. At least, mine does.

ASPARAGUS TIPS

- Buy only spears that appear spanking fresh; any wilted or tired ones will disappoint.
- Wait until the third or fourth week of the season for supplies to become more plentiful and for the prices to come down.
- Don't be put off by woody ends to the stalks – the rest of the spears may be very good indeed – but avoid them if they are cracked.
- Cook the day you buy. If you cannot then wrap the bundles in damp newspaper in the fridge.
- There seems little point to me in trimming the tough bases to the stalks. You need something to hold the vegetable by as you eat.

- Thin sprue can have a fine flavour. Use in soups, for purées or as a vegetable side dish.
- Steamed in a colander for a few minutes till tender, asparagus tips can be stirred into both scrambled eggs and omelettes for a luxurious yet simple lunch dish.
- And whatever you do with your bundle of long, green spears, keep it simple: this is not a vegetable that gains anything by being messed around. In other words, it is wasted in a mousse or terrine, but sublime when served with melted butter.

THE BARBECUE

There is something slightly embarrassing about the barbecue. I don't just mean the hot trolley of flaming coals that comes out once a year. I mean the whole idea of the British trying to cope with cooking in the open air. Every time I am invited to such an event, I usually decline. If I do accept, then I secretly pray for rain.

Food cooked over hot coals varies from the sublimely succulent to the downright inedible. No one would dream of presenting their guests with a blackened lump of barbecued chicken oozing pink juices and coated with ash in the kitchen or dining room. Quite why they should think it reasonable to do so in the garden is just another symptom of the British Summertime. For some of us the very word barbecue sounds the death knell of good eating.

Yet some foods beg to be barbecued. Sardines, which I have cooked over a drum of glowing coals on the banks of the Douro, were made for the job. They cook in a minute or two and are tolerant of inexperienced barbecuers. Their habit of sticking to the hot grill can be overcome by judicious oiling of their skins and a gentle touch with the palette knife.

Small aubergines, no bigger than an egg, available in supermarkets and Middle Eastern shops, turn soft and smoky when cooked over embers. Drizzled with olive oil, yoghurt and chopped mint, the grilled aubergine becomes the most voluptuous of barbecued food. If it is succulence you are after, a leg of chicken, boned and batted out slightly, is difficult to better – especially when anointed with lemon juice and salt after grilling.

Barbecued Sweetcorn

4 corn cobs, complete with their green outer husks
raffia
unsalted butter
sea salt

Peel the husks back carefully, leaving them attached to the corn. Pull away the silky threads that lie between the husk and the corn. Wrap the husks back over the corn and tie with raffia. Soak the entire package in water for half an hour. This will prevent the husks burning and keep the cobs juicy. Shake them dry and place on the barbecue over the hot, grey coals. Cook for 15 minutes, turning from time to time. Peel back the husks (you can use them to hold the cob) and spread with butter and a little sea salt.

Alternatively, you can spread the hot corn with a spiced butter such as this one flavoured with hot chilli. The sweet corn and spicy chilli work well together.

75–100g/3–4oz unsalted butter, softened
1 medium-sized hot red chilli pepper, very finely chopped
a good squeeze of lemon juice
1 small clove of garlic, peeled and crushed

Mash all the ingredients either by hand or in a food processor. Season with a little salt. Chill for half an hour or so before serving. Peel back the husks on the corn cobs and spread the chilli butter over each one as you eat.
Enough for 4–6 cobs

Char-grilled Chicken

A boned leg of chicken has all the flavour of brown meat and stays juicier than a breast. To bone a chicken leg, slice through the sinews that hold the meat to the bone and then cut the flesh with a small sharp knife, working along the 2 bones. Cut around the knuckle, loosening the flesh and cutting through the sinews. You will be left with a rectangular piece of meat which can be grilled as it is or marinated. The operation is easier with a large free range chicken leg than the little ones from the supermarket.

2 boned chicken legs
olive oil
sea salt and coarsely ground black pepper
lemon

Rub the boned chicken legs with a little olive oil. Place them on the barbecue and hold them flat with a fish slice for a minute. Let them cook for 6–10 minutes on each side, brushing once with a little more olive oil, until the skin is lightly charred in patches and the chicken is cooked through. Season with coarse salt and pepper and a squeeze of lemon.
Serves 2

You can cook this on a grill pan in the kitchen if you prefer. One of the heavily ridged, cast-iron ones is best. The cooking time may be slightly less.

You can also marinate the chicken for a while before cooking. I often use a mixture of olive oil, crushed garlic, bay leaf, lemon and thyme leaves, leaving the meat in the marinade for an hour or more. Here are some other ideas for grilled chicken marinades.

Sweetcorn, bought on the cob with its rough-textured leaves to protect it from the heat, is almost better cooked on a barbecue than by the usual method involving pans of deep, boiling water. The short life of a sweetcorn after picking and before its sugar turns unappetisingly to starch seems less critical when the vegetable is cooked over embers. Wrapped in its own wet husk, the sweet yellow niblets inside cook in the steam while taking up some of the smoky notes from the fire.

I prefer barbecued food to the barbecue itself. I have been to some that border on the farcical. The wine is always tepid, there is rarely enough food and people insist on wearing aprons that are too small and shorts showing legs that have not seen the light of day since the last alfresco fiasco. What food there is manages to be both charred and raw at the same time. Worse still, everyone seems so intent on having a good time that they forget how much they have had to drink in the blazing sunshine.

To my mind outdoor cooking comes into its own only when the weather cools. As summer draws to a close and the choice of food changes, ember-cooked food appeals much more. Golden corn almost too hot to hold, dripping with sweet butter and black pepper, huge brown mushrooms with velvet gills, and lamb that has been marinated in olive oil, garlic and spices.

Of course, you can have charcoal-cooked food without suffering the Great British Barbecue. I have just cooked two fat mackerel in a large flowerpot, lined with foil and filled with pebbles topped with charcoal and one of the shelves from the oven. They took on a deep smoky flavour and the skin was crisp enough to eat. The hot, sweet mackerel, which I served with an oniony potato salad and cold cider, seemed all the better for being eaten on a cool late-summer evening.

The real joy of food cooked over embers is the effect the glowing coals have on the flavour and texture of the food. No matter how I cook a boned and flattened leg of chicken, I cannot get it to taste better than when it has sat for a while over the grey coals of the barbecue. The skin turns golden and lightly charred in patches; basted once or twice during cooking with oil and herbs, it remains moist and succulent. Seasoned with lemon juice and sea salt, it is the most savoury, simple and succulent supper imaginable.

There is an art to cooking over embers that goes beyond simply choosing the right ingredients to grill. Whether your barbecue is a fire in a bucket or one of those tasteful trolleys that looks like a cross between the flight deck of a 747 and a Hawaiian cocktail bar, it is only the heat of the coals that really matters. Flames may well mean singed supper. Smoke will mean tears all around. If what you are grilling is to taste really delicious, the coals must be glowing and covered with a thick grey ash. The heat they give off should be steady and hot enough for you to be able to hold your hand over the grill for only a few seconds.

I am happy to grill my dinner on the back step (in my experience even the most powerful extractor fan cannot cope with a barbecue) and then eat the food indoors. I get the flavour I hanker after without the discomfort of eating out of doors – somehow even the most comfortable of garden chairs becomes an accident black-spot the minute you start eating on them. The small investment required for a metal box-type char-grill and a bag of charcoal seems a small price to pay for some of the most delectable food you can possibly eat, yet a large flowerpot may make more sense for those who do not intend to cook this way more than a few times each year.

Teriyaki Marinade

60ml/2fl oz dark soy sauce
50ml/2fl oz groundnut oil
1 clove of garlic, crushed
2 tablespoons dry sherry

Mix the marinade ingredients together. No salt will be necessary after cooking, though a grinding of pepper will not go amiss.

Mustard Marinade

3 tablespoons red wine vinegar
4 tablespoons grain Dijon mustard
4 tablespoons olive oil

Mix the marinade ingredients together in a shallow dish. Place the chicken in the dish and spread with the marinade. Leave for an hour, then grill as above. Scatter with coarsely chopped fresh parsley, salt and freshly ground pepper.

Grilled Apples with Honey and Butter

2 dessert apples
juice of ½ a lemon
30g/1oz butter, melted
1 tablespoon runny honey

Peel the apples and halve them from stalk to flower end. Cut out the core. Brush each apple all over with the lemon juice, then lay the fruit down flat on the grill rack. Brush with the melted butter.

Grill for approximately 10 minutes. Turn them over and grill until the apples start to colour. Pour the honey into the hollows where the cores were, and return to the grill. When the honey bubbles and the apples are tender to the point of a knife, they are done. Eat with vanilla ice-cream or cream.

Alternatively you may prefer to cook these over the barbecue wrapped in tin foil.

Serves 2

Choose a large clay pot. Mine is about 40cm/16in in diameter, balanced on four bricks to give the fire some air, and I have lined it with kitchen foil. One of the shelves from the oven fits neatly over the top. The bottom half is filled with pebbles from the garden path and the top half with charcoal from the local ironmonger. It has cooked chicken, sausages and aubergines, little cubes of lamb marinated in cumin, lemon and oil, and, since a friend showed me how, even corn on the cob.

Once the scorching heat of the summer is over, you can get on with cooking out of doors. I shall burn the aromatic prunings from the lavender, the rosemary and the thyme. I may even add bits of that dead old bay tree if it doesn't show any more signs of life. Cooked outdoors, over glowing charcoal and sweet smelling wood, this autumn's food is going to be more succulent than ever. And without the embarrassment of the Great British Barbecue.

BEANS

'Soak overnight in cold water' is not the sort of line that gets me running into the kitchen, cookbook in hand. In fact, it is almost the ultimate guarantee that I will turn the page and move on to something a little more immediate. A pity really, as I am particularly fond of the mealy, fluffy-textured beans whose recipes invariably start so uninvitingly. Fat and floury butter beans, creamy-white cannellini beans and thin oval flageolet that taste as green as they look provide the basis for some of my favourite winter meals. They fatten and fill, and marry happily with my few cupboard staples, making the possibility of a comforting meal or two without having to brave the cold and damp.

I am not the most patient of cooks. Cake-decorating, making petits fours and constructing nancy little canapés are not on my agenda. Soaking beans for tomorrow's supper is an unlikely event in this household, as I suspect it is in many others. Though even this cannot explain the popularity of those little white beans in sweet, bland tomato sauce that sell in their millions. Of course, there is now a quick way to resuscitate the softly hued, mild-flavoured dried beans that will instantly put paid to such opening lines, and will hopefully herald an increase in popularity of the creamy-brown broad beans, speckled pink pinto beans and diminutive white haricots that are so much a part of every nation's cooking bar ours.

Unless I am unlucky enough to have a packet of beans that has been sitting around for years, my assortment can now be ready to eat in an hour and

BEAN VARIETIES

Flageolet Pale green, long oval beans with the most delicate flavour. Once soaked they take about 30 minutes to cook.

Cannellini Long, oval, creamy-white beans that take about 35–40 minutes to cook after an initial soaking. The inside is fluffier than most others, so they make a wonderful purée.

Borlotti Beautiful beans, dull pink with dark-red marbling. They require a hard initial boiling for 10 minutes before soaking. Ubiquitous in Italy, they are a little harder to find here, though good Italian grocers stock them. Cook for 45 minutes, perhaps longer, depending on the age of the bean.

Brown With their particularly earthy flavour, these are most suitable for comforting casseroles with bacon or mushrooms. Cook for 45 minutes.

China Yellows, Scarlet Runners, Spanish Tolosanas, Steuben Yellow Eyes, Snowcap and *Appaloosa*. Rare, dare I say designer, beans grown in America by specialist farmers. They are particularly tender, each with their own mild, distinctive flavour. The larger Scarlet Runners need a good hour's cooking, but the others are done within 45 minutes. Soaking is not necessary.

Beans with Chilli, Bacon and Cabbage

The bacon is distinctly optional here. A spoonful of coarse-textured mustard wouldn't go amiss at the end either.

350g/12oz dried beans, haricot, flageolet or
   black-eyed peas
100g/4oz fatty bacon, diced
1 tablespoon olive oil
2 medium onions, chopped
2 cloves of garlic, sliced
thyme
bay leaves
dried oregano
1 whole medium-hot chilli, dried or fresh
600ml/1 pint tomato sauce, home-made or good
   quality bottled
100g/4oz finely shredded cabbage
salt and pepper

Place the beans in a deep pan, cover with water and bring to the boil. Keep boiling for 2 minutes, turn off the heat, cover and set aside for 45 minutes, till they have swelled. Drain, cover with more cold water and bring to the boil. Simmer for 30 minutes.

In a large, heavy-based pan cook the bacon over a medium heat until the fat runs and the bacon starts to turn golden brown. If there is plenty of liquid fat, then fry the onions in it; if not, add the oil and then the onions. Cook over a medium heat until the onions are soft and golden, stirring from time to time. Add the garlic, a few sprigs of thyme, a couple of bay leaves, a good pinch or so of dried oregano and the chilli. Cook for 2 minutes then add the tomato sauce and a little water if the sauce is exceptionally thick. Bring to the boil and then turn down. Simmer gently, tasting occasionally and removing the chilli if the sauce is as hot as you want it to be.

a half. I know that most varieties are available in cans and can be ready in 30 minutes, but they seem to lack in texture what they make up for in convenience. I want a bean that gives some resistance when I bite into it, yet is reasonably floury inside. Tinned beans are invariably too soft to cook any further, making them useless in casseroles and bean stews.

Anyway, it's the tiny sweet beans, picked young, that I am after, not the whopping red kidney beans, to my mind altogether too coarse and uninteresting. Modern thinking says that if beans are from a recent harvest, in other words last autumn's, then they can happily forgo the traditional overnight soak – the one thing that puts everyone off cooking with them. Now they need little more than bringing to the boil, leaving off the heat for an hour, then simmering for about half an hour in fresh water.

The length of cooking time depends on what type they are and how old they happen to be. I have to trust my memory and my grocer. I would like to think that they were picked last autumn, but without a packing date on them I frankly haven't a clue. Shopping at busy stores or specialist food shops with a high turnover is as near a guarantee that those beans aren't three years old as I am going to get.

Tipped into a large, deep-sided pan, covered with cold water and brought slowly to the boil, they jump around on the bottom of the pan, no doubt dancing with joy at being released from their long coma. Within two minutes they have floated to the top and are ready to be switched off, covered with a tight-fitting lid and left to drink their soaking water for an hour. This leaves me time to muse over the remaining contents of the cupboard.

There is not usually a lot – a mixture of basics and oddballs, hardly the well-stocked larder of a country house. Olive oil will no doubt offer my pot of mauve-speckled kidney beans welcome lubrication. This may well be the time to use the expensive, deep-green Italian oil that was so peppery as to be barely edible six months ago. Perhaps it has softened a little by now. Of course, there is garlic and there are a handful of deep-red sun-dried tomatoes I am anxious to be rid of. Dried herbes de Provence, a very classy jar of pesto, a lemon, mustard, a jar of thick tomato sauce, sent to me by its manufacturers – that's pretty much all there is that might work with the beans.

Best of all, though, there's a lump of slightly tired, heavily smoked bacon in the fridge. Cured pork of any kind seems to have an affinity with beans, both fresh and dried. Pea and ham soup, *caldo gallego*, the Spanish soup of white beans and paprika-spiced chorizo sausage, Boston baked beans and even *feijoada*, the Brazilian national dish that also includes the animal's ears and trotters, all rely on such a happy marriage. I shall use that block of fatty Italian smoked pancetta, diced into small cubes, in which to soften the onions and then toss the cooked beans, coating them with smoky, savoury fat.

Drained of their cooking liquor and refreshed in cold water, I shall bring them to the boil and turn them down to a simmer while I make something of the rest of my store-cupboard booty. The absolute basics – onions, garlic, chillies, dried herbs and that bacon – will appear with the beans in an hour as a warming, not to mention frugal, hotpot. Even quicker, in just 30 minutes after soaking I can have fresh-tasting green flageolet beans ready to toss with smart olive oil and garlic for a more immediate effect. Hardly fast food, but better than waiting till tomorrow.

When the beans are cooked, drain and tip into the tomato and onion mixture, adding a little stock, water or wine if the mixture is too thick. Add salt and a little freshly ground pepper. Simmer for 10 minutes, then add the shredded cabbage. Continue to cook for 3 minutes until the cabbage is bright green. Serve hot, in bowls.
Serves 4 as a main dish, with rice if you wish

Flageolet with Olive Oil and Garlic

Any of the smaller beans can be treated in this simple way, though flageolet are especially good. A fine accompaniment to baked fish or roast meat.

225g/8oz dried flageolet or other small beans
2 large cloves of garlic
2 tablespoons extra virgin olive oil, the best you have

Prepare and cook the beans following the quick method overleaf. They will need about 30 minutes' cooking time.

Peel the garlic cloves and drop them into boiling water. Cook for 4 minutes, then drain. Cut each clove in half, discard the green shoot and slice the cloves finely. Pour the olive oil in a shallow pan with the sliced garlic and warm over a medium heat till fragrant, about 4 minutes. Tip the drained beans into the warm oil and toss gently. Serve warm.
Serves 4 as a side dish

White Beans with Tarragon and Cream

A comforting dish of creamy, herby beans, to eat either as an accompaniment for grilled or roasted fish or poultry, or as a principal dish with white rice.

a knob of butter
1 small onion, finely diced
1 bay leaf
1 small carrot, finely diced
2 sprigs of fresh thyme
leaves from 4 branches of fresh tarragon
350g/12oz small beans, cooked as opposite
150ml/¼ pint single cream
salt and pepper

Melt the butter in a saucepan and fry the onion gently, until it is soft and golden. It must not burn, or it becomes bitter.

Add the bay leaf, carrot, thyme and tarragon. Tip in the beans, well rinsed and drained. Pour in the cream and slowly bring to the boil. As soon as the mixture starts to boil remove it from the heat, correct the seasoning – it may need a good grinding of pepper – and serve hot.

QUICK SOAKING METHOD FOR BEANS

Place the beans in a roomy, deep-sided pan and cover with plenty of cold water. Bring the pan slowly to the boil. Let the water boil for 2 minutes. Clap on the lid and set aside, off the heat, for 50 minutes. Drain, cover with cold water again, then bring to the boil. Turn down the heat and simmer briskly for 30–40 minutes, topping up with boiling water from the kettle if necessary. Test after 30 minutes. A cooked bean should have a little resistance and bite to it, but must be tender inside.

- Red kidney beans, aduki beans, black beans and borlotti beans must be boiled hard for at least 10 minutes, drained and then cooked in fresh water.
- All beans should be cooked in unsalted water. Salt should be added 10 minutes before the end of cooking – any earlier and the beans will toughen.
- Sodium bicarbonate should not be added to the cooking water as it has a detrimental effect on the vitamin content.
- Most small beans, flageolet, cannellini, haricot and the more rare American beans, will cook in 35 minutes, after an initial two-minute boiling and an hour's soaking.
- If you are serving beans cold, cool them in their cooking water rather than in a colander to avoid the skins splitting.
- Chickpeas, the round, bud-shaped, beige beans used in Middle Eastern cooking, take hours to cook to tenderness. They survive the canning process well and nothing is to be gained by cooking them from dried – except a large gas bill.

BERRIES

Berries and currants are the heart and soul of summer puddings, whether it is a bowl of green and mauve dessert gooseberries to be picked at absent-mindedly after lunch in the garden or a more elaborate confection of raspberries, pastry and cream. The simplicity of these puddings is what appeals to me, in terms of both flavour and effort. It takes little more than 15 minutes to stew a punnet of blackcurrants gently with sugar to make a vivid-tasting dessert. It takes 30 seconds to scatter a handful of tart blackberries over slices of lusciously sweet peach.

Even the most elaborate of summer desserts is not beyond the novice cook. I am talking of home-cooking here, rather than the professional pâtissier's art. Though I suspect even the highest-flying pâtissier would rather tuck into his mum's gooseberry crumble than the coifed cholesterol of his own praline box with pistachio mousse and kiwi-fruit coulis. And who can blame him? This is the time of year when simplicity particularly outshines artifice.

When it comes to summer puddings, there is a certain chemistry that never fails to please. Arm yourself with a slab of frozen puff pastry, a box of ripe scarlet fruits and a bowl of cream and you cannot fail. I know of few who do not love at least one of summer's overload of berries: transparent jewel-like redcurrants or wine-red raspberries served with cream. Who can resist a purple-red salad of loganberries, blackberries, strawberries and golden nectarines or a simpler mixture of white peaches and redcurrants?

Gooseberry and Elderflower Crumble

This is strictly for those who like their crumbles buttery with lots of sweet juice. Those who prefer a drier, more traditional crumble topping should use the classic recipe.

550g/1¼lb gooseberries
90ml/3fl oz elderflower cordial
75g/3oz plus 2 tablespoons sugar
100g/4oz plain flour
100g/4oz cold unsalted butter
cream to serve

Set the oven at 200°C/400°F/Gas Mark 6. Top and tail the gooseberries. They may well need rinsing under a running tap too. Use a little of the butter to rub the dish – a 1.2l/2 pint pudding basin or similar – then add the gooseberries. Pour over the cordial and the 2 tablespoons of sugar. You can add a little more sugar if the gooseberries are particularly sharp.

Put the flour in the bowl of a food processor, add the butter cut into chunks and whiz for a second or so till it resembles coarse crumbs. Take great care not to overmix, which will result in the mixture forming a dough. Stir in the sugar and scatter over the fruit. Alternatively, do the mixing by hand, rubbing the butter into the flour with your fingertips.

Place the crumble in the preheated oven and bake for 30–35 minutes until the crust is golden and the juice has bubbled through in parts. Leave for 5 minutes before serving.

Serves 4–6

Summer Berry *Mille-feuilles*

Mille-feuilles, layers of thin, crisp puff pastry, fruit and cream, are a classic of French pâtisserie. A somewhat wobbly home-made version tastes just as good as a perfectly symmetrical professional one, the home-made version having the added bonus of charm. This dessert is simplicity itself, with minimal cooking required. The trick is to bake the pastry until it is deep golden brown, but catch it well before it burns. Undercooking the pastry will send it rubbery when it meets the cream.

175g/6oz puff pastry, thawed if frozen
300g/10oz berries and currants
240ml/8fl oz double cream, softly whipped
100g/4oz mascarpone cheese
good quality fruit jam or redcurrant jelly
icing sugar

Roll the pastry into a square, 25 x 25cm/10 x 10in. It should be really quite thin. Place the sheet of pastry on a baking tray, lightly oiled if new, and set aside to rest in the fridge for 20 minutes (doing this will prevent the pastry from shrinking during cooking). Bake in a preheated oven at 220°C/425°F/Gas Mark 7 for 8–9 minutes. Check that it is turning golden brown, then give it another minute or so until it is light brown in colour. Take care that it does not burn.

Remove from the oven and cut into 3 strips with a large, heavy knife. Trim the edges if they are very untidy. Cool on a wire rack. Mix the softly whipped cream and the mascarpone gently together.

Place one of the sheets of pastry on a large chopping board or serving plate. Spread with a layer of jam, then a layer of cream mixture. Add some of the fruits. Place a second sheet of pastry, spread with jam and cover with more cream and fruit. Place the last pastry slice on top, press gently, then dust with icing sugar. Leave for 15 minutes before slicing with a large, sharp knife.
Serves 6

To my mind most berries are more delicious when eaten with another fruit – melon, peaches or bananas, for instance. Simple two-note fruit salads such as blackberries with thick slices of banana, salmon-pink Charentais melon with loganberries, or sweet, ripe peaches with raspberries are preferable, I think, to confused mixtures of every fruit you can lay your hands on.

The tenderest of these fruits come together superbly in the traditional Summer Pudding, where layers of thin white bread and raspberries, redcurrants and blackcurrants are left, heavily weighted, overnight to produce a pudding of the deepest purple – the summer's answer to Christmas pudding. A similar mixture of fruits, perhaps with blackberries substituted for the raspberries, can be used for the base of a hot dessert – a crumble, crisp or cobbler, for instance.

Soft, deep-red fruits have an affinity with dough, be it the juice soaked white-sliced of the Summer Pudding or the butter, flour and sugar of the traditional crumble. American cooks use a dough

similar to our scone mixture to make the famous blueberry cobbler, though to my mind it is at its best made with something more piquant, such as blackcurrants.

Cream or soft cheeses are pleasing with the scarlet fruits. Mild, miniature Petits Suisses, cheeses packed individually in old-fashioned wet paper, are my favourites with blackberries, particularly if I pour a slick of yellow double cream over them both. Mascarpone, the thickest and sweetest of them all, is especially good with peaches. A spoonful will fit neatly into the hollow where the stone was, and the peach can then be sprinkled with caster sugar and grilled.

Best of all as a flatterer of fruits is rich, creamy-yellow, untreated double cream. Although more rare than I would wish for, this rich, slightly sharp cream can be found in cheese shops, speciality food stores and some health-food shops. Neither pasteurised nor skimmed, it is the purest cream imaginable and its deep flavour and velvety texture flatter a raspberry like nothing else.

Blackcurrant Cobbler

225g/8oz flour
2 teaspoons baking powder
3 tablespoons cornflour
100g/4oz cold unsalted butter
3 tablespoons caster sugar
2 tablespoons double cream
for the filling
1kg/2lb blackcurrants, removed from their stalks
4 tablespoons sugar
2 tablespoons flour
for glazing
cream and caster sugar

Sieve the flour, baking powder and cornflour into a large bowl. Rub in the butter till it resembles fine breadcrumbs, then add the sugar and bring the mixture together with the cream to form a soft dough. Chill for 15 minutes or so in the fridge.

Heat the oven to 190°C/375°F/Gas Mark 5. In a second bowl mix the blackcurrants with the sugar and flour and place in a large pie dish. Break off pieces of dough and place them randomly over the fruit. Brush them with cream and scatter over a little sugar. Bake in the preheated oven for 40 minutes till the pastry is golden and the fruit bubbling. Serve with cream, or better still, ice-cream.

Serves 6

Beaujolais Strawberries

Slice washed strawberries into a china or glass bowl. Sprinkle with Beaujolais or some other light, fruity wine. Leave in a cool place for half an hour.

Strawberries with Lemon and Basil

225g/8oz ripe strawberries
1 tablespoon lemon juice
1 tablespoon basil leaves finely shredded

Remove the stalks from the berries and cut each strawberry in half. Toss the fruit gently in a large fruit bowl with the lemon and basil leaves. Leave for 20 minutes, then serve at room temperature.
Serves 2

Strawberries with Lime and Mint

450g/1lb ripe strawberries
2 limes
3 small but healthy sprigs of mint

Slice the berries in half and remove their stalks. Put them in a glass or china bowl, then squeeze the limes over the fruit. Strip the mint leaves from the branches and snip them into tiny pieces. Scatter them over the strawberries and toss gently. Eat soon after making to avoid the mint leaves discolouring.
Serves 4

The greatest quality a cook can have is knowing when to leave well alone. I speak as someone who has just eaten a poached strawberry in a celebrated restaurant. A poached strawberry. It slid down, pink and pointless. The similarity to one of those lumps of red slush sulking at the bottom of a can, the tinned strawberry of years gone by, was uncanny. Worst of all, the chef who perpetrated this daft act actually has a gong or two to his name.

The British grow the best strawberries in the world. By the best I mean those with the deepest flavour and with a fair bit of acidity to them. Imported berries either fail to deliver anything in terms of flavour or are hopelessly sweet. Whether it is the varieties we grow, or our climate – I do not know. Perhaps it is the soil. Whatever, we know our strawberries.

June and July is the short British strawberry season, then it is back to the imports till next year. Not that I am against the principle of imported berries – indeed, a Spanish strawberry can perk up a February fruit salad better than anything else – but the deep-red berries have an overdose of seeds and no real acid bite. The Californian berry is good-looking but has little else to offer. And you can forget the Dutch fruit. I remain quite mystified as to what Dutch growers do to their fruit and vegetables. But they keep well. I am far from a patriot, yet remain convinced that no one can grow a strawberry like a Brit.

So why do we treat them with so little respect? It is the sad fate of most strawberries to be smothered in cream, doused with sugar or floated in a silly drink – the most bizarre of our culinary rituals, next to eating Brussels sprouts.

There are only a handful of ways to flatter a strawberry. They do not include putting them in an apple pie or tossing them into a crumble. Neither should a strawberry ever be warmed in a '*soupe de fruits rouges*' with raspberries and redcurrants, unless you particularly like bits of warm red slush in your pudding. But there are ways to improve a ripe berry or make a disappointing one worth eating. Try scattering a little fresh basil, torn into shreds, over the fruit. The peppery edge of the herb is good news to even the best-tasting berry.

Consider a drizzle of red wine, perhaps the remains of the one you drank with your meal – it seems to me a better partner than either cream or sugar. It lifts rather than smothers the flavour. Orange juice, squeezed over the fruit a few minutes before eating, will lift a dull fruit, as will a grating of zest from the orange itself, though take care not to include any of the bitter white pith that lies underneath. Mint, which must be overtaking almost every kitchen garden in the country right now, will add a clean bite to an overly sweet strawberry.

There is even hope for those punnets of berries that look better than they taste. Marcella Hazan, the queen of Italian cookery writers and something of a purist, suggests a dash of balsamic vinegar to brighten the flavour of a dim berry. She sugars them first, then drizzles over a little vinegar just before serving. A saviour to the unripe and uninteresting, though I wouldn't do it to a berry of the first order.

Once the novelty of the great British berry has started to diminish, I am not averse to a little chopping, crushing and slicing. But I will not cook a strawberry. Truly ripe, scarlet berries make a fine fool, though they are more rewarding simply crushed with a fork and stirred into yoghurt or fromage frais than fooled in the traditional sense with custard and cream. They should be ripe enough to pulp easily when pressed against the side

Berries in Beaumes de Venise

450g/1lb ripe strawberries
½ bottle of Beaumes de Venise, chilled

Put the strawberries, halved and stalked, into wine glasses. Top up with Beaumes de Venise.
Serves 4

Strawberry Fool

A fool, lumpy with chunks of fruit and sharpened with fromage frais, is, I think, preferable to the usual concoction of smooth, sweet pink paste.

225g/8oz ripe strawberries
225g/8oz fromage frais
120ml/4fl oz crème fraîche or thick double cream

Crush the berries with a fork in a large pudding basin. Fold in the other ingredients gently but thoroughly. Spoon into glasses or small pots and chill for half an hour before serving. An almond biscuit or shortbread would make a charming accompaniment.
Serves 2

Strawberry Sorbet

Although it is possible to make this sorbet in a normal freezer, the best results will be had from using a sorbet-making machine, serving it straight from the machine.

150g/5oz sugar
450g/1lb strawberries
juice of ½ a small lemon
450ml/¾ pint water

Put the sugar in a heavy-based saucepan with the water and bring slowly to the boil. Simmer briskly for 5 minutes or until it turns slightly syrupy. Stir in the lemon juice. Remove from the heat and cool. I find the mixture cools quickly if I put the pan in a sink of cold water. Chill in the refrigerator.

Wash the strawberries, then pull out the stalks and the leaves (washing them after removing the stalks may waterlog the berries). Whiz the berries to a purée in a blender or food processor. Mix the purée and the chilled syrup together.

If you have a sorbet-making machine, switch it on and follow the manufacturer's instructions, which will, of course, vary from one machine to another. If you are making the sorbet by hand, put the fruit syrup into a bowl and place in the freezer. When the mixture is firm around the edges, probably after an hour or so, beat the outer frozen mixture into the softer middle. Freeze again till firm. Remove from the freezer 15 minutes or so before serving. Machine-made sorbet will have a more luxurious texture and can be served straight away.

Serves 6

of the bowl with a fork. If they resist the fork and bounce around the bowl, then leave them for a day or two. If they are a rich red but have white shoulders, marinate them in balsamic vinegar for half an hour before you crush them.

Strawberries are something of a Shirley Valentine among fruits, often coming to life when coupled with a piquant partner from another culture. A squeeze of passion fruit or a slick of unctuously tart crème fraîche will make them sing like nothing else. A few green peppercorns from a tin may sound exotic in the extreme, yet it's worth a try. The trick of dusting a little pepper over the berries is hardly news, but unless done with care can easily end in tears. The spice must be freshly ground and very fine, but far from dust, and should be used very sparingly. The idea is to be virtually unnoticeable.

If the strawberry must end up in a salad, then it should play a starring role. No good will come from teaming it with chopped apple, orange and pear, as so often happens. Cut each berry no more than once and toss it gently with one other fruit only; blackberries perhaps or blueberries or thick slices of slightly underripe banana. It even works with kiwi fruit. Not being an especially juicy fruit, the strawberry benefits from being included in a bowl of sliced peaches, Charentais melon or ripe and slippery mango. I once worked in a restaurant that soaked the berries in frozen concentrated orange juice and Grand Marnier – a dessert that tasted better than it sounds. At any rate, it was better than poached strawberries.

BISCUITS

There is food that exists simply to amuse rather than satisfy the appetite – the sort of confection you might make to while away a rainy afternoon, such as biscuits, petits fours or old-fashioned sweetmeats. I see nothing wrong with such things, as long as they are treated as nothing more than an amusing diversion: cooking as fun. I am not sure anyone should get too serious about petits fours, though.

This is food to nibble rather than eat, to pass round with the coffee or, better still, to scoff warm from the cooling rack. It's what I call Sunday afternoon food – that is, something to cook for the sheer enjoyment of it rather than the daily task of simply getting food on the table.

I spend far too little time cooking just for fun. Yet every time, I ask myself why I don't do it more often. An hour or two making something just for the hell of it can be surprisingly therapeutic, even to those who put cooking firmly in the chore category. Biscuits (cookies is just too unbearably cute) are something I find relaxing to make – the crisper the better. Afternoons spent making macaroons, brandy snaps or wafer-thin almond biscuits can help to restore the belief that cooking can go far beyond the daily grind.

Rain helps. Water can drizzle down the windows as much as it likes when I have a tray of buttery brandy snaps in the oven. Nothing reassures me that all is well with the world quite like the smell of sweet things baking – or perhaps I should say kids me.

Macaroons

Lovely old-fashioned macaroons are perhaps the easiest of all biscuits to make. The rich, moist version below is from Katie Stewart, and the results are very different from the tired, dry biscuits found in some cake shops. Those whose copy of her much-loved *Times Cookbook* is as tattered and food-stained as mine will be pleased to hear it has now been republished as *Katie Stewart's Cookery Book* (Papermac).

100g/4oz ground almonds
175g/6oz caster sugar
2 small egg whites
¼ teaspoon almond extract
a little granulated sugar
24 blanched almonds

Set the oven to 180°C/350°F/Gas Mark 4. Measure the ground almonds and sugar into a mixing basin, beat in the lightly mixed egg whites, a little at a time, then add the almond extract. Beat well to make a fairly smooth, stiff mixture.

Rub 2 baking trays with a little vegetable oil. Dust with flour, then bang the trays to get rid of any excess. Alternatively, the trays can be lined with rice paper. Spoon the mixture in lumps the size of a 2p piece. Sprinkle with sugar and decorate each with an almond.

Place in a preheated oven and bake for 15 minutes till firm. Cool for a few minutes, then loosen the base of each macaroon with a spatula and lift off the tray.
Makes 24

Brandy Snaps

The crispest biscuits imaginable, brandy snaps can be made as tiny petits fours to serve in a pile with coffee or much larger for serving as a dessert with cream and fruit.

100g/4oz caster sugar
100g/4oz butter
4 tablespoons golden syrup
1 teaspoon brandy
1 teaspoon lemon juice
1 teaspoon ground ginger
100g/4oz plain flour, sifted

Set the oven to 190°C/375°F/Gas Mark 5. Lightly oil a baking sheet.

Put the sugar, butter and syrup in a heavy-based pan and melt over a low heat. Just as the mixture starts to bubble, remove from the heat. Add the brandy, lemon juice, ginger and flour. Stir well until any lumps have disappeared.

At this point the mixture should be smooth but not runny. Place heaped teaspoons of the mixture on the oiled baking sheet, about 4 at a time. Bake in the preheated oven for about 7–8 minutes until they are golden brown. They will have spread considerably.

Remove from the oven and leave for a few minutes to set. Check them every minute or so: they must not be allowed to harden or you will never get them off the tray. When they have cooled a little but are still soft, lift them off the tray with the help of a palette knife. Immediately rest each snap over a rolling pin, pressing gently so that they curl loosely round it. Leave for 2 or 3 minutes, then slide off and place carefully on a cooling rack.

Makes about 15

I have just spent an entire afternoon pottering about making biscuity things. Trapped in my flat. Unable to move in the knowledge that the second I stepped outside to get a newspaper, the guys delivering my new dishwasher (I worked my old one to death) would turn up. I decided to cook simply for the fun of it. Something I wouldn't normally make, something a little frivolous, silly even.

You can't get more frivolous than a brandy snap. Huge lacy curls of butter, syrup and spice baked to a crisp – the stuff of Victorian tea parties. They are not something to knock off in 10 minutes before you put the kettle on – I wish they were – but they are hugely enjoyable to make. Having two baking sheets to cook them on helps, as you can only really cook three or four at a time. They need room to spread. Crowding them on to one sheet will give you one huge biscuit.

As an after-dinner nibble, brandy snaps and almond tuiles are light and less rich than most typical offerings, but you can serve them for tea too. Eaten with softly whipped cream, they provide a gloriously decadent contrast of textures. Add a handful of tart scarlet berries, such as raspberries, blackberries or redcurrants, and you have a pudding that is more than just the sum of its parts: crisp and soft, sweet and tart.

I shall not recommend that you turn such biscuits, warm from the baking tray, over upturned glasses to produce the twee and ubiquitous brandy snap or almond basket. There is something deeply gauche about such affected presentations. To my mind, the simplicity of the crisp biscuits served on a plain plate with a dollop of thick cream and a handful of berries alongside could not be more elegant.

Such delicate cooking is a pleasant enough way to spend an afternoon, and the results are charming

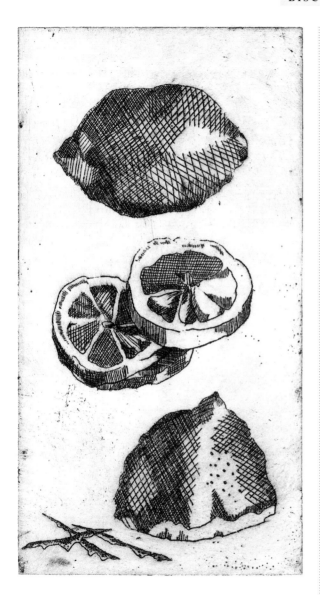

Almond Tuiles

It is sad that so few people make these crisp, light biscuits nowadays. They beat most commercial biscuits hands down and keep just as well in a tin. Like all similar mixtures they are a little bit tricky but are charming as an accompaniment to ice-cream or sorbets. A classic part of French pâtisserie, they deserve to be made more often. Their name, incidentally, comes from the French roof tiles their curved shape resembles.

2 egg whites
100g/4oz caster sugar
a few drops of vanilla extract
a few drops of almond extract
50g/2oz plain flour
50g/2oz butter, melted, but not hot
30g/1oz flaked almonds, plus a few extra

Set the oven to 200°C/400°F/Gas Mark 6. Lightly butter a baking sheet, or line it with Bakewell paper.

Whisk the egg whites with the sugar and vanilla and almond extracts until thoroughly blended. Stir in the flour and the butter until smooth, then fold in the flaked almonds. The batter will be quite thin.

Drop in large teaspoonfuls on to the buttered baking sheet spacing them well apart. Spread the mixture with a palette knife into circles about 6cm/2½in apart. Scatter a few flaked almonds on to each one.

Bake in the preheated oven for 5–6 minutes until the outer rim of each biscuit is golden brown, the centre a pale cream. Remove from the oven and leave for a few seconds, then lift off with a palette knife. Quickly lay each tuile over a rolling pin to set. Leave till almost cool, then slide off and carefully put on the baking tray.
Makes about 30

if inconsequential, almost forgotten classics. True, they demand a slightly delicate hand and a watchful eye once they are in the oven. They burn easily. They can be tricky to lift off the baking sheet and are impossibly fragile when cooked. As I said, cooking as fun.

BISTRO

Coq au vin

a large free-range chicken, about 1.8kg/4lb in
  weight
225g/8oz green (unsmoked) streaky bacon
2 tablespoons olive oil
2 medium-sized onions, peeled and roughly
  chopped
a little flour
bay leaf
thyme
3 tablespoons brandy
1 bottle full-bodied red wine
2 handfuls (about 20) very small white onions,
  peeled
225g/8oz button mushrooms
50g/2oz butter
2 slices of bread
parsley, finely chopped

Cut the chicken into 8 serving joints. Cut the bacon into
2.5cm/1in-wide pieces and dunk into boiling water. Cook
for a couple of minutes then drain and pat dry. (You can
omit this step, but you may find yourself with too much fat
at the end.) Fry the bacon in a little oil until the fat is
golden brown. Lift the pieces out and put them to one side.

Put the chopped onions into the pan and cook until
they are soft and golden, about 20 minutes on a
moderate heat. Lift out the onions and add the chicken to
the pan, with a little more oil if necessary. Cook till
golden, then sprinkle with a little flour, turn them over
and cook on the other side. Return the onions and bacon
to the pan with the herbs and spoon over a little brandy.

The consensus among restaurant critics appears
to be that we have never had it so good. I too
must concede that if I had to pick a restaurant to
eat at tonight, I would honestly be spoilt for choice.
Especially if someone else was picking up the tab.
I suspect that the mid-1990s will, like the 1970s, be
remembered as one of the heydays of British
restaurants.

Right now there is some great cooking around,
and although char-grilled tuna, *pommes
dauphinoise* and lemon tart are 1990s restaurant
clichés, they are good clichés – unlike those of the
1980s such as fanned lukewarm, half-raw duck
breasts and those tortured arrangements on big
plates. But while several restaurant meals are best
forgotten, I should like to put in a plea for the
return of some of the great restaurant clichés of the
past: salmon in pastry with hollandaise sauce for
instance, or duck *à l'orange*, *pommes sautées* and
St Emilion au chocolat, that heady combination of
chocolate mousse and macaroons. How about
chicken tarragon, Stroganoff, hot chocolate soufflé
or perhaps, dare I say, *coq au vin*?

But there are few chefs today with the spunk to
put *coq au vin* on their menu. No matter how
delicious the result. It takes more than guts to fly so
firmly in the face of fashion as to be seen with such
things on your menu. Luckily for me, nostalgia is
the most fashionable ingredient in town, so there is
hope yet.

Few things are so good as a properly made *coq
au vin*, a classic dish of chicken cooked with salt

pork, mushrooms, onions and red wine that must be made with love or not at all. It was the darling of every bistro in the country in the late 1960s and early 1970s. Of course, any cook who was working in professional kitchens in those days will know the reason it tasted so good was that the old bird was cooked in the dregs from every glass and bottle in the restaurant. It was only when that mysterious hybrid 'cooking wine' appeared that it got its bad name. Like other casseroles, such as *bœuf Bourguignon*, pork with prunes and oxtail with grapes, it has been lost to the char-grill and the pan-fry.

If they won't cook it, then we must. Casseroles of this sort are not for the short of time, as they require a good couple of hours' cooking and even then are infinitely better the next day. A little forethought is required. Yet for all the time they take, these are easy dishes, within the scope of even the most inexperienced of cooks. A bit of chopping. A bit of frying. Then a long slow cooking. It could not be simpler.

Or could it? First find your *coq*. Most recipes insist on a cockerel, with the claim that only a bird whose breast bone is no longer pliable (apparently once the cartilage has formed into bone) is suitable. The usual reasoning behind this is that anything younger would turn to sludge during the long cooking. More to the point, I think, is that the bones and sinews of an old fowl will actually enrich the sauce with their gelatine. Young birds, particularly of the intensively farmed variety, lack this quality.

This means locating a bird at least 10 months old – not easy when you learn that most chickens destined for the table are now slaughtered at about 6 weeks. The nearest we can hope to get is a traditional free-range bird, probably just over two months old – frankly, the only chicken worth

Cook on a high heat for 1 or 2 minutes (to burn off the alcohol), then pour in the wine, scraping at the crusty deposits on the pan and stirring them into the sauce as you do so. Cover and simmer very gently – the liquid should on no account boil – until the chicken is tender. This will take from 30 to 50 minutes and can be done either on the hob or in the oven.

While the chicken cooks, fry the mushrooms and the small onions in the butter over a low heat and covered with a lid until they are golden and sweet, about 20 minutes. When the chicken is tender, lift the meat out and put it to one side. Skim as much fat from the top of the sauce as you can. Turn up the heat and cook the sauce at a good bubble till it starts to thicken and shine – a matter of 4 or 5 minutes. Taste and season with salt. Return the chicken to the pan with the cooked onions and mushrooms.

Cover and continue to cook very gently for 15 minutes. Serve with croutes of bread, cut into triangles, hearts or whatever, and fried in butter till golden and crisp and then dipped in parsley.

Serves 4

Classic Green Salad

The perfect accompaniment to a braise such as that described in the next column, a green salad has plenty of soft leaves to mop up the sauce left on your plate. Rather than follow the current fashion of dumping as many unusual baby leaves as possible on to a plate and drizzling them with olive oil, I actually prefer a simple salad of no more than a couple of different leaves, torn into manageable pieces and dressed with a classic French dressing.

per person
2 handfuls of cos or butterhead lettuce
½ a bunch of watercress
for the dressing (enough for 4)
½ a small clove of garlic
a little salt
1 tablespoon mild wine vinegar
6 tablespoons extra virgin olive oil

Crush the garlic to a slush with salt by squashing it with the flat blade of a knife. Scrape this into a small bowl and whisk with vinegar, then whisk in the oil, a little at a time, until all is thoroughly combined.

Tear the leaves into manageable pieces. Pieces too small will turn to sludge when dressed; too large and they will be difficult to eat without the dressing running down your chin. Toss the greens lightly in the dressing no more than a few minutes before you want to eat them.

buying anyway. It will have the muscles to withstand long cooking and the flavour to make our trouble worthwhile.

Technically, *coq au vin* is a braise – in other words, a dish where the main ingredient cooks very gently in liquid that is barely shuddering, either on the hob or in the oven. The process is straightforward: the meat is browned in bacon fat, followed by the vegetables, usually carrots and onions, then wine is poured in and, with the frying deposits in the pan stirred in, left to cook gently for an hour or so. Perfectionists will then strain the cooking liquor of its fat and return it to the meat and vegetables. Real professionals will serve a garnish of heart-shaped croutes of fried bread dipped in parsley.

Whatever, the sauce will need thickening slightly, either by rubbing butter and flour in your fingers to form pellets of *beurre manié* that are whisked into the liquid towards the end of cooking or by reducing the liquid over a moderate heat until it shines and is thick enough to coat the back of a spoon. Lazy cooks like myself will probably prefer the latter.

I would love to be able to say that you can use any old wine, but sadly this is not the case. If it isn't good enough to go in a glass, then it isn't good enough to go in the pot. No one would expect to make a decent casserole with a stock cube, or a rich, shining beef casserole with water, so we cannot really expect a bottle of plonk to give anything but a second-class sauce. The dish's Burgundian traditions would demand Chambertin or some such rich red, but any recipe that insists on the wine of the region is being pretentious – any full-bodied red will do, no matter where it comes from.

Served with bread, preferably of the un-hip white baguette variety, and a bowlful of plain green salad to mop up the winy juices, this classic meal is

Salt-baked Chicken with Thyme and Cracked Garlic

You could use sea salt seasoned with chopped thyme leaves if you prefer. It may appear costly, but you could always use the salt again a few days later.

8 plump cloves of garlic, unpeeled
coarse sea salt
6 free-range chicken pieces on the bone, breasts,
    thighs and drumsticks
6 healthy sprigs of thyme

Squash each of the garlic cloves with the flat of a knife, just enough to crack them open. Place half of the salt in a foil-lined roasting tin. Press the chicken pieces down into the salt, then scatter over the cracked garlic cloves and the thyme sprigs. Cover with the remaining salt. You will probably need about 1.1kg/2½lb, depending on the size of the chicken pieces.

Bake the chicken in a preheated oven at 200°C/400°F/Gas Mark 6 for 35–40 minutes. Remove from the roasting tin by lifting the foil, place on a serving dish and then crack open the salt crust. Serve with the sauce overleaf.

as unfashionable as you can get, yet it is difficult to understand how we have managed to lose such good things in favour of char-grilled tuna. Now who says we have never had things so good?

Tarragon Cream Sauce

1 shallot
75ml/3fl oz white wine
120ml/4fl oz chicken stock
200ml/7fl oz crème fraîche
2 tablespoons tarragon, chopped

Peel and finely chop the shallot. Put in a small pan with the wine and stock and boil hard until reduced by half. Whisk in the crème fraîche and tarragon until the sauce is smooth and creamy. Heat gently, stirring all the time. Season with a little salt and a grinding of pepper. Serve with the chicken.
Serves 2

Chocolate Mousse

If we are having a meal so redolent of the traditional bistro, then we might as well go the whole hog and have the quintessential bistro dessert. The book I turn to for all such classic recipes is Patricia Wells's *Bistro* (Kyle Cathie). A collection of simple bistro favourites such as *pommes boulangères*, *salade de lentilles* and *moules à la provençale*, it has not left the side of my cooker since it came out.

225g/8oz bittersweet chocolate, broken into pieces
3 tablespoons Grand Marnier
2 teaspoons vanilla extract
100g/4oz unsalted butter
8 large egg yolks
100g/4oz sugar
5 large egg whites

Place the chocolate, orange liqueur and vanilla in the top of a double boiler over simmering water and allow to melt, stirring occasionally. Remove from the heat and stir in the butter.

Combine the egg yolks and sugar in a large bowl and beat until thick and pale yellow. Beat in the chocolate mixture while still lukewarm. Place the egg whites in a medium-sized mixing bowl. Beat until stiff but not dry.

Add one-third of the beaten egg whites to the chocolate batter and mix vigorously. Gently fold in the remaining whites. Do this slowly and patiently. Do not overmix but make sure that the mixture is well blended, with no streaks of whites remaining.

Pour the mixture into a large (2l/3⅓ pint) serving bowl. Cover with plastic wrap and refrigerate for at least 6 hours before serving.
Serves 8–10

BRITISH COOKING

Our cooking, by which I mean what has come to be known as Traditional British Cooking, is well suited to our climate and temperament. It is a mild, restrained and soothing cuisine. Its bland flavours do not offend, the way garlic and spices can, the high stodge factor does battle for us against our well-known bad weather and much of our heritage of recipes can be made without spending what we might call an undue amount.

On the face of it, there is little to entice the newcomer to try our national cooking. By newcomer I do not just mean foreigner, I mean any young person who has been brought up on the pizzas, pastas, fish fingers and lasagnes that have become our modern British diet. Does anyone still eat the chops and mint sauce or the rice pudding with a blob of jam that were so much a part of my patriotic, monotonous childhood diet?

If British cooking is held in such low esteem then we have no one but ourselves to blame. Over the last 20 years we have let the rest of the world march over our traditional cooking, filling our supermarkets and restaurants with everything from quiche to quesadillas, crème brûlée to calamari and korma to cannelloni. Can lasagne really be more satisfying than a home-made shepherd's pie? Is Chinese crispy duck so much better than our own crisp-skinned roast duckling with apple sauce? Can anyone hold up their hand and honestly say that a plate of tiramisu is creamier, boozier and more seductive than a properly made sherry trifle?

The roll call of fine British cooking is a long one.

Faggots

A faggot is a bundle of minced meats, herbed and spiced and done up in a wrapping of caul fat, which you will need to order from the butcher. He may have some in his deep freeze. Rinse and dry the fat before you wrap the faggots. This is the ultimate cold-weather food, rich in both meat and fat. If your reason for never making them is the inclusion of liver then try them with some chopped lean pork instead. The recipe below differs from the traditional only in that it includes a handful of chopped fresh parsley, which I think livens the faggots up a bit.

450g/1lb pigs' liver
225g/8oz belly pork
2 large onions, peeled and chopped
1 plump clove of garlic, peeled and crushed
a little crushed savoury or sage
50–75g/2–3oz breadcrumbs
2 eggs
½ teaspoon mace
a good handful of coarsely chopped parsley
bay leaves (optional)
a large sheet of caul fat
about 180ml/6fl oz stock or thin gravy

Chop the liver and pork belly very finely. You can mince it if you wish (that is more traditional anyway), though I prefer a coarser texture. Put it in a frying pan with the chopped onion, garlic and savoury or sage, then cook over a gentle heat for 20 minutes. It should not brown.

There will be quite a lot of juice, which you should drain off and reserve before mixing the meat with the breadcrumbs, eggs, mace and parsley. Stir in a good seasoning of both sea salt and black pepper. You can add 1 or 2 bay leaves, though you will have to fish them out as you eat.

Form the mixture into balls about the size of a dumpling and weighing roughly 50–75g/2–3oz. Roll each faggot in a piece of caul fat as if you were wrapping a parcel, tucking the join underneath and placing the faggots in a buttered roasting tin. They should be just touching, to give them support as they cook. Pour the stock round them and bake at 180°C/350°F/Gas Mark 4 for 50 minutes or until they are cooked through. If the tops have failed to brown then place them under a hot grill for 1 or 2 minutes.

Approximately half-way through the cooking, pour the stock off into the reserved cooking juices, and return the faggots to the oven. Put the mixed liquid into a jug in a cool place (a basin of iced water will do the trick) until the fat solidifies. Scoop it off with a draining spoon, then pour the stock over the faggots and cook till the juices are bubbling. Serve with plenty of garden peas.
Serves 4–6

Londoner's pea soup

A wonderfully warming, satisfying soup, a complete meal in a bowl, named after the thick fogs that blanketed the capital in Victorian times. Good bacon stock can be made using knuckle of bacon, and chunks of meat cut from the knuckle can be used instead of bacon rashers for the substantial garnish. The recipe is from Philippa Davenport's book *Davenport's Dishes*, sadly long out of print but a joy for those lucky enough to have a copy.

An abridged version might include rare roast beef with yorkshire pudding, faggots with peas and gravy, meat and potato pie, fish cakes with parsley sauce, roast potatoes, treacle pudding, sausage and mash, buttered crumpets, blackberry and apple pie and, of course, Christmas pudding. Yet where can you find such food outside the home (or even in it for that matter)? Where can those keen to criticise our kitchens eat such good things when so many restaurant menus are top heavy with bruschetta, grilled peppers and risotto?

Tempted to our table by the smell of roast chicken or a gooseberry pie fresh out of the oven, a discerning newcomer would soon see our weak spots. The chicken is likely to be minus the tarragon or thyme the French have learned to scent it with, the vegetables would be plainly boiled in a way that would bemuse an Italian cook, and the bland white accompaniment of bread sauce and stodgy stuffing would seem pointless to those who have learned to lift a chicken's mild flavour with the juice from a ripe lemon.

We can produce a juicy sausage, yet have no pâté that can hold a candle to the intensely savoury French *rillettes* (the French have the good sense to make them from meat that has first been roasted in a low oven overnight). Good simple fish cooking eludes us, though we can make a mean fish pie. At least we have stopped overcooking the cauliflower. We now undercook the broccoli instead.

The British excel at roasts and slow-cooked casseroles with clear, unthickened juices. There is Lancashire hotpot and Irish stew, one with its layer of sliced potatoes, the other rich with dumplings and pearl barley. Both are frugal to make and soothing to eat, their flavours uncomplicated by cream or herbs. And there is no one more adept at boiling a crab to be eaten from its shell or poaching a piece of salmon to be eaten with boiled new potatoes.

If simplicity is our major trump card, it is also our cooking's greatest problem. When ingredients are of the very best, our no-frills approach works admirably. Things go wrong when we try to stint on the quality of the raw produce – something the British are very good at. If chicken is to be roasted plain, then it has to be a first-class free-range bird for the results to be anything more than merely palatable.

But our simple treatment of good ingredients is not to be overlooked. The uncluttered flavours of our boiled silverside of beef shine out against the sometimes murky amalgam that is an Italian *bolito misto*, with its assortment of veal, chicken, pork and beef. Yet it is the Italian recipe that is to be found on the menus of (our) smart restaurants. Perhaps it is the Italian accompaniment of a bouncing, piquant green *salsa verde* that appeals more than our own bland horseradish, carrots and dumplings. But is the French *pot-au-feu*, where beef is cooked slowly with root vegetables and served with cabbage, mustard and cornichons – the crunchy little gherkins – perhaps better than either? It offers the homely simplicity of our version with the velvety, marrow-enriched broth of the Italian boiled dinner.

The Brits can bake too, though I would argue that we are better at cakes and fruit breads than we are at baking a loaf. We cannot make a thin baguette with a crackling crust and airy crumb to save our lives. I am not sure we understand the importance of the crust, assuming that the white stuff inside is all that matters. Yet we can make cake to die for, be it dark stick-to-your-fingers ginger cake, a fluffy Victoria sponge with home-made gooseberry jam or a fruit-laden Dundee with its neat topping of browned almonds. What gâteaux or *torten* can stand up against my favourite, the sort of coffee and walnut buttercream layer cake now only spotted on cake stalls at the village fête?

1 large onion
1 leek
2 celery stalks
1 large carrot
100g/4oz bacon fat or butter
1 fat clove of garlic
225g/8oz streaky bacon
1.8l/3 pints bacon stock
a large bouquet garni
225g/8oz split green or yellow peas
4 tablespoons oil
6 slices of slightly stale bread, diced
a little mace
4 or more tablespoons each chopped fresh chives and parsley

Chop the vegetables and sweat them in half the bacon fat or butter for 5–7 minutes. Add the crushed garlic clove, the rinds from the streaky bacon (tied in a bundle with a piece of string), the bacon stock and the bouquet garni. Bring to the boil, stir in the split peas, cover the pan with a lid and simmer gently for about 1½ hours or until the peas are completely softened.

When the peas are nearly tender, cut the bacon rashers into smallish pieces. Fry gently over a low heat until the fat runs, then over higher heat until crisp. Remove with a slotted spoon. Add the remaining butter or bacon fat to the frying pan, together with the oil, and fry the diced bread until golden and crisp. Drain well.

Remove the bouquet garni and bacon rind from the soup. Reduce the soup to a purée in a liquidiser. Reheat gently and season to taste with salt, pepper and mace. Stir in the bacon and chopped chives. Sprinkle the parsley over the surface and served accompanied by a bowl of fried croûtons.

Serves 6

Pan Haggerty

A forgotten classic from Northumberland that deserves to be better known.

900g/2lb old potatoes, peeled
2 large onions, peeled
3 tablespoons dripping or butter
175g/6oz Cheddar cheese, grated

Slice the potatoes and onions very thinly. Melt the fat in a large, heavy frying pan and place the potatoes, onions and cheese in layers in the pan. Begin and end with potatoes and season each layer with salt and pepper.

Cover tightly and continue cooking for 15–20 minutes over a medium heat until all the potatoes are tender. Brush some of the juices over the top layer and place under a hot grill till bubbling.
Serves 4

Nowhere will we find a tastier snack than the British 'something on toast', whether the hot buttered bread is topped with grilled mushrooms, a wobbly poached egg or that piquant, mustardy paste known variously as Welsh rarebit or rabbit. Then again, if we cannot decide on its name, how on earth can we persuade a Frenchman that our bubbling cheese and toast snack is infinitely more delectable than his greasy *croque monsieur*?

It should come as no surprise, though, that our menus and chilled-food counters are bulging with foreign dishes: Britain has always had a magpie instinct to cookery. Ideas from India, hints from the Vikings and odds and sods from the Romans have made our cooking what it is, or rather could be, today. The problem is that we have amassed a collection of treasures from afar that has outshone our own. The first to extol the virtues of enriching our diet with good things from elsewhere, even I would hate to see our traditional cookery disappear in favour of peppers *piedmontaise*. It may not be very British, but I think it's time we blew our culinary trumpet a little louder.

CABBAGE

There were wooden crates of cabbages in the market one morning a while ago, a soft purple-green colour and as hard as ice. They were cold to touch, their leaves tightly packed, and were being sold in a pile so high and cheap that I could have been in China, or perhaps somewhere in Eastern Europe, places whose cooks understand and respect this difficult vegetable. I paid less than £1 for two splendid specimens: a crinkly-leaved deep-green Savoy as big as my head and a January King, a heavily veined variety whose leaves were edged in purple and bronze. I carried my trophies home, the two of them bouncing around in my beige string shopping bag like something from a *Viz* cartoon.

This was an impulse buy and I had forgotten how much cabbage you get for your money. Quite where I thought I was going to put them I don't know. In the past I have piled gluts of apples in white china bowls, hung strings of onions from ceiling hooks and stuffed jars of olive oil with cheap and plentiful basil. An embarrassment of cabbages is another matter. People whose homes are featured in glossy magazines seem to keep theirs in the sink. But they usually have two sinks and one cabbage. I had two cabbages and one sink.

If ever there was a misunderstood vegetable, it is the cabbage. The coarse green leaves of this most robust member of the brassica family respond well to both the quick cooking techniques of the East and the long slow cooking of provincial France and Eastern Europe. But boiled in deep water, as is so often the case, it induces the rank flavour and

Cabbage and Green Lentil Soup with Bacon and Sherry

Not a pretty soup this, but it's earthy, frugal and warming. Serve in big bowls with crusty white bread.

a medium-sized onion, chopped
4 cloves of garlic, sliced
1 tablespoon olive oil
75g/3oz smoked bacon, ham or pancetta
100g/4oz mushrooms, chopped
thyme
bay leaves
100g/4oz lentils, brown or green
a wineglass of red wine
2 tablespoons medium sherry
225g/8oz dark green cabbage, shredded
Worcestershire sauce

Cook the onion and garlic slowly in the oil in a heavy-based pan. A good 10 minutes over a low heat should leave the onion soft, golden and translucent. Stir in the chopped bacon and mushrooms and cover with a lid. Leave to cook for 10 minutes or until the bacon fat has coloured a little and the mushrooms are brown and tender.

Add the herbs, preferably in whole sprigs so that you can lift them out later. Rinse the lentils in a sieve under running water, then tip them into the onion mixture. Pour in 1l/1⅔ pints of boiling water and the glass of wine, then bring the pan to the boil. Turn down the heat and simmer for 30 minutes or so until the lentils are tender – eat a couple to find out.

Remove two thirds of the soup and liquidise it, taking care not to include any of the stalks of the herbs. You can use either a blender or a food processor for this. Pour the liquidised soup back into the pan and add the sherry and a careful seasoning of salt and a generous shake of freshly ground black pepper. Bring back to the boil, stir in the shredded cabbage and simmer for 5 minutes until the greens start to wilt. Stir in a little Worcestershire sauce to taste.

Serves 6

Cabbage with Cream and Balsamic Vinegar

The butter and cream have a softening effect on the cabbage, which for this particular dish can be a hard white (or Dutch) one or a dark green one such as January King or Savoy. A suitable accompaniment to virtually any pork or bacon dish, or serve alongside a rice pilau.

1 small, firm cabbage
50g/2oz butter
120ml/4fl oz double cream
1 teaspoon balsamic vinegar

Shred the cabbage finely and rinse thoroughly in running water. Melt the butter in a large, heavy-based pan over a moderate heat. When the butter starts to froth, drop the cabbage in and season with salt and pepper. Continue to cook until the cabbage has wilted and is tender, about 10–15 minutes. Check the heat carefully to make sure the butter does not burn.

Pour the cream into the pan and mix well. Continue to cook for a further 5 minutes. Stir in the balsamic vinegar, check for seasoning and serve while hot.

Serves 4 as a side dish

pervasive smell that hung around every corner at school. In other words, cook a cabbage for five minutes or 50, but never in between.

Shredded and stir-fried with garlic and mushrooms, those cabbages made a robust, earthy lunch. Some of the leaves chopped and fried with bits of fatty bacon were even better. Best of all was the supremely comforting soup made with slate green lentils and dark mushrooms, the cabbage adding bulk and brightness to a seriously worthy broth. There were enough leaves to stuff, and enough to shred, blanch in boiling water for two minutes, then drain and fry in butter, as an accompaniment to grilled pork. There was plenty, if I could have been bothered, to cut into fine hair-like shreds and deep-fry twice to give crisp little shards like the so-called seaweed in Chinese restaurants. And there was certainly enough to mash with potatoes for a bubble and squeak breakfast.

There are really two parts to each cabbage. First, the large and slightly coarse outer leaves, ideal for rolling round a nutty spice-and-rice filling, and then the inner, tender young leaves. Packed so tight that not even the most determined caterpillar could squeeze a way in, the young leaves of the January King are good enough to eat raw. Shredded very finely and coated with a mustardy dressing, they make a surprisingly good side dish for, say, pork pie, though it is not for the faint-hearted.

Tempering a cabbage's strong flavour can be something of a challenge. I find earthy, mealy things like lentils, beans and nuts good for that, and smoked flavours too. The intense heat of stir-frying, not to mention dousing with salty soy sauce, seems to soften its rough edges too, as does dipping it in boiling water before you toss it in melted butter and grated lemon. Walnut oil, gently warmed with a few caraway seeds and crushed black pepper, and olive oil sizzling with thinly sliced garlic will both knock the wind out of its sails.

Long, slow cooking will bring out the brassica's well-hidden sweetness, especially when served with a cream-based sauce. Or try the large leaves blanched, stuffed with cream cheese and nuts, and baked with a soothing tomato sauce. And if all else fails, you can always beat its strong flavour into submission with copious amounts of garlic, or mash it to a pulp and braise it with cream, or simply smother it in melted butter. Each way, you get a lot of cabbage for your money.

Stir-fried Pork with Savoy Cabbage

A straightforward stir-fry, and as easy a supper as it is possible to get. Fierce heat tempers the forthright notes of the cabbage.

350g/12oz boneless pork
2 tablespoons rice wine or medium sherry
1 teaspoon sesame oil
1 tablespoon light soy sauce
1 teaspoon cornflour
2 tablespoons groundnut oil
3 spring onions, chopped
½ a firm, small Savoy cabbage

Cut the pork into cubes or strips about 1cm/½in in diameter. Toss the pork with the wine or sherry, sesame oil, soy and cornflour – don't worry too much about the lumps. Set aside for 20 minutes. Meanwhile shred the cabbage finely.

Heat a wok or large, deep-sided frying pan until it is really hot. Add the groundnut oil and gently swirl it about a bit. Just as it starts to smoke, which will be a matter of seconds, add the pork, but not its marinating juices. Cook quickly, stirring around with chopsticks for a couple of minutes till brown around the edges. The pork must be slightly brown if it is to be good.

Add the spring onions, a good grinding of pepper and some salt, then the shredded cabbage. Cook, stirring and frying, for about 4 or 5 minutes till the pork is done right through and the cabbage is bright green and just starting to wilt. Tip in the marinating juices from the pork, bubble once or twice and eat while hot. Pass the soy sauce at the table.

Serves 2

Stuffed Cabbage with Mushrooms and Pine Kernels

To reduce the risk of any stuffing leaking during steaming, you may prefer to wrap the cabbage in muslin first.

2 large onions, peeled and chopped
3 cloves of garlic, peeled and sliced
1 tablespoon olive oil
450g/1lb mushrooms, finely chopped
10–12 large cabbage leaves
225g/8oz raw cabbage
100g/4oz rice, lightly cooked
50g/2oz pine kernels, toasted
2 tablespoons chopped parsley
1 tablespoon chopped fresh tarragon
3 tablespoons crème fraîche

In a deep, heavy-based pan cook the onions and garlic in the olive oil till golden brown. A long, slow cooking, covered with a lid, for 15 minutes is preferable to cooking them quickly. When they are golden and sweet, add the chopped mushrooms and continue to cook until the mushrooms are brown and tender, about 10–15 minutes.

Meanwhile, blanch the cabbage leaves in boiling water for a couple of minutes until they start to wilt. Their colour should still be bright. Chop 225g/8oz of leaves from the rest of the cabbage and add to the mushrooms and onions. Cook until tender, turning up the heat to evaporate any extra liquid that may form. The filling should be moist but not wet.

Stir in the cooked rice, nuts, herbs and crème fraîche and season with salt and pepper. In a metal or wooden steamer basket, lay 2 pieces of string in the form of a cross. (Or, if you plan to wrap the cabbage in muslin, lay a double sheet in the steamer now, with enough hanging over the sides to draw up round the cabbage and tie.) Place 3 of the large blanched and drained leaves on top to form a base. Lay half a dozen or so other leaves around the sides, radiating from the centre to form, for want of a better expression, a flower shape. Pile the stuffing in the centre and lay another leaf on top. Bring up the string (or muslin) around the edge, at the same time pulling the leaves gently together to cover the stuffing. Tie firmly, then place the steamer on to its base to steam, covered with a lid, for 20 minutes or until the filling is thoroughly hot.

Untie and cut into slices like a cake. A couple of slices per person will look better than a quarter of the cabbage each.

Serves 4

If all this sounds rather a lot of fuss, then take the easy option: fill the leaves individually and roll them up, tucking the sides in to form a neat package, then pack them into the steamer tightly and steam as before.

CHEESE

She has just found out what I do for a living. I know what is coming next. The questions are always the same: one of the three classic enquiries that invariably follow such a discovery. One, have I ever met Delia? Two, what is my favourite restaurant? Three (and the one I dread), what is my favourite thing to eat? I have often wondered what would happen if I said I was a doctor. 'And what's your favourite disease?' But I must answer.

'It depends,' I offer pathetically. 'On the season, the time of day, or my mood.' It is obviously not going to be as easy as that. It never is. I am going to have to commit myself. Should I say 'mashed potato' and risk yet another mashed-potato conversation. I have had about 50 and it's beginning to sound like a recorded message. I try to sum up my inquisitor.

If I say roast grouse, I know she will be a hunt saboteur. If I declare a passion for omelettes, I will have to listen to yet another tirade against 'the veggies'. Say caviare and I will be élitist, offal and I will be a pervert, grilled chicken and I can guarantee she will be a hard-line vegetarian. Rice pudding from the tin and she will know I am a slob. Give in to the temptation of a slightly risqué reply and I might get more than I had bargained for. Panic sets in.

'It must be crisp, voluptuous, deeply savoury and hot. It must be quick to make, not extravagant and I must be able to pick it up and eat it with my fingers. I love licking my fingers. It must smell warm and friendly, be slightly messy to eat and

Baked Camembert

Bonchester, a melting, creamy English cheese from the Borders, is as suitable as Camembert for this treatment. It is not yet as easy to find as the French version, though I think it deserves to be, but your local cheesemonger, if he is a good one, should stock it.

225g/8oz puff pastry, thawed if frozen
1 small Camembert or Bonchester cheese
a little beaten egg

Get the oven really hot, 220°C/425°F/Gas Mark 7. Cut the pastry in half and roll out 2 circles, about 4cm/1½in larger than your cheese, one circle slightly larger than the other. Lay the smaller circle on a baking sheet, then take the cheese out of its wrapping and lay it on top of the pastry

With a pastry brush or your fingers, wet the edge of the pastry thoroughly with beaten egg. Place the larger disc of pastry on top of the cheese. Press the overhanging top pastry on to the base pastry, then trim both to give a 2cm/¾in border. Seal the pastry, to stop the cheese leaking, with the prongs of a fork. Push down hard to seal but not so hard that you slice through to the baking sheet.

Brush all over with beaten egg and cut 2 small slits in the top to let the steam out. Bake in the preheated oven for 15–20 minutes until the pastry is golden brown and puffed up. Leave the pastry to cool for 10 minutes before cutting it so that the cheese oozes rather than pours out. Eat with a leafy salad.
Serves 2

Goats'-cheese Tarts

I find the little cylindrical goats' cheeses marketed under the name of Capricorn just the right size for this. They are well distributed, but there are plenty of other suitable cheeses around. Those with a white bloomy rind are best; the rind seems to help keep the cheese in place. A large goats' 'log' can be used also; simply cut off slices about 5cm/2in thick instead.

350g/12oz frozen puff pastry, thawed
**3 soft, barrel-shaped goats' cheeses, or 2 goats'-
    cheese logs**
1 egg, beaten
few sprigs of thyme or rosemary

Preheat the oven to 220°C/425°F/Gas Mark 7. Cut the pastry into 6 equal pieces. Place them on a floured board and roll each into a 13cm/5in square.

Cut the cheeses in half, or into 5cm/2in pieces if you are using a log. Place each piece of cheese on a square of pastry. Brush the edges of the pastry with egg. Draw the sides of the pastry up to form a pyramid. Press the pastry edges together half-way up the sides, leaving the centre open. Add a small sprig of herb to each of them.

Slide on to a baking sheet and bake for 15 minutes or until the pastry is golden and puffed up and the cheese has softened. Eat while the cheese is still warm.

Makes 6

must look handmade.' It was time to commit myself. 'Something that involves the pairing of a hot, crisp crust with melted cheese.' Phew! Not only politically correct but true.

'Toasted cheese sandwiches come pretty high. So do pizzas whose topping involves nothing more than piquant melted cheese and salty, herby olives. But if I had to put my finger on one thing, it is the utterly sexy combination of warm cheese and hot pastry. It must be the perfect edible marriage. Flaky, crumbly pastry with voluptuous, melting cheese. It could be a slice of goats' cheese wrapped in buttery pastry, or a whole molten Camembert trapped inside a layer of puff pastry; a pasty of creamy Gorgonzola, or a tiny tart of melting Fontina.

In desperation, a croissant warm from the grill with melted Cheddar. Anything that involves this sublime, tantalising and unctuous partnership.

'The problem is that cheese behaves unpredictably at the best of times. Not every cheese melts seductively. This is a matter not simply of ripeness but of variety. Some, like very fresh, soft goats' cheeses, become grainy rather than satisfyingly molten. Others, particularly some blue cheeses, are inclined to separate, while the very hard cheeses need finely grating if they are not to just sit and sweat in the oven. Worst of all are the plastic-wrapped "block" cheeses which release vast amounts of greasy oil, which then burns in the oven, producing clouds of black smoke.

'Mozzarella, the pizza cheese, melts into strings, which can be mildly annoying or fun depending on your predicament. But texture rather than flavour is the point of that particular cheese. Tomme fraîche de Cantal, the young cows'-milk cheese, melts smoothly and predictably, though is easier said than found. Creamy, ripe Italian Gorgonzola can melt so smoothly as to become a sauce. Springy, golden Fontina melts beautifully enough to be the Italian's premier fondue cheese. Cheddar, the mainstay of British cheeses, can melt satisfactorily if grated or sliced finely. But none matches the sheer unctuousness of warm Camembert or goats'-milk cheeses.

'It is not just the contrast of melted cheese and crisp pastry that is so good. Think of the deeply savoury marriage of hot cheese and crisp toast in a Welsh rabbit, or melting mozzarella on a crisp based pizza. Any crisp, savoury crust will do the trick. But the trick is to know when both the cheese and the crust are at their best. The real point is this: if it is to be really good then the crust base must be slightly charred (think of the best pizza you have ever eaten) but the cheese must not.

'Cheese, any cheese, toughens if it is overcooked. In the case of goats' cheeses or mozzarella, this is a comparatively short time, and infuriatingly less time than it takes to cook the crust to a perfect ratio of gold and black. The trick is to use the crust to protect the cheese. Covering the cheese with pastry ensures that the pastry browns successfully while keeping the cheese protected, allowing it to soften and melt without toughening. The perfect edible marriage.'

I have done it. I have committed myself. And she wishes she had never asked. It would have been quicker to say offal.

Toasted Croissants with Mushrooms, Onions and Melted Cheese

A cheat's version.

2 small onions, peeled and thinly sliced
1 tablespoon olive oil
4 croissants
French mustard
6 medium-sized mushrooms, sliced
100g/4oz good melting cheese, thinly sliced

Fry the onion in a little oil till soft and transparent. It will take a good 10 minutes to turn soft and golden. After 5 minutes or so, add the mushrooms and cook for a further 5 minutes.

Split the croissants horizontally. Spread them generously with mustard. Scoop the onions and mushrooms from the pan with a draining spoon and place on the bottom halves of croissants. Arrange the cheese on top and place under a hot grill till melted. Add the warmed top halves and eat while still hot.

Makes 4 – a snack for 2

Christmas . . . a whole Stilton. It seemed such a good idea at the time. I followed all the rules, choosing my supplier with care, asking his advice and telling him when I intended to eat it. I took it home carefully, stored it in the coolest place in the house (my bedroom, would you believe?) and gave it as much tender loving care as it is possible to give. Or at least to give to a cheese.

I cut the top off carefully in one piece, so as to provide a natural lid. The cheese had no contact with the cling film which would have made it sweat, or with the fridge that could have dulled its sharp-edged richness. The magnificent cream and blue-green flesh never met the port which would have turned the cheese sour and the port undrinkable, and my buttery, ivory velvet cheese never even glimpsed the shine of the dreaded Stilton scoop, famous for leaving vast craters of exposed cheese to go dry and crusty.

But what shall I do with it now? Perhaps I should have bought a large hunk rather than a whole cheese. Or maybe I should have been tempted by one of those dinky little numbers sold in two-tone earthenware pots and sealed with wax – the ones I have been reliably informed never mature thoroughly. Whatever, I now have a goodly amount of cheese, slightly smelly though far from rank, that is no longer in fine enough a condition to eat with the juicy golden Orléans Reinette apples I have wolfed all season.

I have read some very sniffy comments about cooking with the King of British cheeses – especially a regal Colston Basset, whose dry, crinkly rind hides such a rich, fudgy, creamy flesh. But it is past its best now, and I have to admit I am eager to try some of the other fine British cheeses that are around. No, I shall cook with it! Perhaps I could toss little cubes of it into scrambled eggs, or stir fine shavings of it into a risotto. I could wrap hunks of it in leaves of the now *passé* filo pastry to make little parcels, but someone might see me. Maybe I could grate it for a soufflé that would be so good with a spinach salad. I shall stuff it into baked potatoes, grill it on top of toast, stir it into pasta sauces and melt it over pears. I may even attempt a version of the often disappointing Stilton soup. Anything really, just to get it out of my bedroom.

Pork Steaks with Stilton Sauce

A rich and voluptuous dish which needs nothing more than raw shredded hard cabbage or frisée dressed with lemon juice and pepper as an accompaniment. The parsley is an important addition, somehow rescuing the dish from cloying.

a little olive oil
2 pork steaks, about 1cm/½in thick
60ml/2fl oz Marsala
100g/4oz Stilton
3 tablespoons double cream
2 tablespoons chopped parsley

Warm the olive oil in a sauté or frying pan. Season the meat with a little salt and pepper. When the oil is hot, add the pork and fry quickly till golden brown, then turn and cook the other side. Meanwhile, pour the Marsala into a small, heavy-based pan. Bring it slowly to the boil, then turn down the heat so that it is barely simmering and add the cheese, crumbled into small pieces. Add the cream. Stir continuously until the cheese has melted into the cream and the sauce shows some sign of thickening. Stir in the parsley. Take care not to overheat, or it will separate. Serve the sauce with the pork immediately.
Serves 2

Stilton with Warm Potato Salad

A robust warm salad for a cold night. I found myself accompanying this with even more starch in the form of bread, and can recommend it. A spinach salad, perhaps with a few grapes tossed in, would be a splendid partner.

12 medium waxy potatoes, wiped clean
2 teaspoons red wine vinegar
1 tablespoon walnut oil
2 tablespoons not too finely chopped parsley
225g/8oz Stilton, cut into roughly 2.5cm/1in chunks

Boil the potatoes in salted water till tender to the point of a knife, about 15–20 minutes. Mix the vinegar, oil and parsley in a salad bowl. Grind in a little black pepper. Drain the potatoes and slice them thickly, say 3 or 4 slices from each potato. Add them to the dressing while still hot. Stir in the crumbled Stilton and toss the salad gently. Leave for 10 minutes or so, then serve with chunks of soft white bread.
Serves 2

Stilton Rabbit

I am slightly reluctant to call this a rabbit as my instructions are distinctly unorthodox, but they do avoid the curdling that is so often the result of following the traditional recipes.

225g/8oz finely crumbled Stilton (even the driest
  bits will do)
30g/1oz butter
1 tablespoon Worcestershire sauce
1 tablespoon English mustard
2 tablespoons beer
2 English muffins, split and toasted on the cut side

Mix the crumbled cheese to a rough paste with the butter, Worcestershire sauce, mustard and beer. Spread the mixture over the muffins and toast under a hot grill for a minute or so until it bubbles and singes in patches. Eat with the rest of the beer.
Serves 2 as a snack

Pan-fried Pear and Stilton Salad

A useful supper dish in which I have used all manner of cheeses that might have seen better days. The cheese will soften rather than melt over the pears. Use whatever decent salad leaves you can find, depending on the season.

1 large or 2 small pears
juice of ½ a lemon
1 tablespoon walnut oil
2 tablespoons broken walnuts
a handful of salad leaves
90g/3oz Stilton

Wipe the pears, but do not peel them. Cut them in half and then into quarters. Remove the core and cut into thick slices, probably about 8 per pear. Squeeze lemon juice on to the flesh to prevent it discolouring.

Heat the oil in a large, shallow pan, place the pear slices in the hot oil and scatter over the broken walnuts. Cook the pears until golden and sizzling, turning them once.

Place a few salad leaves on 2 plates. With a palette knife, remove the pears and place them on top of the salad leaves.

Crumble the cheese into small pieces about the size of a walnut half. You can do this while the pears are cooking. Divide the crumbled cheese between the plates, scattering it over the hot pears. It should soften a little, but not melt. Squeeze any remaining lemon juice into the pan and, over the heat, stir well to scrape up any residue left by the pears (there won't be much but don't waste it). Drizzle over the cheese.
Serves 2

CHILLIES

I am new to chillies. In fact, I have spent most of my life deliberately avoiding them and was hardly grateful when a huge bag of dried ones dropped through my letter box. There were a dozen different varieties, resembling everything from giant black cherries to dead mice. But the labels intrigued: 'Little Rattle – heatscale 4/10, nutty and woody' or 'Ancho – heatscale 5/10, sweet and fruity with coffee and liquorice tones, indispensable for *moles*'. I broke off a piece of 'Little Raisin – 3/10' and knew that my illusions about chillies (they bring you out in a sweat and burn a hole through your stomach) were probably about to go up in flames.

The Cool Chile Company's intercom warped 'Nigel Slater for Dodie Miller' into 'Mr Slater from the *Daily Mirror*'. Once up the stairs to her ochre and turquoise and chilli-filled flat, I was then sidetracked by a bag of orangy-yellow fruit. Wonderfully tart and piquant, they were the first sun-dried yellow tomatoes I had ever seen – a real find, their flavour poised between dried apricot and tomato but without the smoky tones of the ubiquitous red ones. But this was not what I had come for.

Dodie Miller, with her partner David Bashford, is hoping to change the way some of us think about chillies, used on a daily basis in most of the developing world but used, if at all, with caution in most British kitchens. Her passion for these fiery peppers has led her to track down supplies of dried chillies not often available here in quantity and her line 'some are hot and some are not' is testament to

New Mexican Mild Red Chilli Bread

Food writer Marlene Spieler has a passion for chillies and had been bringing them back from Mexico herself when she discovered Dodie Miller's original stall in Portobello Road market decked with Mexican chillies. This recipe from Marlene's fun, lively and chilli-packed book *Hot and Spicy* (Grafton), uses chilli powder; good though it is, it is even better with the Chimayo powdered chilli. Crusty and fragrant, with the flavourings melting into the hot bread, this is a chilli version of garlic bread.

3 cloves of garlic, chopped
30g/1oz coriander leaves
1 spring onion, thinly sliced
2 tablespoons mild chilli powder
100g/4oz unsalted butter
2 to 3 tablespoons olive oil
salt
450g/1lb loaf French bread, cut in half lengthways
50g/2oz Parmesan or other hard cheese, coarsely grated

Purée the garlic in a processor or liquidiser. Add the coriander, spring onion and chilli powder, and process until finely chopped. Add the butter, olive oil and salt to taste. Blend until smooth.

Place the bread on a baking sheet, then spread with chilli butter and sprinkle with Parmesan cheese. Bake in the oven at 230°C/ 450°F/Gas Mark 8 until the edges are crispy, the top lightly browned in spots, and the butter melted. Serve immediately.
Serves 2

Chilli Purée

A deep rust-red, slightly smoky purée.

12 medium to large dried chillies such as Guajillo

Toast the chillies gently over a low heat in a frying pan until they soften slightly, and smell warm and roasted, about 5–7 minutes depending on the heat. Toast them slowly, turning from time to time, taking great care not to burn them, even in small patches, or they will become inedibly bitter.

Put the chillies into a basin and pour over enough boiling water to cover. Keep them under the surface with another smaller basin if necessary. Soak for 20–30 minutes till soft and flaccid. Pull away the stalks and remove the seeds. Tear into smaller pieces and place in the bowl of a food processor or blender with 3 tablespoons of the soaking water, provided it is not bitter, in which case use tap water.

Whiz to a smooth purée. Push through a sieve if the skin has failed to completely work smooth.

- Stir 1 or 2 tablespoons into mayonnaise.
- Use as a relish for any grilled fish, vegetables or meat.
- Add small amounts to soups and stews or to salad dressings.
- Add to a stir-fry at the end of cooking.

her mission to expel the widely held myth that there is nothing more to a chilli than heat. It is also the line that tempted me to beat a path to her door.

Ms Miller started me off on a mild note. More of a wafer than anything else, the dried Pasado is my kind of chilli. Crisp fruity and tasting distinctly of stewed dried apples, this is a dried green chilli from New Mexico. I munched away gratefully at this blissfully mild 'chilli-biscuit'. Later, reconstituted in warm water, it had more of a bite.

We progressed through the liquorice and tobacco tones of the dried Poblano, just as pronounced whether dried or fresh, to the long, black, raisin-flavoured Pasilla that later turned into a chocolate-brown snake in my bean stew. I fought hard to locate some of the deeper notes Ms Miller sensed, though the green-tea flavour of the rich, red Guajillo was clear enough, as were the tobacco notes of the Ancho. Like apricots or tomatoes, they had the intensity of flavour that comes with being dried in the blistering hot sun. It is this array of flavours rather than their heat that she is using as ammunition in her one-woman crusade for the chilli.

It is only right that we should be behind many other nations in our appreciation of the chilli. By the time the plant first reached our shores in the late fifteenth century, it was already well established as part of the daily cooking of the Mayas and Aztecs, and is now probably the most widely used spice in the world. Certainly it is much appreciated in poor countries for livening up a dull diet. The real bringer of heat is capsaicin, which lives in the flesh and the seeds but is present in greatest force in the white membrane, or placenta, inside the pepper.

Dodie Miller offered me a jar of smooth red gunge. I wasn't sure how much to taste. I didn't want to appear a complete wimp, but nor did I want to embarrass myself if it turned out to be lethally hot. This was a smoky, rich, brick-red sauce, made really for pasta. There was no intense heat, no burning throat, just a wonderful rush of adrenalin, followed quickly by a glowing, tingling warmth that went right down to my toes. I spent the next 10 minutes feeling as high as a kite.

Tasting my way through my new collection of chillies, from the minuscule and red-hot Birds'-eye I picked up from a Thai shop to the leathery, glossy and mild Pasilla, I am starting to see what I have been missing. Some, particularly the large, wrinkled, black-maroon Ancho, taste richly of fruit, while others, such as the mild Mulato, taste overwhelmingly of liquorice.

I suddenly spotted a bag of rich, almost luminous, red powder, more like a brilliant red-ochre pigment than spice. This was Chimayo, one of three chilli powders that the company imports. Its rich sweetness was a revelation to someone used to coarse, fiery versions. Rich and moist, with a deep earthy sweetness familiar to anyone who has grilled sweet peppers, this is some of the finest Mexican chilli powder available. So fresh and rich in the chillies' volatile oils that it has stuck together in soft lumps, it has become the most exciting addition to my spice shelf for years.

Ms Miller then opened a huge plastic sack and told me to inhale. This intense heat belonged to the brown and orange Habanero chilli (heatscale 10/10). Glowing like little lanterns, they gave off a viscous heat and powerful yeasty smell, with more than a whiff of the locker room. Eyes stinging, and my nose starting to run, it was time to go. Somehow I had known it would all end in tears.

Linguine with Chilli Tomato Sauce

A spicy sauce for pasta. You can add toasted sunflower or pumpkin seeds or pine kernels if you wish.

linguine or other ribbon pasta for 2
6 medium-sized tomatoes, halved
6 tablespoons of the chilli purée above
juice of 1 lime
2 tablespoons extra virgin olive oil
salt and freshly ground black pepper
2 tablespoons fresh coriander leaves, chopped

Cook the pasta in plenty of boiling, salted water till tender, about 7–10 minutes if dried, 2–3 if fresh.

Place the tomatoes on a grill pan and cook under a medium grill till slightly charred. Scoop into the bowl of a food processor or blender, skins and all, and whiz till smooth (you can scoop out the seeds first if you wish, but I never do). Add the chilli purée, lime, olive oil and salt. Season with a good grinding of black pepper to really bring out the flavour of the chillies. Scoop into a saucepan, bring to the boil then toss with the hot, drained pasta. Scatter with the coriander leaves and serve.
Serves 2

CHILLI VARIETIES

Guajillo Deceptively coloured a deep wine red, this long thin chilli turned my vegetable soup a vivid orange. Mildly hot, it tastes overwhelmingly of sweet green tea.

Pasado A roasted and peeled New Mexican chilli, dried to beautiful red, ochre and brown crisps. I have been eating them like wafers ever since. Its apple and herb notes seem less obvious after soaking. Even I would describe this one as very mild.

Ñoras Spanish. A rich Rioja-red globe. Turning a bright scarlet when reconstituted, its tough, unyielding skin has little flesh beneath it.

Mulato A soft, leathery consistency when dried, this mild, mahogany brown variety has a deep, smoky, liquorice flavour with a distinct whiff of tobacco. Sweeter than most. After half an hour in water it plumps up like a huge toad.

Cascabel Beautiful, round chillies that resemble huge black cherries. Their loose seeds rattle.

Ancho These are dried Poblano chillies. Similar in shape but smaller than the Mulato, they have a rich, reddy-brown glow to them. With prune and liquorice notes, and generously fleshy, this is one of California's most popular chillies.

Bird's-eye Very small and very hot, these tiny, brittle, rusty-orange chillies are popular in Thai and Chinese cooking.

Pequín From Texas. Round, orange-red and barely 1cm/½in in diameter, this is one of the hotter varieties.

Pasilla Long, shiny, black chillies with a clear raisin flavour.

Chipotle A crisp, smoked Jalapeño. Resembling a little brown mouse, this hot, deeply flavoured chilli is for those who like their food hot rather than spicy. Its smell, rather like the barrel of a pipe, is a clue to its flavour.

CHINESE GREENS

A snap of frost can change the diet overnight. Out go tomatoes and mozzarella and in come baked onions and goats' cheese; off with crab salad and on with braised lamb shanks, bye-bye basil, hello rosemary. And there is no more dramatic evidence of the shifting seasons than the vegetable rack.

You know that winter is truly on the way when the ripe and tender vegetables make way for parsnips, fennel, celeriac and swedes – hard vegetables for slow cooking. This is also when cabbage comes into its own. The strident flavours of deep-green Savoys and rock-hard, tight white cabbage are more suited to the cold evenings, but so too are the softer-leaved Chinese greens that our greengrocers and supermarkets have recently taken to stocking. Refreshing, crunchy, tender and neat, pak choi and its sisters, the mustard greens, have the qualities of our better-known cabbages plus the bonus of tender flesh and mustardy undertones.

Pak choi is easy to identify among the myriad greens on offer. Short and stocky, these tender-leaved cabbages are recognisable by the shape of their leaves which appropriately enough, resemble Chinese soup spoons – they are sometimes referred to in such terms. The soup-spoon cabbages, often quite squat, have fleshy white or green stalks full of juice and tender, dark-green leaves. In supermarkets they are generally packed in fours or sixes and are caught when very young, and at the most tender, barely 3 inches high. Piled up in Chinatown, the bunches are big enough to require both hands.

Blanched Pak Choi with Oyster Sauce

An exception to the hot-water rule.

450g/1lb pak choi
3 tablespoons oyster sauce
1 tablespoon groundnut oil

Plunge the pak choi into boiling water and leave them there for 30 seconds. They will wilt slightly. Drain carefully, so that all the water is removed, then place them on a hot serving dish. Pour over the oyster sauce and oil and serve immediately as a side dish.
Serves 2

Chinese Greens with Raisins and Vinegar

Sweet, mellow and piquant, a quick accompaniment which I have been known to eat as a light supper, with a rich pudding to follow.

450g/1lb choy sum, pak choi or mustard greens
3 tablespoons olive oil
2 cloves of garlic, peeled and chopped
2 tablespoons balsamic vinegar
a handful of golden raisins

Cut the greens into large bite-sized pieces. Heat the oil in a shallow pan and fry the garlic till pale gold in colour, then add the balsamic vinegar and raisins. As soon as the raisins plump up, throw in the greens. Fry for a minute, till they wilt, then season with salt and freshly ground pepper. Serve immediately as a side dish.
Serves 2

Gingered Mustard Greens

450g/1lb mustard greens or assorted Chinese greens
2 tablespoons groundnut oil
5cm/2in knob of root ginger, peeled and finely
   shredded
1 tablespoon sesame oil

Roughly chop the greens and rinse them under running
water. Heat the groundnut oil in a hot wok until it is very
hot, then add the ginger with a generous pinch or so of
both salt and freshly ground black pepper. Stir fry for a
few seconds, then add the washed leaves. Moving the
greens around the pan, cook for 2 minutes and then add
2 tablespoons of water. When the greens are hot, add the
sesame oil and serve immediately as a side dish.
Serves 2

A first attempt to cook these resulted in mild
disappointment. Like celery, rhubarb and that other
fleshy stalk chard, these Chinese cabbages are best
kept away from boiling water. The direct heat of a
hot wok will do wonders for such mild members of
the brassica family; a spell in boiling water, on the
other hand, dilutes their flavour. There is but a thin
line between the subtle and the tasteless.

Pak choi, also known as bok choy, bak cai and
Chinese celery cabbage, is just one of the subtly
piquant greens for those with access to Chinatown

or an imaginative market gardener. (They are easy to grow, but that is another matter.) Farmers in Hong Kong grow up to 20 different varieties. There are, in the words of Joy Larkcom, whose book *Oriental Vegetables* (John Murray) is a delight to both cook and gardener, 'jungles of Chinese vegetables – with different vegetables often called the same name, the same vegetable called by several names and botanists still arguing about what is the correct name'.

The most common of these oriental brassicas is what is often referred to as Chinese flowering cabbage, or choy sum. Anyone who has ventured into their local Chinese quarter cannot fail to have spotted these soft-leaved vegetables with their thin stalks, bright-green leaves and tiny yellow flower buds. Anyone who has bought a bunch out of curiosity only to pick out and discard the flower buds has rather missed the point. Unlike our own broccoli, this variety does not turn bitter when the buds open. It is said that the best flavour is to be had just when the flower heads appear. Whatever, the Chinese cook them for no more than two minutes.

Choy sum is not widely available yet, but I suspect it may be high on the lists of 'the powers that be', or should it be 'the powers that buy'? as a user-friendly alternative to their customers lugging home a huge cabbage.

The earliest (in historical terms) of cultivated greens are the excitingly flavoured mustard greens – the gai choy, or gaai choy. They are grown mostly to be pickled, though the escapees may end up being simply stir-fried – to my mind a better fate. The point of these, like any other cabbage, is their earthy astringency. Once tasted it is not difficult to believe that they were initially grown for their seeds, which form the mustard oil used in much oriental cooking. While the obvious flavourings of

Soy Choy

My inauthentic title for the savoury greens that grace my plate at least once a week. I have used pretty much every green going, and that includes lettuce.

450g/1lb pak choi, or other greens
1 tablespoon chilli oil
1 tablespoon groundnut oil
8 spring onions, finely chopped
1 tablespoon light soy sauce
1 tablespoon dark soy

Cut the greens, leaves and stems, into 5cm/2in lengths. Rinse them. Heat the two oils in a hot wok till very hot, almost smoking, then throw in the spring onions. Cook for 30 seconds, moving the onions around the pan all the time. Add the greens and stir and fry for no longer than a minute. Tip the light soy over the greens, give them a few seconds' more cooking, then tip on to a warm plate. Sprinkle with dark soy and eat immediately as a side dish.
Serves 2

Mixed Greens and Smoked Bacon

Mustard greens are great with bacon. Throw in pak choi too, or spinach or even Savoy cabbage. A fine accompaniment for sausages.

per person
100g/4oz fat, smoked bacon
1 tablespoon groundnut oil
350g/12oz assorted greens, chopped
ground black pepper

Fry the bacon in the oil in a shallow pan till it starts to crisp. The fat should be golden. Add the greens, and toss in the bacon and its fat. Fry for 1 or 2 minutes or till the greens have wilted and soaked up some of the smoky bacon fat. Season with pepper and serve while very hot.

the Chinese kitchen spring to mind as partners in the pot, northern ingredients such as cream, juniper and cheese successfully broaden the leaves' use in our kitchens.

Neither should the stalks be discarded. Unlike those of other European cabbages, they are a delicacy. I am always amazed that the Chinese manage to get broccoli stalks to taste so good. I am convinced it is as much in the cutting as the cooking. Slicing a stalk across the diagonal, as in Chinese roll-cutting, seems to render it magically tender. No doubt it is all in the wrist. With pak choi and the mustard greens, so unaccustomed to juicy brassicas are we that the stalks may well seem the best bit.

Those who have a taste for such things may like to try sprinkling mustard greens with salt, pouring off the resulting liquid, then packing the limp stems jarred with boiling vinegar, sugar, chillies and more salt. Frankly I'd rather have Britain's purple-red wimp's version.

As much as I find the big heads of our better-known brassicas an essential part of cold-weather cooking, I have rather taken to the soft, spicy, juicy leaves of the Chinese greens. I like the way they need nothing more than a quick rinse, their lack of fat slugs hiding between the leaves and their ability to be on the table in three minutes. I applaud their neat, chirpy posture ('bonny' is Joy Larkcom's superbly accurate term) and the fact that they don't take up my entire shopping bag like a crinkly-leaved Savoy. But best of all, I have got something soft and tender for my vegetable rack.

CHOCOLATE CAKE

I would kill for chocolate cake. I'm not fussy what sort. It could be the rich truffle cake of a famous chef or a home-made chocolate Victoria sponge from a cake-stall. It might be a *passé* chocolate roulade or a trendy chocolate tart. In desperation, it could even be a chocolate-flavour Swiss roll from the corner shop. But it must be chocolate cake.

I still remember my first one. Taken home from a childhood birthday party, its buttercream frosting sticking to the paper-serviette wrapping, mottled with the leaked colour from the Smarties on top. Crude though it was, and no doubt made with cocoa powder and milk chocolate, it would be as welcome today as some obscenely rich truffle cake.

There followed years of department-store teas, with tinkling china and waitresses in black dresses and white aprons, dispensing slices of cake from heavily laden trolleys. Sponges, covered in thin chocolate that shattered at the touch of pastry fork. If we were lucky, there was a tiny log of chocolate flake on top too. At home there was something called mini-rolls, made by Cadbury's and devoured quicker than you could peel off their thin gold wrappers.

But then the chocolate cake grew up. In the 1970s there was the flourless chocolate roulade, rolled around a thick core of whipped cream. The darling of every dinner party and the guest of honour at every wedding buffet, the roulade replaced the Black Forest gâteau, with its sublime marriage of black cherries and dark chocolate – though even in its heyday it was considered slightly common.

Chocolate Roulade

A classic chocolate cake that is worthy of a revival.

175g/6oz fine chocolate, broken into pieces
3 tablespoons hot water
5 eggs, separated
150g/5oz caster sugar
icing sugar
300ml/½ pint double cream

Line a shallow baking tin approximately 30 x 23cm/12 x 9in with tin foil or Bakewell non-stick paper. Melt the chocolate in a bowl over simmering water, stirring very occasionally. Remove from the heat and stir in the hot water. Beat the egg yolks and sugar with an electric whisk until thick and fluffy, then beat the chocolate mixture into the egg yolks and sugar.

Beat the egg whites until stiff and fold them gently but thoroughly into the chocolate mixture. Do not overmix, which will knock the air out. Scoop into the lined tin and bake in a preheated oven (180°C/350°F/Gas Mark 4) for 15 minutes. Remove from the oven and cover with a clean, slightly damp tea-towel.

Dust a sheet of greaseproof paper thickly with icing sugar. Tip the roulade out on to the icing sugar and carefully peel off the foil. Lightly whip the cream so that it stands in soft peaks and spread it over the roulade. Roll the cake up with the help of the sugared paper. Transfer to a long serving dish.

Serves 6–8

Chocolate, Prune and Roasted Almond Cake

The richest of all chocolate cakes, with the texture of a chocolate truffle, this should be served in thin slivers with whipped cream or ice-cream.

350g/12oz plain chocolate
200g/7oz unsalted butter
100g/4oz shelled hazelnuts
100g/4oz shelled brazil nuts
100g/4oz shelled almonds
2 eggs
100g/4oz soft dried prunes

Line a 20cm/8in-square cake tin, or its rectangular equivalent, with non-stick cooking parchment. Melt 225g/8oz of the chocolate and all the butter together in a heavy saucepan over a low heat.

Spread the nuts on a baking sheet or grill pan and toast in a hot oven or grill till the skins start to blister. Rub the nuts with a cloth, discarding the skins, which flake off, and return the nuts to the grill till they are golden brown.

When the chocolate is melted, remove from the heat and stir in the nuts. Beat the eggs lightly with a fork and add to the chocolate and nuts along with the fruit. Spoon the mixture into the lined cake tin and leave to set in the fridge overnight.

When completely set, remove from the tin and peel off the paper. Melt the remaining chocolate in a basin over simmering water, then pour over the cake and return to the fridge to set. With a large, heavy knife, cut the cake in half, then cut each half into 6 slices. Or keep in the fridge and cut as you wish.
Makes 12 slices

The mid-1980s brought with it something called truffle cake. A wedge, or sometimes a disc, of the richest imaginable cake. The texture was not dissimilar to butter, and was probably the least suitable ending for a meal, yet no restaurant menu was complete without it. The slice was usually accompanied by a heart-shaped slick of raspberry sauce. In line with the times, it was a case of 'let's see how rich we can get'.

Round about this time, a new sort of chocolate cake was appearing in American cookery books: shallow and dark with bitter chocolate, this was caky round the edges while almost molten in the centre. Like a chocolate Brie. It is easy to cook, but only a success if you remember to remove it from the oven while the middle is still wobbly. It sets on cooling. As far as 'smart' chocolate cakes go, this oozing disc of chocolate, eggs and ground almonds remains a favourite, despite some professional competition from the pâtisseries that seem to spring up like sponges in the night.

There are chocolate-cake extravaganzas too. The American food companies tempt us with their triple-choc layer cakes. Sweet and sickly, these layered confections of sponge and buttercream are really for those who prefer the taste of sugar to cocoa, but are better than no chocolate cake at all. And frankly preferable to the slice I recently ate from a very posh London pâtisserie that seemed to have involved a lot of work on the part of the cook (sponge, buttercream and a shiny glaze) to little effect. A sure case of style over substance.

Which brings me to the chocolate itself. Go for broke. Spending money on good chocolate for cooking is not a waste. The better the chocolate, the better the cake. A fine chocolate with a high cocoa-butter content (at least 60 per cent) will give a longer-lasting flavour and a denser texture than the cheap and cheerful types. I have also had trouble melting the household-name brands, probably due to the enormous quantity of sugar in them. Chocolate of this quality (high cocoa-butter content and very little sugar) does not come cheap.

But even the best chocolate cakes need a contrast. The sharp bite of Morello cherries (not the gobstopper sweet black jobbies), or the crunch of roasted nuts, or the tang of fresh raspberries. Strawberries and chocolate are not, at least in my mouth, a marriage made in heaven. Roasted nuts offer a warm bitterness, particularly almonds, and a crunchiness to add interest to the chocolaty goo. Hazelnuts and pecans are sublime with dark chocolate too. Less so walnuts – although I wouldn't say no to a walnut whip.

Not all cakes are demanding of the cook. A rich shallow cake with a fudgy centre can be whipped up in 15 minutes and takes little more than that to cook. A refrigerator cake, made by melting the mixture before setting it in the cool, is an option for those who want their cake but can't be bothered to cook it. It is a sound recipe, rich with butter, dark chocolate and nuts, more akin to a truffle than a cake, but has sadly been debased by horrid commercial versions piled high in delicatessens. The recipe opposite should put things to rights.

As with anything that is good to eat, there are rules about chocolate cake. The result must be moist, if not positively gooey, so don't overcook it. It must have an unwavering richness, so don't stint on the other ingredients, such as butter and eggs (it is supposed to be a treat, after all), and the flavour must be deep and long – which means using good-quality chocolate.

At the risk of sounding distinctly piggy, there are few better accompaniments to a slice of chocolate cake than a ball of ice-cream. Cold, hard ice-cream and soft, gooey chocolate cake. Vanilla or coffee seem the best match. Chocolate ice-cream would be a case of overkill – if not a case of death by chocolate.

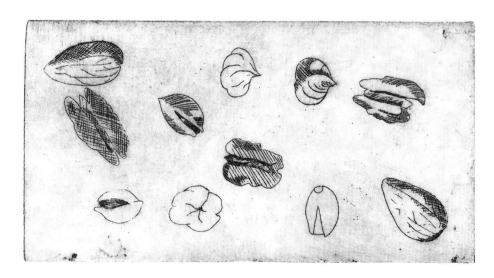

A Quick Chocolate Cake

A fudge-centred shallow chocolate cake. Accompany with vanilla or coffee ice-cream or crème fraîche.

150g/5oz fine chocolate

75g/3oz shelled hazelnuts

30g/1oz butter

2 tablespoons double cream

5 eggs, separated

3 tablespoons caster sugar

75g/3oz flour

25g/1oz cocoa powder, plus a little for dusting the finished cake

You will need either one of those spring-clip shallow cake tins or a deep tart tin with a tight-fitting removable base. Whichever, it should be about 20cm/8in in diameter, buttered and dusted with a little flour.

Set the oven to 180°C/350°F/Gas Mark 4. Break the chocolate into pieces and set it in a small bowl balanced over a pan of simmering water. Put the hazelnuts on a baking sheet and put them in the oven till the skins crack and flake. Rub them with a tea-towel; most of the skins will flake off. Chop them roughly, either with a large knife or in a food processor. Return them to the oven till they are golden brown.

When the chocolate has melted, stir in the butter, in little chunks, and the cream. Remove from the heat. Beat the egg whites till they stand in peaks; this will take seconds with an electric mixer. Fold in the sugar with a metal spoon. Do this tenderly but thoroughly.

Stir the egg yolks quickly into the chocolate, butter and cream. Fold in the flour, cocoa and hazelnuts. Fold this in turn into the egg whites and sugar. You must be careful here – the point is to mix the chocolate and egg-white mixtures scrupulously so that there are no streaks of white but the mixture is still light and full of air. Be thorough and gentle; a large metal spoon will help. The result will be rather like an unset chocolate mousse.

Pour it into the tin, scraping every little bit out of the bowl with a rubber spatula. Bake in the preheated oven for 15 minutes. The outer edges of the cake will be firm, like a sponge cake, the middle rather wobbly. If you take it out now, the cake will have a creamy soft centre. If you prefer something more cake-like, then leave it in for another 5 minutes. Any longer and you might as well have made an ordinary chocolate sponge cake.

Let the cake cool for 10 minutes or so, then slide a palette knife around the edge and remove the cake tin. Leave the cake on its base to cool further. Dust with cocoa powder if you wish, but this is not essential. Serve in small pieces on large plates, perhaps with crème fraîche.

COCONUT

Many Hindu rituals start with the offering of a broken coconut to Lord Ganesha, the elephant-headed god and the remover of all obstacles. And well they might. It has just taken me the best part of 20 minutes to break into this armour-plated nut and release its thin, sweet juice and moist, rich meat.

A coconut's existence must be one long holiday. The sandy beaches, blue skies and shady palm leaves of its tropical habitat must be the envy of our apple trees as they shiver under a covering of frost. It has even been known to take a dip in the warm tropical waters, and it is generally accepted that *Cocos nucifera* made its way round the tropics by the sea route, taking root easily in the salty, sandy coastal soil. Recipe books feature them in curries, creams and cakes, though I know them best as reasonably accurate sound-effects for cantering horses, and I remember my father smashing them in half and hanging them up for the blue tits in the garden. I shall never forget once being presented with an extremely embarrassing cocktail set in the hollowed out shell, complete with pink straws and a silly little paper parasol in an expensive hotel bar. But as one of India's largest exports, there has to be more to them than that.

I have never bought a coconut before, only won one, and I had no idea how long the row of coconuts had been sitting in the greengrocer's, on the shelf above the shallots. They all looked pretty much the same, offering no clue as to which was ripe or rotten. I asked for the heaviest, reckoning

HOW TO MAKE COCONUT MILK

There are two ways. First, using a fresh coconut, pierce the coconut through two of its three eyes with a skewer. They are wobbly things, so take care not to skewer yourself. An electric drill might appear to be going over the top, but it will do the job in seconds. Drain off the coconut water into a small bowl. Put the coconut into a hot oven and bake for 15 minutes. This will loosen the flesh from the shell without drying it out. Break the nut open with a hammer and remove the flesh.

Peel the thin brown skin away with a vegetable peeler or small knife. Cut the white flesh into small chunks and whiz in a food processor with the coconut water and half a pint of cold water. No food proccessor? Then grate large coconut pieces on the fine side of the grater before adding the waters.

Refrigerate for an hour. This is essential if the best of the flavour is to be extracted. Strain the liquid through a clean kitchen cloth – a new J-Cloth will do – squeezing hard to extract all the flavour. Discard the flesh and refrigerate the milk.

The second way involves using a block of creamed coconut. Make sure that the block you have is unsweetened. Slice it into chunks and dissolve in hot but not boiling water in a jug. Check the recommended ratio on the packet, but it should be about 75g/3oz of creamed coconut to 150ml/5fl oz.

Quick Coconut Chicken

A simple chicken sauté in a spiced coconut sauce.

1 tablespoon groundnut oil
4 chicken pieces (thighs and drumsticks have the
    best flavour)
1 medium onion, finely chopped
2 cloves of garlic, sliced
2.5cm/1in knob of ginger, grated
1 cinnamon stick
2 small hot chillies, seeded and chopped
½ teaspoon ground turmeric
75g/3oz creamed coconut
2 tablespoons coriander leaves, chopped
rice to serve

Heat the groundnut oil in a shallow-sided pan, add the chicken pieces and cook till the skin is golden. Turn down the heat, cover, and continue cooking until the juices run clear when the flesh is pierced with a skewer, about 20 minutes. Remove chicken and set aside.

Cook the onion in the same pan till translucent. Add the garlic and ginger and cook for 2 minutes, stirring so that the mixture does not stick. Add the cinnamon stick, broken in half, the chillies and the turmeric and continue to cook for 2 minutes. At this point the onions should be tender but not browned and the mixture golden.

Dissolve the coconut in 240ml/8fl oz hot water. Stir into the spiced onions and cook over a low heat, stirring all the time, till warmed through. Add the chicken and cook, without boiling, for 10–15 minutes. Correct the consistency of the sauce with a little more coconut milk or, if it is thinner than you would like, with 1 or 2 lumps of creamed coconut from the block. Stir in the chopped coriander leaves and serve with rice.

Serves 2

on the same clue to quality as with other tropical fruit such as passionfruit and pineapples. The liquid sloshing around inside must mean the flesh is moist and far from dried out.

The textbook method of breaking into a coconut involves a vice, a drill and a hammer, only one of which I possess. I barely know which end of a screwdriver to use, let alone how to set up a coconut in a vice. But I know I want the liquid from inside and that I shall lose it if I attempt to smash the nut without draining it first. Pierce two of three eyes, say my instructions. These lurk under the thick tuft of coarse fibres on top, but no one tells you that. Then it's a question of prising the tough little tuft away from the shell with a blunt knife. No wonder they are the principal ingredient in a doormat. Piercing the shell through the weak spots gives me a small glassful of thin, opaque liquid.

Store it in the fridge and use in cocktails, I read. I am not really a cocktail sort of person, so I'll just store it in the fridge. This somewhat disappointing liquid is coconut water, and not the famed coconut milk I am really after. Entry to the inner core of white flesh was provided by a couple of swift blows of the blunt end of a hammer. I wish I had put it in a plastic bag first – I may be picking up coconut shrapnel for the next week. The flesh pulls away easily from the shell with the help of a small knife. I am supposed to peel the thin brown skin off with a potato peeler but cannot wait to taste.

I can think of nothing that has the same texture as a slice of white coconut flesh. It is crisp and moist, dense and delicate, tender and chewy. And nothing whatsoever like the white sawdust that masqueraded as coconut throughout my childhood on sandcastle-shaped sponge cakes covered in jam, or mixed in with the chocolate coating for favourite shaving-foam marshmallows.

Every tropical cuisine exploits the rich flesh of the coconut: in Sri Lanka they flavour custards with it; in Pakistan they use it to make a fresh chutney with coriander and chillies; Malaysian cooks spread coconut over fish fillets with garam masala, lemon and coriander, and steam them; and in Thailand they make a green curry scented with basil and lemon. Here in Britain we have the Bounty Bar.

The real joy of the coconut is the fabulously rich, creamy milk extracted from the grated flesh. This is the stuff that mellows the spice notes in an Indian curry and softens the sometimes harsh effect of chilli-hot dishes from South-East Asia. There are three ways to prepare it: by steeping flakes of desiccated coconut in water; by diluting a block of prepared creamed coconut; and by grating the fresh nut and making a mulch with water.

I am not convinced of the revived desiccated-coconut method, even though experienced Asian

Coconut Rice

I first encountered this on a plane in a little plastic tray. It smelled good but was a little dry. This, I think, is a better version.

400g/14oz long-grain rice
750ml/1¼ pints coconut milk
1 tablespoon coriander leaves, chopped

Put the rice and coconut milk into a heavy-based saucepan with 1½ teaspoons of salt. Bring the mixture to the boil, then turn down the heat to a low simmer and stir to mix. Cover with a lid and simmer for 15 minutes. Lift the lid to see if the coconut milk has been absorbed. Cook for a few minutes longer if it has not. Stir gently with a fork and serve.
Serves 2–4 as an accompaniment

Broccoli and Coconut Soup

A light yet rich soup, soothing and mildly aromatic. Finding it difficult to think of coconut without coriander, I would add a tablespoon as the soup is served, but that is purely optional. An unusual soup to be served in small amounts.

120ml/4fl oz coconut milk
2.5cm/1in knob of ginger, peeled and finely
  chopped
2 stalks of lemon grass, cut into fine shreds
600ml/1 pint vegetable stock
450g/1lb broccoli, broken into small florets
1 teaspoon of sugar
2 tablespoons light soy sauce
2 small, mild green chillies, finely chopped
juice of ½ a lemon

Place the milk, ginger, lemon grass, vegetable stock and broccoli in a large saucepan and bring to the boil. Turn down the heat immediately and simmer till the broccoli is tender, about 15–20 minutes. Add the sugar, soy, chillies and lemon juice.

Serves 4

As a quick snack with drinks, peel hunks of coconut and sprinkle them with sea salt.

cooks recommend it. It lacks fragrance and body, no matter how high the ratio of flakes to water. Having just made my own coconut milk I would be grateful for a short cut. I have baked the whole nut till the flesh popped cleanly away from the shell, then peeled and chopped it, whizzed the little pieces of white flesh in the processor and steeped it in water for a couple of hours. The worst part was squeezing the liquid through a clean J-Cloth, twice. The result was a sweet scented white milk. But not a lot of it for the effort.

Creamed coconut, on the other hand, is one of the better culinary short cuts I have come across. At its best it has nothing added in the way of oils and sugars, but that is something you will have to check on the side of the packet. I cannot think why anyone would add sugar to anything so naturally sweet and unctuous, but they do. But in its purest form, the hard white block, slightly greasy to the touch, is something of a godsend. I quickly learned to break bits off and stir them into an enthusiastically spiced chicken sauté, and to mix lumps of the cream in the blender with double cream to give an instant coconut sauce. I have mixed the grated fresh nuts with bananas, chillies and yoghurt as an accompaniment to grilled chicken and have even made a coconut gravy for soaking up fluffy rice. Everything, in fact, except covered it in chocolate.

COFFEE

I am high in the Andes and desperate for a drinkable cup of coffee. Despite Colombia's reputation, everything I have drunk so far has been uniformly filthy. It would appear that finding a fine cup of coffee here is on a par with tracking down a decent Sunday lunch in England.

Colombia exports most of its best coffee. And its best is very good indeed. The average cup of coffee drunk here in Colombia is made with beans that are sound, but far from the very best. If you want a coffee that is exciting you have to know where to look or buy it at home. Which explains why I am 1800 feet above sea level, slightly dizzy and short of breath, in search of the finest high-grown coffees this beautiful, tropical and exhilarating country has to offer. The steep hillsides, spiked with banana trees and coffee bushes that seem to be holding on for dear life, drop hundreds of feet below me. (Much of the coffee is harvested by pickers tied on to ropes.) I ate no supper last night. Heights, humidity and hunger are not really my thing.

I am not doing this alone. I have a guide whose place in the coffee trade goes back three generations. Sandra Marshall has accompanied me over hundreds of miles in the back of a Land Rover, bumping and jolting along, swerving round the rockfalls that litter the path, dodging the dusty 1950s Dodge trucks festooned with fairy lights and piled to the gills with bulging coffee sacks. I am wondering if her bottom is as bruised and numb as mine is. Sandra is the antithesis of the power-smug woman coffee buyer on the television advert, the

Coffee Mascarpone Trifle

A cross between a classic layered trifle and a creamy, liquorous and indulgent tiramisu.

225g/8oz mascarpone
3 eggs, separated
3 tablespoons caster sugar
1 tablespoon espresso coffee
120ml/4fl oz strong coffee
3 tablespoon brandy
100g/4oz boudoir biscuits (sponge fingers)
120ml/4fl oz double cream
1 tablespoon very finely ground coffee
1 tablespoon cocoa powder
a few coffee beans for decoration

With an electric beater, mix the mascarpone till soft, then beat the egg yolks and sugar together till just creamy and mix gently into the mascarpone. Pour in the tablespoon of espresso coffee and stir till thoroughly mixed.

Stir the brandy into the strong coffee. Break the sponge fingers into chunks and put them in a serving bowl. Pour over the coffee and brandy. Beat the egg whites till stiff, then fold into the mascarpone mixture. Fold gently into the coffee-soaked sponge fingers and mix lightly. Leave to set in the fridge for 1 or 2 hours, covered with cling film or a plate.

Gently whip the cream. It should form soft waves rather than stiff peaks. Smooth the cream on top of the trifle. Sift the coffee and cocoa together and dust over the cream. Serve immediately, or at least within the hour. *Serves 6*

Chocolate-covered Roasted Coffee Beans

**75g/3oz dark chocolate, at least 54 per cent
  cocoa solids
30g/1oz medium roast coffee beans**

Melt the chocolate by breaking it into squares and warming it in a small basin over a pan of hot water. When the chocolate is liquid, stir gently once or twice, then add the roasted coffee beans. Stir to coat the beans, then lift them out with a fork and drop them on to a plate or marble slab covered with non-stick baking parchment. Separate each bean with a skewer, then leave to harden. Remove the beans with a palette knife and keep in an air-tight jar.

Alternatively, and I think better, drop the wet chocolate coated beans on to a plate or slab covered thickly with sieved good quality cocoa powder. Separate as above and leave to harden.

Creamy Iced Coffee

You never quite know what to expect when you order iced coffee. The name means different things to different people. This version is light and creamy but with a deep coffee flavour. The better the coffee, the better the result.

**240ml/8fl oz strong, fresh coffee, chilled
1 tablespoon caster sugar
240ml/8fl oz crushed ice cubes
3 tablespoons double cream**

Pour the coffee, sugar and crushed ice into a blender or food processor. Mix until light brown and frothy. Stir in the double cream, pour into 2 glasses and serve immediately.
Serves 2

one who runs her hand through sacks of dark roasted coffee and buys them all for 'instant' – an absurdity, I suspect, as I notice coffee is usually roasted only in small amounts for buyers to taste. It is normally shipped green and unroasted.

We are heading for a farm that grows a particularly fine coffee, arguably the finest in Colombia. I am hot and sticky and pretending that I am enjoying myself. As the coffee bushes, healthy with their gleaming leaves and red, green and orange berries, get thicker on the ground and the cries of parakeets get louder, we turn along the roughest track of all. I am going to protest. I have already been woken by an explosion too close for comfort, searched at gunpoint by some seriously dodgy guys in combat gear, who may or may not have been soldiers, and spent a night unconscious on the bathroom floor, too sick even to crawl into bed. And I could kill for a cup of coffee.

The farm is a small single-storey building with a flat roof. The pretty cottage garden has a horse, pigs and children running amok, and a turkey I wouldn't turn my back on. The view over the mountains is literally breathtaking – lush, warm and staggeringly beautiful. From the hearth in the kitchen comes the smell of coffee. A dark, rich smell, quite subtle at first, gradually getting stronger. The smell is of beans being roasted in a pan over the coals. The coffee beans I usually see are dark brown, so it comes as something of a surprise to see them slowly changing from a soft sage green to a rich deep brown. They are constantly tossed and moved around the pan so as to roast evenly.

Within minutes they are ground and I am drinking the result: a fragrant, velvety cup with a long, bright flavour. Perhaps it is my imagination, but could this be the best-tasting cup of coffee I have ever had? Or could my senses be overwhelmed

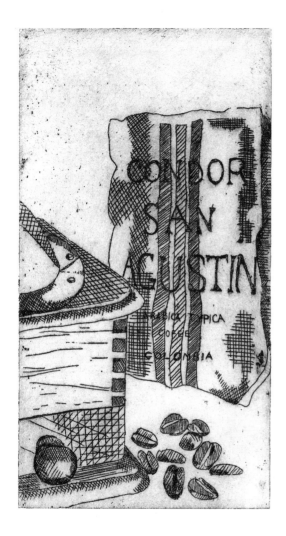

Coffee Granita

A granita is nothing more than sweetened, flavoured ice crystals. It is a refreshing alternative to ice-cream and can be made with fruit juice, wine or coffee. Even frozen, you will get the true coffee flavour.

1.2l/2 pints freshly made, strong black coffee
6 tablespoons sugar
6 tablespoons softly whipped double cream or
   crème fraîche

Sweeten the coffee with the sugar and stir until the sugar has dissolved. Pour the coffee into a large, shallow container – a plastic one will be easier to work with. Allow to cool, then freeze overnight.

Next day you will have a coffee-coloured block – its high sugar content will ensure that it has not frozen like a brick. Using a blunt knife, smash the coffee ice into crystals, then stir and spoon into 6 chilled glasses. Spoon the double cream or crème fraîche on top of each glass and serve immediately.
Serves 6

by the view, the thin air, the squawking wild life and the aroma coming from the hearth? Or could it be that only a few minutes ago the beans were drying on the flat roof of the farm in the blazing Colombian sun?

These beans are part of the tiny 2 per cent of Colombian coffee from around San Agustín. They are grown on an old variety of bush rather than the new disease-resistant, heavy-cropping strains that are being introduced all over the country. Although you get less beans per bush and a careful watch must be maintained for disease, the resulting coffee is far finer than that from the modern hybrid bushes.

Hacking away at the undergrowth and shaded by the huge banana palms overhead, I feel like Indiana Jones – though I look more like Alan Bennett. A few feet in front of me is Felipe Isaza Piedrahita, a coffee exporter passionate about the rare coffee of San Agustín and determined to make it better known. Picking oranges on the way and delighting in the jasmine smell of the coffee blossom, I am trying hard not to think about the snakes that no doubt lie underfoot. I spot the pickers in their vivid purple, pink and green bandannas with their collecting sacks around their waists. They are working the bushes, carefully picking only the ripest 'cherries', as the beans are known at that point. Coffee bushes boast flowers, immature and ripe beans all at once, making picking slow and labour intensive.

I am mesmerised by the machine into which these freshly picked cherries are dumped. It sucks them down like a whirlpool into the well-worn drum that strips the beans of their claret-red flesh, then spews them out into concrete fermenting tanks. Soon the green beans will be on the roof, drying in the baking sun. Which is pretty much where I came in.

I am not sure I can live without my morning kick start of coffee. I use the stuff in cooking too, finding that most of the coffee flavourings and essences I come across lack a true flavour. Once the weather warms up, I take to making coffee milk shakes, iced coffee and even sparkling granita. I have dipped roasted coffee beans in dark bitter chocolate for an after-dinner treat and occasionally indulge in a creamy coffee-scented trifle.

And anyone who likes the clear, winy, velvety notes of Colombian coffee will be pleased to know that a small quantity of rare San Agustín beans can now be found here in Britain – especially good news for those who cannot face vertigo, guns and food poisoning before their morning coffee.

CROISSANTS

The croissants I buy in my local shops are often better than those I have eaten in France. By better I mean flakier, lighter and more buttery (the thin dough they are made from is lightened with yeast and made rich with butter). Even the major chain stores, not renowned for their pâtisserie, can turn their hand to a croissant, even though the shape is less well defined and they need a spell in the oven before consumption. But then the croissant is not French.

The croissant hails from Budapest, which may explain why a French woman once told me, 'Only tourists eat croissants for breakfast; we all eat corn flakes like everyone else.' In France they are now more often consumed as a snack, split and filled with anything from warm spinach and cheese to fried onions and thinly sliced ham.

In 1686, when the Turks were besieging Budapest and were digging underground passages to reach the hub of the city, it was the town's bakers on night-shift who discovered and foiled their plans. The bakers were then granted the privilege of baking a pastry in the form of the crescent on the Ottoman flag – which would be akin to our bakers being permitted to produce a crumpet in the shape of Princess Anne.

These light, rich pastries, washed down with coffee and preceded by a little glass pot of yoghurt, form my daily breakfast. My constitution can no longer tolerate bacon and sausage at the start of the day (though I do like porridge in the depths of winter and would add that you really haven't lived

Chèvre, Thyme and Sun-dried Tomatoes

2 large croissants
2 sun-dried tomatoes preserved in oil
100g/4oz goats' cheese, preferably cut from a 'log'
a few fresh thyme leaves, chopped

Preheat the grill. Slice the croissants horizontally and place under the grill and lightly cook both cut sides. Slice the tomatoes into thin strips. Remove the croissants from the heat and scatter the tomatoes over the bottom halves with a little of their oil. Sprinkle with a few chopped thyme leaves and cover with the cheese, in thin overlapping slices.

Return the laden halves to the grill, leave till the cheese melts slightly and then cover with the upper half. Eat immediately.
Serves 2

Parmesan Croissants

A life-saving snack when there is little else in the house to eat.

Split a large croissant horizontally, butter both cut sides generously then cover with a thick layer of finely grated Parmesan. Add 1 or 2 dots of butter to each half, then place under a preheated grill till the cheese colours lightly. Watch that it does not burn, which it is inclined to do the moment you turn your back.

Eat the halves of cheese croissant while they are still hot, perhaps with a little salad. A croissant should be enough for 1 person.

Camembert Croissants with Green Peppercorns and Tomato

1 teaspoon bottled green peppercorns, rinsed of
  their brine
40g/1½oz butter at room temperature
2 large croissants
75g/3oz ripe Camembert
1 ripe plum tomato

Preheat the grill. Crush the peppercorns, then mash with
the soft butter. Slice each croissant in half, toast the flat
sides under the grill till lightly coloured and then spread
with the peppercorn butter. Cover with thin slices of
Camembert and grill till bubbling. Serve with slices of
ripe plum tomato, seasoned with a little black pepper.
Serves 2

Stuffed Croissants with Mozzarella and Onion Chutney

Split and toast the croissants, then spread the bottom half
of each with a spicy chutney. It could be tomato or onion
chutney, but should be well spiced to balance the bland
milky cheese. Cover the chutney with thinly sliced
mozzarella, overlapping the slices here and there, then
grill till bubbling but not brown (when the cheese would
go tough, just as it does on an overcooked pizza).
Replace the top half and eat while warm.

till you have eaten a dish of cold trifle at 8 o'clock
in the morning). I shop for food daily but venture
in the direction of the croissant shop only every
other day, which means that my croissant is
sometimes fresher than others. I do not butter it –
the butter is already in there, though I am partial to
a spot of jelly or jam.

The croissant makes an elegant, satisfying snack.
You can use a slightly stale one, as they crisp up
well enough in a hot oven. Slice them in half
horizontally, toast them under a hot grill and stuff
them with something that flatters their flaky
texture. Their inherent crispness is a suitable
partner for melting cheese and crisp bacon, pan-
fried mushrooms with butter and garlic, and
raspberries and softly whipped cream. Unlike the
soft, doughy texture of a sandwich, what you end
up with is a light, crisp holdall for those things too
hot, creamy or sticky to hold in your hand.

Some of the most bizarre-sounding fillings for
hot croissants have proved themselves worthy of
note. Sweet mincemeat and sharp crème fraîche for
instance, or mozzarella cheese and hot onion
chutney – the mild white cheese softening into the
spicy chutney in the heat.

In a moment of bare-cupboardness, I made a
perfectly acceptable snack by splitting a croissant
and spreading both halves with a little butter,
sprinkling with grated Parmesan and grilling till the
cheese turned slightly golden. This little snack, born
out of desperation (it was raining and I was
hungry), served me well and has now become a
favourite light lunch to eat while I am working.

Another adaptation is a quick version of the
croque monsieur, the French snack involving thin
slices of ham and Gruyère cheese on hot toast.
Using a croissant instead of bread adds a crisp
element and allows you to dispense with knife and
fork. The French have been stuffing croissants for

Croissants with Hot Apples and Crème Fraîche

generous 30g/1oz butter
1 large dessert apple
2 tablespoons caster sugar
2 large croissants
3 tablespoons crème fraîche

Melt the butter in a shallow pan. Halve and core the apple and cut into about 10 segments. Cook the apple in the butter till tender, turning once to cook the other side, then add the sugar and cook over a high heat until the mixture caramelises (it should turn a rich golden colour; if the edges of the apples catch slightly then so much the better).

Split the croissants in half and warm under the grill. Spoon crème fraîche and some of the hot apple slices on to the bottom halves, then pour over the remaining buttery sauce and replace the top halves.
Serves 2

years, though thankfully with more suitable fillings than I have spotted recently in sandwich bars here in Britain. Taramasalata and salad is one of the least appealing I have encountered to date. The best was salty Roquefort cheese and crumbled walnuts.

Such a snack, if it is to be really good, needs a little care in preparation. The croissant itself should be as good an example as you can find outside, presumably, Budapest. It should be of reasonable size if the filling is to be confined in a tidy fashion, and the pastry should not be so stale that you can barely cut it. Slice it horizontally and lightly toast both sides. Lay a suitable filling on the bottom half (otherwise the finished sandwich will wobble) and return that half only to the grill or oven. Place the top half on the hot filling and press gently. The filling should ooze slightly from its flaky pastry shell.

Like all the best food, this sort of snack must be eaten as soon as it is ready; such fare loses all interest once the filling becomes tepid. Anything that can be as simple and sumptuous as a croissant stuffed to the gills with unctuous cheese and spiced chutney deserves more, in my kitchen at least, than to be squandered early in the morning on the hurried and the barely conscious.

A FEW OTHER THINGS WITH WHICH TO STUFF A CROISSANT

Figs and Clotted Cream

Slice a couple of croissants in half and lightly toast both cut sides. For each croissant, warm 2 tablespoons of fig jam in a small non-stick pan, slice a ripe fresh fig and place the slices on a toasted half. Put dollops of clotted cream (about 2 tablespoons) over the fig, then drizzle over the warmed fig jam. Top with the second half and serve hot.

Roquefort and Walnut

Crumble a generous quantity of Roquefort (or Cashel Blue, Gorgonzola or Stilton) over the bottom half of a split and toasted croissant. Scatter a few broken walnuts on top and place in the oven or under the grill until the cheese has started to melt. Take care that the nuts do not burn.

Creamed Eggs and Grilled Onions

For each croissant, toasted as above, brush 2 small spring onions with olive oil and grill until golden. Prepare scrambled eggs for 1 with a little butter, then fold in 1 or 2 spoonfuls of fromage frais while the eggs are still creamy. Spoon the creamed eggs, carefully seasoned with salt and black pepper, on to the bottom half of the toasted croissant and top with the grilled onions. Place the remaining half on top and serve warm.

Chocolate and Vanilla Ice-cream

Crisp flaky pastry is just the thing to hold rich melted chocolate and a creamy vanilla ice. Melt some dark fine chocolate in a small bowl over hot water. Split and toast 1 or 2 croissants. Sandwich the croissant halves together with balls of good quality ice-cream and pour over the melted dark chocolate. Replace the top half of the croissant and eat just as the ice-cream starts to melt into the hot chocolate.

CURRY

Fragrance comes second only to flavour in my book. This is what brings me to the table. It is true to say that some cuisines are more fragrant than others; Thai cooking, with its fresh, clean waft of ginger, limes and chillies, is as inviting as the warm, sweet notes of the caramelising onions and garlic of French country cooking. Indian cooking, with spices as its heart and soul, is perhaps the most fragrant of all.

Although all spices add to the combined flavour of an Indian dish, some in particular are added simply because of the aroma they lend to the food. I am unaware of any other cuisine that adds an ingredient purely for its olfactory interest, with the possible exception of the orange-blossom and rose-water used by Persian and Moroccan cooks.

Garam masala, the personal mixture of spices used by all Indian cooks, is a prime example of the attention paid by them to the matter of aroma in a dish. The flavour it adds is the same whether fried at the beginning of a recipe with the onions and spices that provide the flavour base of the dish or scattered over the finished result just prior to being served. But in most cases, garam masala is stirred in at the end, contributing dramatically to the aroma of the food.

Camellia Panjabi's 50 *Great Curries of India* (Kyle Cathie) lists several spices used by Indian cooks for adding aroma to food. They include cardamoms, both green and black, nutmeg, cinnamon leaf, mace, star anise, rose petals and saffron. Five of these are on my spice shelf, though

Chicken Dopiaza

A Bengali dish from Camellia Panjabi's book. The onion-rich dish is particularly aromatic – with cinnamon, cardamom, cloves and garam masala. It gets its name from *do*, meaning 2, and *piaz*, the Hindi for onions. If your onions are anything larger than the size of a table-tennis ball, either cut them in quarters rather than halves or cook for a little longer. The cups used for liquid measures contain 200ml/7fl oz.

1.25/2½lb small roasting chicken
9 medium onions
8 small potatoes (optional)
3 teaspoons red chilli powder
½ cup full-fat yoghurt
½ cup oil
6 plump cloves of garlic, finely chopped
2 cinnamon or bay leaves
5cm/2in cinnamon stick
6 cardamoms
1½ teaspoons peppercorns
12 cloves
3 whole red chillies
2 tablespoons ginger purée
½ teaspoon turmeric
2 tomatoes, chopped
1 tablespoon butter
¾ teaspoon sugar
1½ teaspoons garam masala powder
salt

Cut the chicken into 8 pieces on the bone. Cut 3 of the onions in half. Chop 2 of the onions coarsely. Extract the juice from the remaining 4 onions by grating them and squeezing out the juice through a cheesecloth, discarding the pulp.

Peel the potatoes, if using. Mix the chilli powder to a paste with a little water. Whisk the yoghurt.

Heat the oil in a heavy pan and fry the chopped onions until light brown. Remove, drain on kitchen paper and set aside. In the same oil, fry the garlic with the bay leaves and, after a couple of minutes, add the cinnamon and cardamoms. Then, 2 minutes later, add the peppercorns, cloves and whole red chillies.

After 30 seconds, add the ginger purée, chilli paste and turmeric and stir continuously. Add the chicken, potatoes and tomatoes, followed by the butter, yoghurt and sugar. Cook for 10–12 minutes, stirring so that the spices do not stick to the bottom of the pan, and add a little water if necessary.

Now add the onion halves, followed by the onion juice and salt to taste. Stir for 2–3 minutes, then transfer to a baking dish and cook in the oven, preheated to 160°C/325°F/Gas Mark 3, for 20–25 minutes. When the chicken and potatoes are done, add half the fried onions and sprinkle over the garam masala powder. Sprinkle over the remaining onions just before serving.
Serves 4

A Quick Lamb Curry

A straightforward curry recipe for those who have little time to cook. The juices, though rich with cream and yoghurt, are unthickened, so serve the dish with rice to soak them up.

700g/1½lb cubed lamb
2 tablespoons groundnut oil
2 medium onions, chopped
4 cloves of garlic, finely sliced
4cm/1½in knob of fresh root ginger, peeled and
   grated

not cinnamon leaf, which is not quite what it sounds, actually the cinnamon-flavoured leaf from a tree similar to that from which the long, aromatic scrolls of cinnamon come. I long to sniff this leaf, sadly difficult to locate at present in the West.

This book contains the first reference I have seen to adding ingredients purely for their effect on the smell of a dish; it is also the first time I have had the thickening, souring, colouring and spicing agents used in Indian food explained to me with such precision. It will delight, educate and inspire anyone who longs to make authentic curries at home. The first 50 pages of introduction to the subject make particularly fascinating reading: 'Curry powder in the form it is known now in the West was invented in Madras, to be exported to England for use by the English who had become addicted to curry.'

I am happy to use highly fragrant spices such as cardamom and cinnamon in my cooking just for their smell alone. Saffron too, its golden filaments collected from the purple crocus fields of Kashmir. I will also try the sun-dried petals from the miniature and intensely scented Indian rose, ground to a powder, in my next creamy chicken Korma.

But the most tempting fragrance of all is when freshly ground spices are warmed in butter and stirred into the dish at the last moment. This spice-perfumed butter is known as *tadka* and is one of the simplest ways to aromatise food. For some dishes, nutty clarified butter, warmed with cumin seed, cayenne pepper, garam masala and chopped fresh coriander, is poured over steaming dhal, the lid clapped on tight, then lifted off, minutes later, at the table. The spiced and perfumed butter, inhaled by the diner as the lid is removed, is the gastronomic answer to aromatherapy.

Sad, really, that such a magically smelling and warming embellishment is confined to Indian food.

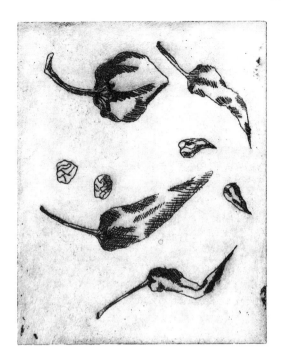

1 medium-sized, medium-hot chilli pepper
8 green cardamom pods
1 teaspoon coriander seeds, freshly ground
1 tablespoon ground turmeric
1 teaspoon ground cumin
240ml/8fl oz good chicken stock
120ml/4fl oz yoghurt
90ml/3fl oz double cream
1 tablespoon lemon juice
1 tablespoon coriander leaves, chopped

Lightly brown the lamb in half of the oil in a deep-sided pan over a high heat. Remove the lamb and set aside. Cook the onion, garlic, ginger and chilli in the remaining oil. Remove the black seeds from the cardamom pods and crush them using a pestle and mortar. When the onion is soft, add the coriander and cook for 3 minutes over a moderate heat, stirring. Add the turmeric and cardamom and stir for 1 minute, then add the ground cumin. Cook till all is fragrant, about a minute longer, taking care that the spices do not burn.

Return the lamb to the pan and stir to coat with the onion and spices. Pour in the stock and bring to the boil. Season with salt and pepper, then cover and simmer till the lamb is tender, about 25 minutes at a low simmer. When the lamb is done to your liking mix the yoghurt and cream and stir in. Simmer gently, then stir in the lemon juice and coriander leaves and serve.
Serves 2 with rice

If Indian cooks can add such a delectable potion to their dhals, then why don't we use it to add interest to vegetable purées or thick soups? Stir it into chopped cabbage or spinach or, probably best of all, into a thick mash of root vegetables, such as parsnips or carrots. Mash them to a pulp, then pile them into a hot dish, pour over the hot spiced butter then cover tightly until you take off the lid to eat. The smell will hit you long before you begin, teasing and tempting, making it impossible not to dig in.

To deliberately add fragrance to your cooking in this way is to create a dish which truly delights all the senses, heightening the pleasure of eating even before you start. More than just a bonus or accident, more than just a by-product of the cooking process, it is an essential part of the meal, second only to flavour, and is one that Indian cooks seem to have down to a fine art.

A Deeply Fragrant Spiced Butter

100g/4oz ghee or clarified butter
1 teaspoon cumin seed
225g/8oz finely chopped onions
2 cloves of garlic, finely sliced
2 bay leaves
¼ teaspoon cayenne pepper
2 tablespoons coriander leaves, finely chopped

Heat the butter gently in a frying pan over a low heat. When it is hot add the cumin seeds. Fry them in the butter for about 15 seconds or until they darken slightly. Take care that they do not burn. Add the onions, garlic and bay leaves and cook until deep golden brown, stirring from time to time. This will take about 15–20 minutes, by which time the kitchen will smell wonderful.

Stir in the cayenne pepper and the coriander leaves and pour over lentils or whatever. Close the lid then take to the table. Serve hot.

Use this spiced butter on any of the following:

- yellow or red lentils, cooked till tender then whipped into a purée with a wooden spoon (the above mixture is enough for 300g/10oz lentils);
- mashed potatoes, creamed with only a little butter, the spiced butter poured over, then stirred in at the table;
- a purée of any of the following: swede, carrot, parsnip or beetroot;
- lightly cooked and chopped spinach, cabbage or greens;
- rice, steamed or simmered;
- soft scrambled eggs, the spice butter stirred in when the eggs are still creamy and served immediately, though not for breakfast;
- tinned butter beans, warmed, drained and mashed to a purée.

Or, after adding the *tadka* to any of the above, pour over about 120ml/4fl oz of double cream, finishing with more coriander. Especially good with potatoes and root vegetables.

DUMPLINGS

I long to taste my landlady's dumplings again. At 19, the smell of her beef stew, albeit more carrots than meat, was the only thing that would get me out of bed on a Saturday morning. The boys, as she referred to her lodgers, ate after the family, while her husband marked exercise books and she marched off to do the church flowers, leaving us all to fight over the remaining gravy-saturated lumps of flour and suet.

If the next few years are to be, as I suspect, good years for British cooking, I may be seeing more of those comforting dough-balls. They are already on the menus of several of the country's better restaurants, so it is only a matter of time before the stubble-chin brigade catches on. Born to fill hungry families before they got a chance at the beef ('no broth no ball; no ball no beef,' wrote Cranford), dumplings may now find themselves the next in line for the stodge crown.

I have not tried the earliest and crudest of dumplings, made with leftover bread dough from the day's baking, dropped into the pot for lunch. These might be good time-saver for those who bake their own bread, but they are not really the dumplings I hanker after. Neither are the tiringly fashionable gnocchi, made with potato, egg and a little olive oil. I am after something lighter, yet with enough body to soak up juice from its mother dish without dissolving into it.

A traditional suet dumpling contains half as much fat as flour. Unless you are grating your own suet, the mixing of the flour, fat and herbs with

Parsley Dumplings

Traditionalists do not need reminding that a classic dumpling must contain suet but may be interested to know that dried vegetable suet, made from palm oil, is available as an alternative. Fresh suet needs grating and chopping finely so that no large pieces remain.

100g/4oz flour
salt
50g/2oz shredded suet
2 tablespoons parsley, finely chopped
stock or broth

Sift the flour into a large basin, add salt and stir in the suet and parsley. Mix gently with a little water to form a soft but not sticky dough. Roll into balls about the size of a small egg. Bring a deep pan of stock to the boil, turn down to a rolling boil and drop in the dumplings. Cover and cook for 15–20 minutes till cooked right through.
Makes 8–12 dumplings or 16 smaller ones

Thyme and Bacon Dumplings

These are my favourite addition to a rich chicken soup. I ate them last night with nothing more than a bowl of home-made chicken stock – a soothing supper indeed. They have the advantage of turning a bowl of soup, home-made or a decent commercial brand if you can find one, into a substantial supper in minutes.

3 rashers of smoked fatty bacon, diced
1 small onion, finely chopped
the leaves of 4 small sprigs of thyme, chopped

Heat the diced bacon in a small pan till the fat runs. (If you cannot find any fat, then add an ounce of butter.) Fry the onion with the thyme in the fat until the onion is soft and golden. Season with salt and pepper and add to either of the above dumpling mixtures. Cook in lightly boiling stock as above if using suet, if not they can be added to any casserole or soup.

GOOD THINGS TO ADD TO THE BASIC DUMPLING RECIPE

- chopped fresh thyme
- lightly browned, chopped onions
- chopped mushrooms, cooked in a little butter
- fried smoked, diced bacon
- creamed horseradish and chopped parsley
- chopped toasted walnuts

GOOD THINGS TO WHICH TO ADD DUMPLINGS

- chicken soup or clear broth
- vegetable stew or soup
- classic stews and casseroles: Irish stew, Hungarian goulash, *coq au vin*
- onion soup (one without the bread topping), minestrone or clear Japanese miso broth

enough water to make a stiffish dough will take all of five minutes. Cooking the balls of dough in boiling stock, or in the gravy itself, will take little more than 15 minutes. The result will be rib-sticking in the extreme and as comforting as a hot-water bottle.

Flavour, for once, isn't really the point. It is the dumplings' duty to act as a spoiler to the precious meat and sponge up its juices. Parsley, thyme, bacon bits and black pepper are welcome extras rather than essentials. Those for whom saturated fat is a worry will delight in the knowledge that among the dumplings I have just concocted, those made with only flour, herbs, milk and egg were nicer than the suet ones. True, they lack the proper stickiness and weight of a classic dumpling, but they are lighter and carry out the rest of their duties impeccably.

Lifting the lid on my bubbling stew, I see huge creamy-beige clouds bobbing around among the vegetables. They are better than Mrs P's. They are fluffy and light, or as light as a dumpling ever gets. They have free-range eggs. They have Parmesan. They have basil. They have no suet. Technically they are not really dumplings, and I made them out of longing rather than frugality. Yet they have still turned stew for two into stew for four and chicken soup for one into chicken soup for two. But, of course, that is the whole point, isn't it?

Winter Vegetable Stew with Cheese and Herb Dumplings

A comforting and frugal dish for deep midwinter. Rather than the traditional winter herbs such as thyme and rosemary, I have taken advantage of the imported tarragon and basil.

4 medium-sized leeks, trimmed
4 carrots, scrubbed
2 parsnips, peeled
1 bulb of fennel
225g/8oz broccoli
1 large potato, peeled
225g/8oz mushrooms
70g/scant 3 oz butter
2 bay leaves
10g/1 small handful of dried mushrooms
1 tablespoon chopped tarragon
2 tablespoons chopped parsley
2 tablespoons flour
salt and pepper
for the dumplings
200g/7oz flour
2 teaspoons baking powder
1 teaspoon salt
4 tablespoons grated Parmesan
2 tablespoons basil leaves, finely chopped
4 tablespoons parsley, chopped
1 egg, beaten
about 120ml/4fl oz milk

Chop the leeks, carrots, parsnips and fennel into 2.5cm/1in-thick rounds, the broccoli into large florets and the potato into 2.5cm/1in-thick pieces. Cut the mushrooms into quarters, unless they are very small. Melt the butter in a large, deep pan and add the leeks. Cook over a medium heat till they have started to soften, then add the bay leaves and the vegetables you have just prepared, except the broccoli. Cover with a lid and cook over a medium heat till tender but with a little bite left in them. This will take about 30 minutes.

Meanwhile pour 1.2l/2 pints of boiling water on the dried mushrooms and set aside. When the vegetables are tender, sprinkle the herbs and flour over. Cook for 2 minutes. Pour in the dried mushrooms and their soaking water. Add the broccoli. Stir thoroughly but without breaking the vegetables and bring slowly to the boil, then turn down the heat and simmer for 20 minutes, adding salt and black pepper and stirring from time to time.

Make the dumplings by sieving the flour (yes, you must sieve it if they are to be light) with the baking powder and salt. Add the grated Parmesan cheese and the herbs. Mix the egg into the dry ingredients with enough milk to make a soft but not sticky dough, just firm enough to form into 8 balls. Slide them into the stew. Cover with a lid and simmer for 10–12 minutes.
Serves 4

FIGS

Baked Figs with Honey and Thyme

6 fat purple figs
4 tablespoons runny honey
juice of ½ a lemon
a few sprigs of fresh thyme

Put the figs in a shallow baking dish; they should nestle up against each other. Pour over the honey and lemon juice. Strip the thyme leaves from the stalks and scatter them over the figs.

Bake for 20 minutes in a preheated oven, 200°C/400°F/Gas Mark 6, occasionally basting the fruit with the juices in the dish. Serve warm, spooning over the warm juices, with clotted cream or thick yoghurt.
Serves 2

Figs with Ciabatta

A simple and surprisingly good weekday lunch is ciabatta, the holey, chewy Italian loaf, torn into large chunks and eaten with ripe figs. The bread should be very fresh and the fruit very ripe.

Grilled Figs

Place whole figs on a heated griddle and cook them till they char in places. Eat them while they are still hot. No butter, cream or honey. Just plump, warm, ripe figs.

No sooner has autumn arrived than the traditional Christmas fruits are being piled high in the markets and greengrocers' shops – the regal pomegranate with its jewelled interior, the easy-to-peel satsuma and its more interesting, tight-skinned sister, the clementine, not to mention the majestic, sweet-smelling pineapple with its spiky crown. Good eating though these classics of the festive fruit bowl are, none can match the sheer sexiness of the fig. Flown in from Turkey, the bulging, dark-purple fruits are in the shops until the New Year and are, for me, the ultimate festive fruit.

In terms of sensuous eating, nothing save a dribbling peach comes within a stone's throw of a ripe fig. Even the names of the varieties are a joy to read: Negronne, Negro Largo and Violette de Bordeaux; there is even one named Madonna. Sadly, the figs we buy are unlikely to be labelled, but that should not lessen their appeal.

A fig ripe for eating is not difficult to discern. It will bulge and be soft and tender to the touch. Its velvety bloom may ooze a sticky bead of nectar from its base. It will beg to be eaten. Shopkeepers should not be expected to sell such a soft, easily damaged fruit in perfect ripeness. We must choose them earlier than we need them, then ripen them off at home – or risk returning from the shops with a bag of red slush.

There is something particularly luxurious about the fig to us here in our cold climate. Its royal colours, purple without and rich red and gold within, belie the fact that in its natural home,

Turkey, Greece and Egypt, it is a cheap and staple food. There can be few edible pleasures that rank higher than eating a warm fig straight from the tree. Lost in a national park in what was Yugoslavia, I have scrumped figs so ripe they were almost molten inside. Warmed by the sun, the fruit and its little seeds, which are actually miniature fruits themselves, about 1,500 to each fig, kept me going as I tried to retrace my steps before nightfall. Warmth is a friend to the fig and even a short spell in the sun before serving them seems to concentrate their flavour.

The popular black figs, in truth the deepest purple, are mostly imported from Turkey. Plump and squat, they have a good flavour and ripen sweetly. They are an excellent dessert fruit and good to cook with, keeping their shape while taking on a melting quality in the heat of the oven. Many prefer the amber-coloured Smyrna figs, similar to those cultivated in Asia Minor 2,000 years ago, because of their mild walnut flavour. The majority being dried, they are far from easy to track down here in their fresh state. The ubiquitous black fig is good enough for me.

Baked Figs with Mascarpone and Walnuts

12 ripe figs
50g/2oz shelled, broken walnut pieces
3 tablespoons honey
2 tablespoons Marsala or medium sherry
100g/4oz mascarpone cheese

Cut a cross in the top of each fig and gently push the sides to open a hollow.

Toast the walnuts lightly under a preheated hot grill till fragrant but barely coloured. Rub off the skins that have come loose. There is no need to be too pernickety about this. Mix the broken nuts with the honey, alcohol and mascarpone cheese and fill the figs with this mixture.

Bake in a preheated oven, 200°C/400°F/Gas Mark 6, until bubbling, about 15–20 minutes. Serve warm.
Serves 4

Figs with Blackberries and Clotted Cream

Big purple figs, as sweet and ripe as you can get, are glorious with juicy blackberries or raspberries and thick cream. When the figs are in season, you will still be able to get berries in the major supermarkets, flown in from somewhere warm.

Place the figs on a large plate, allowing 2 per person. Break open the figs so that they are like water-lilies. Place a scoop of clotted cream, softly whipped double cream or thick yoghurt in the centre of each fig, then scatter over the berries.

With the fig, ripeness is all. Unlike the pear, an unripe fig cannot even boast a certain crunch, offering nothing at all to the impatient eater. At their peak they will have a melting, jelly-like flesh and a little sweet juice, though it must be said that copious juice is not the point of this fruit. It is the texture that intrigues as much as flavour. No other fruit can offer us flesh that is at once soft, velvety and crunchy.

Cooks will know the fig's worth already as the most superior of jam fruits, yet few seem to remember that it is just as good baked as you would an apple, with honey and a surprise seasoning of thyme leaves. A plate of roasted figs served with a spoonful of sweet mascarpone cheese melting on top is surely the most seductive of dishes. Pleasing enough on its own, the texture of the hot fig's red interior becomes positively ambrosial when topped with clotted cream or crème fraîche.

Figs are good-natured in the oven, producing a delicious juice without collapsing. Writing in her book *The Gastronomy of Italy* (Bantam), Anna Del Conte mentions a recipe from Agnoletti in Montello in the Veneto, where ripe figs are simmered in water and lemon and left to cool up to three times before being packed into glass jars. They are then served with rum.

The skin can be good too. Occasionally I come across a fig with skin too tough to eat, but not as often as I see instructions to discard it. Poached or baked it is tender enough and peeling is generally unnecessary. The skin also plays a part in the ritual of eating a raw fig: the fig is pulled gently in half, then each part is eaten by pushing the fruit carefully inside-out, while at the same time sucking the flesh from the skin, losing as little juice as possible.

The fruit from the second crop, in the shops around late autumn, is as finely flavoured if not better than the first. Most of the major supermarkets will carry some until the turn of the year. As a light lunch or first course they are sublime with the savouriness of Parma ham and the crunchy golden seeds are a good contrast to the soft, sweet fat. For dessert it is hard to beat a ripe, perfect fig served in all its glory on a plain white plate, though it is utterly wasted when chopped into a fruit salad.

Deeply savoury foods, such as cured meats, are good with figs. Blue cheese and figs is a fantastic combination. Bizarre though it sounds, a salty, creamy blue cheese such as the Irish Cashel Blue or the French Bleu de Causses is a fine match for the rich subtlety of the fig – and as easy a snack as you can imagine.

Whatever way we are going to eat our figs, cooked, or raw and heavily ripe, we should avoid chopping or slicing them. Tease and pull them gently apart, rather than cutting them flat with a knife, and the texture of this luscious, sensuous and enchanting fruit will be much more of a joy to eat. Just don't ask me why.

FILO PASTRY

Pity the poor sheet of filo pastry that finds itself wrapped around a lamb noisette and spoonful of chopped peppers at a Home Counties dinner party. Sitting in its pool of smooth tomato sauce and surrounded by polite chatter, it must be so desperately homesick for its Middle Eastern friends, the pistachios and almonds, butter and honey, saffron and cinnamon, not to mention the sticky orange-blossom and rose-scented syrups with which it is traditionally associated.

This delicate, wafer-thin dough has been well known in the Middle East since the time of the Ottoman Empire and in Britain for about 10 years. For centuries, sheets of this fine, almost transparent pastry have been layered with butter, nuts, spices and, in some parts, pigeon or chicken to make a vast array of Persian, African and Mediterranean delicacies. Sold in cafés, on street corners and in tantalising pastry shops in huge circular trays, they are usually offered warm as a snack with glasses of tea or thick, sweet coffee.

Far away from home, filo has been hijacked by that most dangerous of creatures, the creative cook. The thin leaves now find themselves wrapped around anything that will stand still for long enough: fillets of Scottish salmon, Chinese beanshoots and Thai mini-sweetcorns, lamb and redcurrant jelly, even prawns with mango mayonnaise. I will concede that the light and crackling pastry works exceedingly well as a crunchy case for warm, melting goats' cheese and is a better than average partner for mussels or scallops in a creamy sauce. But ratatouille?

Pistachio and Rose Baklava

I would normally suggest that pistachios taste fresher when bought in the shell, but shelling large quantities is tedious in the extreme, so ready-shelled ones can be used here. Ignore all offers of help to shell the nuts; your helpers will probably eat at least half of them. I would like to acknowledge Claudia Roden's *A New Book of Middle Eastern Food* (Penguin) for help with the method, though the quantities and spicing are my own.

20 sheets filo pastry
175g/6oz unsalted butter, melted
1 teaspoon ground cinnamon
275g/10oz shelled pistachio nuts, very finely chopped
rose-water syrup (see below)

Butter a rectangular baking dish approximately 30 x 20cm/12 x 8in. Set the oven at 180°C/350°F/Gas Mark 4. Lay half of the pastry in the tin, a sheet at a time, brushing each sheet with butter. Mix the cinnamon with the chopped pistachio nuts and sprinkle all but 4 tablespoons of them over the top layer of pastry.

Add the remaining pastry, sheet by sheet, brushing each one with butter as before. Scatter with remaining pistachios and cut diagonally into diamond shapes. Bake in the preheated oven for 25 minutes, then turn up the heat to 200°C/400°F/Gas Mark 6, and bake for a further 15–20 minutes till pale golden brown.

As soon as the pastry comes out of the oven, spoon over the chilled rose syrup, and sprinkle with more pistachios if you like.
Serves 10, at least

Filo Pastry with Cream Cheese and Orange-blossom Syrup

There is a delectable Eastern sweetmeat filled with a fruit, nut and custard mixture. It is a bit of a drag to make the custard filling with the traditional ground rice and cream, so I have substituted mascarpone, the Italian cream cheese – not as unorthodox as it might sound, as many Middle Eastern pastries are often filled with sweetened ricotta cheese. Of the several of these I have made lately, one in which I replaced the walnuts with an equal amount of dark chocolate chips was unexpectedly delicious, especially when eaten slightly warm.

450g/1lb mascarpone
100g/4oz ground almonds
50g/2oz walnuts, chopped
grated zest of an orange
50g/2oz sultanas
100g/4oz raisins
400g/4oz pack filo pastry
50g/2oz unsalted butter, melted
2 tablespoons shelled pistachios
orange-blossom syrup (see p.78)

You will need a 30 x 20cm/12 x 8in baking tin, at least 2.5cm/1in high, though a cake tin or even a roasting tin will do.

Set the oven at 200°C/400°F/Gas Mark 6. Scoop the mascarpone into a basin and stir in the almonds, walnuts, orange zest and dried fruit. Mix thoroughly. Cover the base of the baking tin with 2 pieces of filo pastry, brush them with some of the melted butter and lay another 2 sheets on top.

Lay the remaining sheets of pastry, 1 by 1, in the baking tin, each piece half covering the base of the tin and half hanging over the sides. Work round the tin till you have pastry hanging over all of the sides. Brush with butter and repeat so that each piece is now at least 2 sheets thick. Brush again with butter.

I have enjoyed it too wrapped around chicken spiced with ginger and saffron in Marrakesh, with honey and walnuts in a Tunisian café in Paris and layered with spinach and wonderfully salty feta cheese in Athens. Filo, fila or phyllo as it is known in Britain, the Middle East and Greece is also known as *yufka* in Turkey and *brik* in Tunisia. Made from nothing more than flour and water, it can be rolled, after a good deal of practice, into large sheets thin enough to read a newspaper through. Thinness is what counts.

I have, of course, made sheets of the stuff myself. Once. It took about an hour and looked more like a pair of fishnet tights than a sheet of pastry. Now I buy my filo from the supermarket, or from the Turkish shops down the road, in neat rectangular boxes from the deep-freeze. Each box contains a plastic roll of precut, unbelievably thin pastry sheets, so easy to use and silky to touch as to be almost addictive.

Eaten on their home territory, filo pastries have a texture like no other. Light and crisp, sweet and sticky, with a magical perfume to them born of crisp, hot pastry drenched with cold, thick blossom-scented syrup. Baklava, the best known of the Middle Eastern pastries, contains chopped pistachios or walnuts trapped between syrup-soaked layers of pastry – a mysterious balance of crisp pastry and sweet syrup. Even the savoury versions manage to retain their crispness while being soaked in butter.

I am not sure filo pastry was ever meant to be used as it is here – a couple of sheets stuck together with olive oil and used as edible wrapping paper. Its success surely lies in generosity. Layer upon layer of pastry, each lavishly buttered, then filled and covered with further layers is how it is used in Turkish, Greek and Moroccan cooking. Even as the hot pastry leaves the oven, a chilled syrup is poured over, cooling to a breathtaking sweetness.

Looking at the dozen or so thin and pale pastry sheets rolled up inside the box, it's hard to imagine how they can end up as a voluptuous sweetmeat. Sheet sizes vary but are generally about 12 x 18 inches, and will tear easily to fit whatever tin you use. Initially easy to handle, they will dry to a crisp in minutes, though keeping them covered with a damp cloth will help. There is no doubt that filo is fun – you need no flour on the table and it does not stick unless you get it wet. Precision is of little importance – a couple of layers too many here and there will not hurt, and tears and holes can be patched up with another sheet. It takes little more than 30 minutes to cook and the preparation is a doddle.

A packet of filo pastry will make an entire baklava or a dozen parcels of goats' cheese. You can make a decent sized *spanokopitta*, the Middle Eastern feta and spinach snack, or a handful of smaller ones. You can keep a pack of filo leaves in the freezer for three months, defrost them in 20 minutes and then return the unused pastry to the freezer. And you can even buy it at your local major supermarket. Just keep it far away from creative cooks.

Spoon in the mascarpone mixture and smooth level with the back of a spoon. Now lift each double piece of pastry hanging over the sides and fold it into the middle, twisting it into a large curl as you do so. The top of the pie should be pretty much covered with pastry. Brush with any remaining butter and scatter with the shelled pistachios. Bake in the preheated oven till golden brown, about 20 minutes. Drizzle with the hot syrup. Leave for 30 minutes before serving.
Serves 8

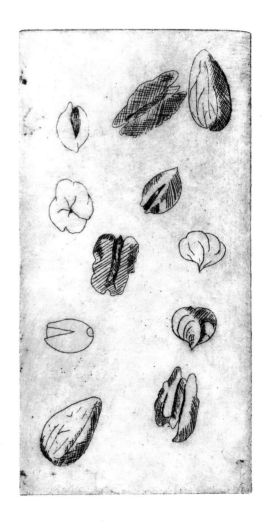

SCENTED SYRUPS

The thick, uncompromisingly sweet sugar syrups are an essential part of many such pastries. They are invariably scented with distilled water made from rose petals or orange blossoms. Once made, they will keep in the fridge for several weeks. Both orange-blossom-water and rose-water are available at the grocer's, though the most fragrant seem to come, not surprisingly, from Middle Eastern food shops, along with the fattest and freshest pistachio nuts.

Orange-blossom Syrup

150g/5oz sugar
1 tablespoon lemon juice
1 tablespoon orange-blossom-water

Put the sugar into a small, heavy-based saucepan with 120ml/4fl oz cold water. Add the lemon juice and simmer till quite thick but remove before it starts to colour. Stir in the orange-blossom-water. Cool, then refrigerate till cold and thick.

Rose Syrup

225g/8oz sugar
2 tablespoons lemon juice
1 tablespoon orange-blossom-water
2 tablespoons rose-water

Put the sugar in a heavy-based pan with 300ml/½ pint of water and bring to the boil with the lemon juice. Simmer hard until it is thick enough to coat the back of a spoon. Stir in the orange-blossom- and rose-water, heat for a further 1 or 2 minutes, then refrigerate till cold and thick.

FISH

Fish always tastes better in restaurants. There is a certain magic that happens between a piece of fish, a good chef and a hot pan, a magic that simply cannot be repeated at home.

I have used this pathetic line for years as my main excuse for not cooking more fish than I do, and frankly it doesn't really wash any more. I am somewhat ashamed that I leave such a simple task as frying a fillet of fish to the professionals. If I can fry a steak, grill a chop or stuff an aubergine, I can surely cook myself a decent piece of fish. Besides, some of my most memorable meals have been piscatorial. The round, flat pomfret fried in a rusty pan over an open fire in India (and served with nothing more than half a lime and a beer), a clear, coriander-flecked fish broth eaten one spring on the terrace of a Paris restaurant, the huge wedge of battered cod at Islington's Upper Street Fish Shop, wolfed from its paper, and the handfuls of hot, crisp whitebait pinched on their journey from kitchen to dining room during a student job as a waiter. So why, then, do I cook so little fish at home?

Of course, fish is expensive. Well, yes, some is. Turbot, for instance, or wild salmon. Monkfish can be a bit dear too. But that is only one end of the spectrum. Choose carefully and it won't cost you any more than a standard British meat-and-two-veg supper. Haddock, lemon sole and hake are not going to break the bank. Mackerel is a positive bargain. Mussels too. So it cannot be the price.

Fish has bones. Except that so many people

Fried Whitebait

Tiny fish, generally young herring or sprats, eaten whole. Little more than a fishy crunch, whitebait had their day in the late 1960s, when they were often found in pubs, served 'in the basket'. I have never tired of eating them, even if I now have to buy them frozen from the fishmonger. Supper in seconds.

450g/1lb whitebait
milk
flour, seasoned with salt and pepper
oil for frying
lemon

Toss the whitebait, still frozen, in the milk and then in the seasoned flour. Deep- or shallow-fry them in hot oil. (After years of deep-frying them, I recently found that they crisp up just as nicely in a frying pan in about 1cm/½in of oil.) After 3 or 4 minutes, maybe less, in the hot fat their thin batter will turn golden in patches. Serve when crisp, with thick wedges of lemon, and eat while hot.
Serves 2 (just)

Mackerel with Bacon

Cooking rich-textured fish such as salmon or herring in bacon fat is an old tradition that sadly seems to have died out. The saltiness of the bacon is what makes this way of cooking mackerel work so well.

oatmeal
4 medium-sized mackerel fillets
a large lump of lard or butter, about 50g/2oz
a handful of diced bacon or lardon
lemon

Cover a large plate with oatmeal and press the mackerel fillets down into it. Make sure that most of the fish is well covered. Melt the fat in a shallow pan over a medium heat. Fry the diced bacon till the fat becomes golden, then push the pieces to the side of the pan and add the mackerel fillets.

Fry until the oatmeal changes colour, removing before it turns brown. Lift out with a fish slice on to warm plates, then scatter the bacon over. Eat with plenty of lemon and crisp, slightly bitter leaves such as frisée or chicory.
Serves 2

Baked Mackerel in a Sea-salt Crust

The whole fish is baked in a crust of salt. The crust is broken away to reveal moist, subtly seasoned mackerel. The fish should be spanking fresh.

1 medium mackerel per person or 1 large mackerel
   between 2
sea salt

Cover the base of a roasting tin with salt. It should be about 1cm/½in thick. Put the fish, thoroughly cleaned, on the salt, then cover it with more. For 2 fish set close together but not touching; you will need about 900g/2lb. The body of the fish should be covered with salt. The

detest fishbones, most of the fish we buy is ready boned (at the supermarket) or boned as a matter of course (at the fishmongers). In fact you almost have to beg for the bones.

Fish smells. No, only stale fish smells. Fresh fish smells of the sea rather than what we might call 'fishy'. Well, OK, but it smells when it cooks. Nothing is worse than the smell of cooked fish pervading the house, especially when it wafts upstairs and lurks in the bedroom. But I live in a flat and have a state-of-the-art cooker hood that extracts the tiniest piscine pong at the click of a switch.

Fish is difficult to find. No, most major supermarkets have a reasonable supply of fresh fish. Most dodgy fishmongers went out of business years ago. Because fish smells so disgusting when it is not fresh, a bad fishmonger is his own worst advert. My local fishmonger has a 10-foot display of extraordinarily fresh fish. On just one day he had silvery, pearl-white cod, some slippery, spotted plaice and huge pinky-white wings of skate. There were tight mussels and glistening sprats, silvery-blue mackerel and some juicy, sticky cod-flaps that I brought home for the cat. Under the counter there was a couple of huge blue lobsters. There were neat shoals of red mullet, an orderly row of cod fillets and a jumble of oysters in their woven wooden box. Outside, a smartly dressed woman was attempting to settle the crustacean from hell, a huge pink spiny creature armed with menacing tentacles, on the back seat of her car.

Fish is a hassle. Not necessarily so. Any fishmonger will happily bone, skin and fillet for you, rid you of the yucky bits, and hand you a neat parcel of pristine fillets ready for the pan. Or, of course, if you are really squeamish, you can buy it in the supermarket, sealed in cute little blue trays with a sprig of parsley and a serving suggestion.

Cooking fish takes time. Er, no. A fillet of salmon, sautéd in butter then sauced with a little cream and some chopped tarragon, takes about 10 minutes from start to finish. Baby squid can be floured and fried in hot oil in what amounts to little more than seconds, while a huge hunk of cod can be roasted in less time than it takes to fry a sausage. Sorry, it can't be that either.

Truth be told, there is no particular reason why I do not buy more fish than I do. Like most Brits, I think of fish as a treat rather than a twice-weekly opportunity to eat healthy, tasty food. No doubt like the rest of us, I have been conditioned to think that fish is expensive, smelly, difficult to cook and best left to the professionals, whether they be fish-fryers at the local chippie or a Michelin-starred chef.

As it happens, fish is absurdly easy to cook. You heat a little butter, lightly flour a fillet, then dip it into the foaming butter. Cook it for a couple of minutes, less if you wish. Then turn it over with a palette knife. Cook the other side, then lift it out on to a plate. Add fresh butter to the pan, a few chopped soft-leaved herbs (tarragon, parsley or dill), then let it foam, squeeze in the juice from half a lemon and zap it over the fish. Supper in seven minutes. If you feel like getting fancy, then add a little cream or wine to the pan.

Of course, if you want to get clever, you can tackle some of the more complicated recipes around, though I am not sure there is much to recommend them over fresh fish simply cooked.

Now is the time to dust off or replace the best of the fish books, *Jane Grigson's Fish Book* (Penguin) and Richard Stein's *English Seafood Cookery* (Penguin), both packed to the gills with good ideas. There is fresh, interesting fish in the shops, and the fishmongers will welcome you with open arms. They will do anything you want – they will chop off head and tail can poke out. Press the salt down with your hands.

Bake the fish in a preheated oven, 230°C/450°F/Gas Mark 8, for about 25 minutes. Remove the fish from the oven, crack open the salt and serve the fish. Boiled potatoes and plum-tomato salad are a good accompaniment. If the dressing has a little more lemon juice or vinegar in than usual, it will be all to the good.
Serves 2

Roast Cod with French Beans and Mayonnaise

Perhaps the simplest way to cook a piece of fish, but the fish must be very fresh and moist and should be cut from the thick end of the fillet.

2 large, thick fillets of cod, about 225g/8oz each
a little flour
a good knob of butter, about 50g/2oz
1 tablespoon olive oil
2 large handfuls of lightly cooked French beans
extra virgin olive oil
home-made or good quality bought mayonnaise

Get the oven hot, about 200°C/400°F/Gas Mark 6. Dust the cod with flour and a good seasoning of salt and finely crushed black pepper. Heat the butter and the oil in a shallow pan and let it start to froth, then add the fish, skin side down. Cook for no more than 2 minutes, then remove and place in the hot oven until tender enough for you to be able to pull a huge flake of fish away easily, about 8–10 minutes' cooking.

Lift the fish out, place on a warm plate with the freshly cooked French beans and then drizzle over a little of your best olive oil. Serve with a large spoonful of stiff mayonnaise.
Serves 2

Salmon with Cream and Dill

Another easy recipe that requires little preparation, the majority of the work being done by the fishmonger. Dill works best of all the herbs in this instance, I think, though you may like to try it with tarragon and parsley. The lemon juice is essential to brighten the flavour of the sauce.

450g/1lb salmon fillets, about 2.5cm/1in thick
6 tablespoons fresh dill, chopped
50g/2oz butter
1 clove of garlic, squashed flat
4 tablespoons crème fraîche
lemon

Cut the salmon fillets into strips, about 4cm/1½in wide. Scatter the dill on a plate and roll the salmon in it, pressing down firmly so that the herb adheres.

Melt the butter in a shallow pan over a moderately high heat. Add the garlic and cook gently until its fragrance rises. When the butter starts to foam, add the herbed salmon to the pan. Cook until the flesh of the fish becomes opaque, about 3 minutes. Stir in the crème fraîche and leave it to melt into the butter. Season with salt and black pepper and a squeeze of lemon.
Serves 2

A Mediterranean Fish Soup

This is a substantial meal in itself. It is based on the famous Marseilles bouillabaisse, though I have chosen to pour the broth on to the fish rather than serving it separately (this is a simple supper) and I have cooked the potatoes separately as I prefer them thickly sliced and they take a little longer to cook than the rest of the ingredients.

the head, chop off the tail and give you the bones for stock, they will scale and clean, gut and skin, fillet, roll and slice.

No more excuses. Let's make this the year of the fish.

Fish Soup

The Scots make a simple and sustaining soup of local smoked haddock called cullen skink. Thickened with mashed potatoes, and occasionally embellished with cream, it boasts a velvety texture and mild smoky flavour for very little outlay. Good eating it may be, but it is absurd that this is our only offering to the world of fish soups.

Spanish peasant cooking is rich with fish soups, from the slow-simmered Basque *purrusalda*, a frugal broth of salt cod, garlic and potatoes, to the extravagent Catalan *suquet*, thick with rock and monkfish, sea bass and halibut, and sometimes brandy.

A French kitchen may produce the famed mixed-fish bouillabaisse, made with the obligatory inclusion of the elusive and spiky rascasse, or perhaps *aigo-sau*, a more relaxed affair of seasonal fish, tomatoes and potatoes. Easier perhaps for British cooks to copy is *bourride*, with its loose ingredients of mixed white fish made orange-bright with saffron and strips of bitter orange peel. All three would be served with a plate of crisp croutes of fried bread and accompanying ointment (red-pepper *rouille* or the garlicky aïoli) to first float and then sink childishly into the thick soup.

Thailand has its clear white-fish soups flavoured, as you might expect, with aromatic lemon grass, coriander and the juice and leaves of the kaffir lime. These soups are soothing and easily digested, lacking the cream and brandy of some of the richer offerings from Europe. Their clarity of flavour is welcome after the fishy muddles from elsewhere.

The Mediterranean is arguably the best hunting ground for those looking for fishy broths, creamy soups and more substantial stews. Although the fish will vary according to coast and catch, the basic flavours are olive oil, garlic, fennel and tomato; in some cases orange peel and saffron are used, and invariably there's a hot garlic sauce and grated cheese. Such soups can either be served with the fish pieces in place and the vegetables left in chunks or be sieved to give a smooth result.

Lindsey Bareham, author of the encyclopedic *A Celebration of Soup* (Penguin), feels it could be our aversion to bones that explains Britain's lack of fish soups. (It may also explain our love of the fish finger.) The answer, she believes is to carefully sieve the soup, rather than just whizzing in a blender which may leave bits of finely chopped bone in the soup, giving a 'furry' texture.

I suspect our reticence to produce fish soup at home may also be something to do with fishy smells that linger long after the soup has been supped. Even the most enthusiastic of fish cooks is unlikely to welcome the imposing aroma of boiling fish coming back to haunt them the next day. Adding aromatics to the broth – lemon grass, bay leaves, fennel and olive oil – helps, but it is hardly pot-pourri.

Much of this intrusion can be cut down by simply cooking the fish stock for less time. Lindsey Bareham says that 20–30 minutes is long enough for a simple stock of bones scrounged from the fishmonger, parsley, thyme, fennel and finely sliced carrot, celery and shallots. A light chicken stock, she adds, is also surprisingly successful in fish soups.

The long list of ingredients preceding most recipes for fish soup can be truly daunting, but it is

1kg/2¼lb prepared mixed fish (I suggest an assortment from whiting, cod, eel, bream, sea bass, red mullet, mussels and prawns)
2 potatoes, peeled and thickly sliced
1 medium onion, finely sliced
4 ripe tomatoes, cored and quartered
3 plump cloves of garlic, crushed
1 small bulb of fennel, finely sliced
peppercorns
a few sprigs of thyme
a handful of parsley, coarsely chopped
120ml/4fl oz olive oil
bay leaf
a good pinch of saffron threads
to serve
toasted croutes
rouille or garlic mayonnaise
grated cheese, preferably Gruyère

Wash the fish and remove any bits that your fishmonger has failed to notice, such as scales and the odd innard. Cut each piece of fish into roughly 5cm/2in pieces. Put the potatoes into boiling, salted water and cook till tender, about 10 minutes depending on the thickness of your slices.

Place the onion, tomatoes, garlic and fennel in a large, heavy saucepan, add a few peppercorns, a generous seasoning of salt and thyme, parsley and the bay leaf. Add half the oil and cook for 5 minutes until the onions soften. Place the prepared fish (reserving the shellfish) on top of the vegetables. Pour over the remaining olive oil, the saffron threads and about 1.2l/2 pints of boiling water. Cover with a lid and boil hard for about 10 minutes. Add the prawns and mussels and cook for a further 2–3 minutes until the mussels have opened.

Place the potato slices in 4 large, deep soup bowls, then remove the fish and vegetables with a draining spoon and place them on top of the potatoes. Ladle over the fish broth and serve with croutes, *rouille* and cheese. Serve the broth and fish separately if you prefer.
Serves 4

A Quick Fish Soup

1 shallot, finely chopped

2 cloves of garlic, squashed flat

1 tablespoon olive oil

3 tomatoes, seeded and chopped

bay leaf

450ml/¾ pint hot fish or chicken stock (or at a
  pinch, water)

100g/4oz boned white fish (cod, skate or hake)

8 small clams, cleaned and sorted

8 mussels in their shells, cleaned and sorted

100g/4oz shelled prawns

1 teaspoon saffron strands

flat leaf parsley, if you like

Cook the shallot and garlic in the olive oil till soft and just turning gold. Add the tomatoes, bay leaf and fish stock. Bring to the boil. Turn the heat down to a simmer and add the fish. Add the clams 4 or 5 minutes later, simmer for 2 minutes, then add the mussels and prawns. Stir in the saffron strands. Cook for a further couple of minutes, till the clams have opened.

Taste the broth; it may need salt and pepper. Throw out the bay leaf. Add some chopped parsley if you have any. It will add freshness and make the colours sing. Serve hot, spooning broth, fish and shellfish into large, warm bowls. Offer bread for dunking.

Serves 2

worth remembering that such things as John Dory, dogfish, monkfish, conger eel and gurnard should be taken as suggestions rather than gospel. Any writer who insists you follow their ingredients to the letter is being impractical, not to say more than a little precious.

Refinement is all well and good, but before cooks get too carried away with embellishment it is worth remembering the origin of such fare. Fish soup began its life as nothing more than a working lunch for fishermen, an assortment of their catch, made on board ship or perhaps at the quayside – an impromptu and varying meal. And here, I think, is the crux of the matter: the recipe depended on the catch. Of course, this would vary from season to season, even from trip to trip, which is part of the joy of such soups. No fish-soup recipe should be carved in stone. Recipes should be used only as a vague shopping list.

The line between fish soup and fish stew is pretty thin. I tend to prefer something in between the smooth fish purées and the broths piled high with a dazzling/daunting heap of seafood. An aromatic fish broth with small pieces of fish and potatoes in it is very much to my taste. It is also perhaps the easiest for the home cook to contemplate.

Standing at my local fishmonger's slab, as it glistens with ice and sparkling fish, I am faced with something of an embarrassment of riches. It is autumn – a fortunate time for the fish trade when so much is so good – and the prices reflect the high quality around at the moment. I need a sturdy white fish, gelatinous enough to give the soup some body, some shellfish (prawns look the cheapest bet) to lend a little sweetness, and something delicate to float in the soup along with the croutes and garlic mayonnaise.

It's not cheap making fish soup. At least the fishmonger cannot bark at you when you beg for the bones, though you should push for a head. There is a lot of flavour in a fish head, particularly cod, and it will give a bit of body to the whole. But there are plenty of interesting fish at not too grand a price if you look closely, and a good fishmonger will sort out something not too dear for a regular customer if you explain what it is for.

I long to make a truly British fish soup, using only fish from our waters, leeks, carrot and celery, and flavouring it with bay, thyme and parsley. Perhaps I should top it with grated cheddar and toast. But just one whiff of a bubbling pot of fish leaves me longing for the garlic, saffron and fennel of the Mediterranean, or the lemon grass and lime leaves of the East. And having spent a little too much on the ingredients (there is not much on offer for less than £1 a pound) and a little too long on the preparation, I can perhaps see why our cookery lacks a traditional fish soup. That British cookery has been shaped by home cooks rather than by chefs has something to do with it too. Home cooks often hold the purse strings, and well know the cost of feeding a family with a properly made fish soup. Which brings me back to cullen skink.

A Quicker Fish Soup

This is something of a cheat, but I have been doing it for years and few have noticed.

400g/14oz tin good quality fish soup
420ml/14fl oz bought fish stock
100g/4oz defrosted prawns
100g/4oz squid rings
a pinch of saffron threads
brandy
to serve
slices of baguette
mayonnaise
bottled pesto
grated Gruyère cheese

Tip the soup into a saucepan with the stock. Add the fish and gently bring the whole lot to the boil. Stir in the saffron and a good slug from the brandy bottle. Turn the heat down to a simmer.

Make some croutes by toasting slices of baguette and spreading them with a half-and-half mixture of mayonnaise and pesto. Scatter grated cheese over the croutes and tip the soup into warm bowls. Float the croutes on top of the soup, sinking them until the bread goes soggy and the cheese melts into the soup.
Serves 2

Brandade of Salt Cod

A creamy, fishy, savoury paste served warm with toast. It doesn't take a great deal of time, though the dish does seem to produce more washing up than expected. If you have no food processor, you can smash the fish flakes using a pestle and mortar, though in my experience that takes a bit of doing.

450g/1lb salt cod, soaked in several changes of cold water for 24 hours
1 clove of garlic
150ml/5fl oz olive oil
150ml/5fl oz cream
lemon

Give the cod a final rinse and put it into a large pan of cold water. Bring it slowly to the boil, then, just as the water reaches boiling point, turn off the heat and slap on the lid. Set aside for 15 minutes.

Remove the fish with a draining spoon and break into flakes. Take care to remove all the bones. The fish will split easily into large flakes, some of them huge. Drop them with the grey skin (which will give body to the *brandade*) into the bowl of a food processor. Whiz for a few seconds until the fish is a coarse mush. Do not overprocess, which will result in a purée, spoiling the consistency of the finished dish. Tip the mashed fish back into the saucepan.

Squash the garlic clove flat and put into a small saucepan with the olive oil. Warm it gently over a low heat. Warm the cream in a separate pan. Put the fish pan over a very low heat. When the oil, cream and fish are warm, but not hot, add the liquids to the fish alternately, beating them in with a wooden spoon. When the mixture is a rough creamy mass, with the consistency of porridge, it is ready. Season with black pepper and a little lemon juice. Check for salt, although it is unlikely to need any.

Serve warm, spread on thick rounds of hot toast. I like a squeeze of extra lemon juice on mine.

Serves 4 as a starter

Salt Cod

Had it not been for the flat, whole fish swinging like tea-towels on a washing line outside, I would have thought I had just arrived at an old book shop. Stacked floor to ceiling with parchment-coloured blocks, many tied up with string like ancient manuscripts, this food shop was one of the most curious I had ever seen. A shop selling nothing but preserved fish. A shop that smelled like a cross between Patum Peperium (Gentleman's Relish) and the sea. Here was shelf upon shelf of glistening, salted fish, in a shop painted long ago the same colour as its wares, tucked down a side street in Oporto.

Each shelf held a different cut, type or vintage of fish. This is where the local shoppers come to buy their comforting *bacalhau*, the salted and dried cod which has been a part of their everyday eating since medieval times. To ask simply for salt cod here is probably akin to asking for a book in a bookshop or a house in an estate agent's. The creamy-white kites of dried fish may look like something long since washed up on the shoreline and parched in the sun, but to the Portuguese cook *bacalhau* is a thing of joy.

There are prime middle cuts, a sort of loin if you like, tongues and cheeks (a reference to their shape), wafer-thin strips (can't be much meat on those) and magnificent whole fish like pteradactyls hanging from the ceiling. Some is wind-dried in the traditional manner, while even more is dehydrated in large, modern, commercial drying rooms. And some, wafer-thin and as stiff as a board, looked as if it had been in the shop since it was built.

Intrigued by some that looked thick, moist and fresh, though still heavily salted, I asked for a little out of curiosity. Whatever it was, I was denied it

Salt Cod with Tomatoes and Pesto

I offer this as a simple, somewhat unorthodox, version of some of the more complex and time-consuming Portuguese dishes where the fish is cooked with tomatoes and garlic. A deeply savoury dish best accompanied with unbuttered, unskinned boiled potatoes and a little more wine than usual.

2 steaks of salt cod about 200g/7½oz each
flour
1 clove of garlic, peeled
2 small, dried chillies
4 tomatoes, seeded and chopped (you can skin
    them if you wish, it makes little difference here)
2 tablespoons pesto sauce from a jar
a small glass of white wine

Pour 4 tablespoons of olive oil into an ovenproof dish and place the soaked cod steaks skin side up in the oil. Set aside for at least half an hour.

Preheat the oven to 200°C/400°F/Gas Mark 6. Put a layer of flour on a flat plate and press the cod steaks into it so that they retain some of the flour. Pour the oil in which the fish has been sitting into a shallow-sided pan and fry the fish steaks on both sides till golden and crisp.

Lift the fish back into the ovenproof dish. Wipe the flour and oil from the inside of the shallow pan – there is no need to be too scrupulous about this – and add a little more oil. Add the clove of garlic roughly crushed (you can squash it flat with the blade of a knife) and the chillies, crushed. Warm the oil over a medium heat until the garlic turns pale gold, then add the tomatoes, cook for 2 minutes, then stir in the pesto and the wine. Allow to bubble for a couple of minutes then season with freshly ground black pepper.

Slosh the sauce – actually it is more of a gunge – around the fish and cook in the preheated oven for 15 minutes, a little longer if the steaks are really thick. When the sauce is bubbling and the fish cooked right through it

with a 'No, you don't want that'. Certainly the flies seemed to be enjoying it.

Up until this point I had a take-it-or-leave-it attitude to salt cod. And even then I would probably have left it. I spent an hour in the shop, watching customers buying it with the same sort of passion that some of the French reserve for cheese. They obviously knew something I didn't, even though I had cooked it before and was deeply unimpressed. At last I chose my fish, an assortment of cuts, and took it away in a brown-paper parcel tied up with string.

Now, never, never, never pack salt cod in your suitcase. It has certainly left its calling card in my old Globetrotter. Next time I'll pack it in my hand-luggage and trust my fellow passengers to be wearing enough duty-free perfume to get the better of it. Or better still, I shall pick it up in chunks at my local Spanish, West Indian or Italian grocer's, or in neat, rectangular packets in the supermarket.

Once home, the fish must have its salt removed, and the only way to do this is by soaking in cold water. I am not the sort who knows what I will want to eat the day after next and there are few lines more off-putting in a recipe than 'soak for 36 hours'. Why bother with the dried version at all when there is so much fine-quality fresh cod around anyway? Well, the soaking was not a great problem, in fact I enjoyed watching the emaciated slices of fish firm up into juicy steaks, and it was no big deal to change the water every few hours. But the great surprise was that the resuscitated fish was quite different from the fresh thing altogether.

The salting and drying process changes the taste of the fish in much the same way as curing alters the flavour of pork to ham. It has the same huge, meaty flakes that make the cod so special, and the same firm texture, but the real joy of salt cod is in the fish's deep savouriness, similar to that of cured meats. A rich but moreish flavour with an appetising tangy, piquant aroma – unless, of course, it's in your suitcase.

A FEW NOTES ABOUT SALT COD

- Salt cod is the very devil to cut. Buy it ready cut in practical-sized pieces, no matter how beautiful the whole dried fish will look hanging in your larder.
- The thicker pieces offer the best value. There is little of interest on the thin scraps.
- Avoid the brown- or yellow-stained pieces, or anything that looks ragged; it will only fall to pieces during soaking.
- If you do need to cut the dried fish before soaking, i.e. to get it into your soaking bowl, then use a sharp serrated knife.
- Soak the fish for no less than 24 hours, changing the water at least half-a-dozen times.
- The only way to test if the fish has soaked for long enough is to break off a tiny piece and taste it – it should be savoury, not salty.
- Once hydrated, treat as fresh fish, i.e. keep it cool.
- Although soaking should remove much of the salt, go easy on the seasoning of the cooked dish.

is ready. Serve simply with boiled rice or, better still, plain boiled potatoes.

Serves 2 as a main dish

Salt Cod and Scrambled Egg

Fry a steak of soaked salt cod in a little olive oil till golden on both sides. Break it into flakes and carefully remove all the bones. Meanwhile, fry a sliced onion until soft and translucent. Let it catch appetisingly at the edges. Scoop the onion out of the pan and add to the fish.

Add the above mixture, seasoned with a little black pepper and some chopped parsley if you have it, to your breakfast scrambled eggs. Stir in the fish and onions just as the eggs have started to turn creamy, cook very lightly and eat immediately.

FOCACCIA BREAD

Focaccia

Fresh yeast is getting increasingly difficult to find, but dried yeast is available in packets in grocers' shops and supermarkets. I find the quick-acting variety works well. Check the sell-by date though.

300g/10oz unbleached plain flour
1 teaspoon sea salt, crushed
2 teaspoons easy-blend yeast
a generous 180ml/6fl oz warm water
2 tablespoons extra virgin olive oil
for baking
1 tablespoon extra virgin olive oil
1 tablespoon sea salt (Maldon crystals are the best for this)

Sift the flour and the salt through a fine sieve into a large mixing bowl. Add the yeast granules and stir them in. Mix the warm water – it should be about blood temperature but no hotter – with the olive oil and pour into the flour. Mix with a wooden spoon until the dough comes together. It will be slightly sticky at this point but keep mixing until it comes clean away from the sides of the bowl.

Sprinkle a large, clean surface lightly with flour. It can be a wooden chopping board, table or kitchen work-surface. Knead the dough with your hands, holding it flat on the board and pushing it away from you with the heel of your palm, then pull it back into a ball and turn slightly clockwise. Continue stretching, rolling and turning for 10 minutes. The dough should feel springy and elastic.

There is something that annoys me about people who say they always bake their own bread. It's not just that it is virtually impossible to make such a claim without sounding ever so slightly smug, nor is it that it reminds me that the state of suppressed chaos I live in forbids such good housekeeping. I suspect it is simply that I know what I am missing. That wonderful buzz, albeit a slightly self-righteous one in my case, that you get when you take your own loaf from the oven.

I do bake my own bread as it happens. At least once a year. And always in the spring. No doubt it has something to do with some primeval force, the same one that makes me lust for long walks in the countryside or steers me towards the garden centre. In the past I have toyed with rich golden brioche, slaved over politically correct organic wholemeal loaves and even amused myself with fruit-laden German Stollen.

Focaccia, the excruciatingly fashionable Italian bread, has been baked since before there were ovens. It is a hearth-bread, cooked for thousands of years on flat stones in the hearth, covered by hot ashes. The name comes from *focus*, the Latin for hearth, the focus or hub of the household. I shall not attempt one of these ashbreads in my hearth. I lack the thick *schiacce*, the flat rough stone kept in the embers that gives rise to *schiacciate*, the Tuscan name for focaccia. And I am not sure what my Coalite is actually made from.

I am slightly suspicious of the 3-inch-thick slabs of focaccia on sale at the moment. Can this somewhat cake-like bread, topped with herbs and sun-dried tomatoes and rich with extra virgin oil, be true to its name? A rather grand version I am sure. I want mine to be the epitome of a true Ligurian country hearth-bread, baked in the embers – or as near as I can get in a 1990s designer oven.

Making the dough is reassuringly simple. The yeast is thrown in with the flour, mixed with warm water and olive oil, then pummelled about a bit. After an hour of being ignored, the dough rises dutifully and is ready to be bashed about again and baked. It is as simple as that.

The real joy is in the kneading. I love the feel of the warm dough in my hands. It is soft and warm yes, but it is also alive. The warm water and flour goad the yeast into producing the carbon dioxide that makes the dough rise, literally making it come to life. On the table, which is covered in flour, I continue stretching the dough and gathering it back into a ball until it softens. In the space of 10 minutes my tense ball of dough has become soft, springy and relaxed. It has come to life.

Put the ball of dough back in the bowl and cover with a clean tea-towel. Place the bowl in a warm but not hot place for an hour. I leave mine in the kitchen near the cooker, though I would use an airing cupboard if I had such a thing. If you leave it in a cool place it will still rise but will take a while longer.

After 30 minutes or so the dough should have doubled in size. It should be light and airy to the touch. Push your fist gently into the dough and turn out on to the floured board again. You may have to pull the dough away from the bowl with your fingertips. Knead the dough again for 1 or 2 minutes, then lift it on to a lightly oiled and floured baking sheet.

Gently push the dough with your fist into a rough rectangle about 25 x 20cm/10 x 8in. You can make a round loaf if your prefer. Cover with a tea-towel and leave in a warm place for a further 25 minutes, in which time the dough will rise and spread slightly. If it is spreading alarmingly, push it back into shape. Press your finger down into the dough in several places to make deep holes. Brush the dough with the olive oil and sprinkle with sea salt. Some of the oil will settle in the holes but no matter.

Bake in a preheated oven at 220°C/425°C/Gas Mark 7 for 25 minutes or till golden. Slide the focaccia from the baking tray and eat while warm.
Makes 1 loaf, enough for 4

Focaccia with Bacon

You need slab bacon for this, which can be bought at Italian grocers' and food halls.

Cut 75g/3oz slab of bacon into small dice, about the size of Dolly Mixtures. Knead two-thirds of these into the dough and continue as above.

When you come to brush the focaccia with olive oil, scatter the remaining bacon over the top, press lightly into the dough and bake as above.

Focaccia with Onions, Garlic and Olives

2 tablespoons olive oil
1 small onion, peeled and sliced
6 cloves of garlic, unpeeled
1 tablespoon rosemary leaves
12 black olives

Warm the oil in a shallow pan and cook the onions in it till soft and golden. Blanch the garlic cloves in boiling water for 4 minutes, drain and peel.

Follow the basic focaccia recipe up to the second rising. Just before you put the bread in the oven, spread the onions and their cooking oil over the dough. Dot with the garlic cloves and scatter over the rosemary leaves and olives. Season with a little sea salt and bake as above.

Pecorino Focaccia

During the second kneading work 50g/2oz finely grated Pecorino or Parmesan cheese, a grinding of black pepper and a tablespoon of dried oregano into the dough. Bake as above.

In the ancient tradition of hearth-breads, I shall embellish mine just enough to take it beyond the utilitarian. A handful of chopped bacon, a dozen black olives or a sprinkling of rosemary has been the customary addition to focaccia since antiquity. I decide on a generous scattering of coarse sea salt instead of the bacon and a little red onion. A handful of green olives and a few mauve and grey sage leaves would have been acceptable, as would a couple of spoonfuls of grated sharp Pecorino cheese.

The bread is a success. It is cooked in half an hour, crisp on top with a pleasing open texture. My kitchen smells too good to be true.

I can see why people bake their own bread. Sure, it tastes good, but there is more to it than that; it also makes you feel good. It feels better to me than simply cooking, almost like I have just given birth. It must be spring.

TO ACCOMPANY HEARTH-BREADS

The simple hearth-breads above can be eaten as bread with a meal or better still with salami, prosciutto and cheeses. Accompanied by a salad of rocket and tomato, dressed with olive oil, you have a substantial supper for two.

GAME

Licking my fingers clean after eating something hot and deeply savoury is one of life's great pleasures. And I find the gamy, salty juices from roast birds, hot from the oven, perhaps the finest finger-licking food of all. It is only when the juicy, tender breasts of quail, partridge and pigeon have been sliced away and eaten with some degree of elegance that I can pick up the toothsome carcass and really start to enjoy myself.

Small poultry and game are maddeningly difficult to eat. Once you have removed the breast meat the rest is virtually impenetrable with a knife and fork, and many a quail must have ended its days on the carpet. Though not as tender as other parts, the legs of pigeon and partridge have a succulence and flavour which are altogether too good to waste. Fingers are the only answer and often the point at which my meal will go from the good to the sublime.

I remain convinced that food eaten with my fingers tastes better, just as that eaten out of doors in sea air seems infinitely more tasty than the same food eaten elsewhere. Perhaps it is the primitiveness of it all that appeals, I don't know. I thoroughly enjoy meat that has a bit of fight left in it. The leg meat of small game is far from the most tender cut, so is unlikely to interest those to whom melting tenderness is all. Sinews are hardly good to eat but are pleasantly resilient and succulent to suck on. Meat that 'melts in your mouth' is to my mind as overrated as that which is lean and fat-free. What I can say is that there are few meals I enjoy more

Grilled Quail

Tiny, tender birds cooked under a medium-hot grill will be ready in 15 minutes or less. A couple per person is generous but far from excessive. A salad of spinach leaves and grapes with a simple dressing of walnut oil and lemon juice would be my accompaniment, and bread to soak up the meagre juices from the pan. Forget knives and forks: quail is finger food.

4 quails
olive oil
a sprig or two of thyme
lemon

Heat the grill. Rub each of the quails with a generous amount of olive oil, then scatter thyme leaves over them. Place under the hot grill, a good 15cm/6in away from the heat.

Cook for 5 minutes on each side, then turn breast up and cook for 2 or 3 minutes till golden brown. If they show any sign of drying, then anoint them further with olive oil. Remove them from the grill, season with salt and a little coarsely ground black pepper. Squeeze a little lemon juice over the meat as you eat.
Serves 2

Roast Partridge with Juniper and Mushrooms

Birds for roasting are invariably sold with a strip of bacon over their tender breasts to prevent their drying out. If your birds are baconless, then wrap a rasher of unsmoked bacon around each one before roasting. Plain pork fat, if you can get hold of some, may do the job even better.

2 partridge, ready for the oven
75g/3oz butter
100g/4oz mushrooms, any variety
12 juniper berries
thyme
bay leaves

Preheat the oven to 220°C/425°F/Gas Mark 7. Put the birds in a roasting pan, not too close together, and place a knob of butter, about the size of half a walnut, on each. Add the mushrooms, halved if large. Season each partridge with a little salt and pepper. Squash the juniper berries lightly and scatter them over and inside the birds. Add a few herbs to the dish, 1 or 2 sprigs of thyme and a few bay leaves will suffice, then dot a little butter over the birds and mushrooms. Roast in the preheated oven for about 20 minutes.

Baste all with the pan juices at least once during the cooking. Remove the bacon from the birds' breasts and return them to the oven for a final 5 minutes. Check that the birds are done to your liking, then serve with some of the pan juices, mushrooms, bacon, bread and a green salad. A blob of fruit jelly, redcurrant or bramble, would not go amiss.

Serves 2

than a small game bird, roasted till lightly crisp on the outside and only faintly pink within, eaten without the hindrance of knife and fork. A puddle of old-fashioned bread sauce for dipping and something better than usual to drink could be the only improvements.

Partridge has much to recommend it, though it is one of the more expensive birds. There are often two types on offer: the red-legged and the grey. Game dealers and supermarkets charge more for the grey, or English, partridge, and well they might. It is smaller than the red-legged or French variety and has a particularly fine flavour. The French, though a chubbier bird, has a darker, less subtle flesh and is generally considered inferior. I am not sure that I would turn my nose up at either – whatever colour socks they are sporting, though a dealer at Leadenhall market in London told me that he has little call for the French even though he sells them at half the price.

Pigeons are the least sophisticated of all the small birds. Their flavour varies from the mild to the piquant, depending on their age, diet and no doubt what mood they were in when they died. If you are lucky you will get something like the one I bought a while back from the supermarket: succulent, tender and without the bitterness you sometimes get in the leg meat. It is very much a matter of luck. I have had a number of disastrous attempts with slow cooking and now prefer to flash roast them for minutes rather than stew them slowly into unconsciousness.

Quails are almost entirely farmed and are tiny enough for me to eat two as a main course. There is little meat on them, but they have the sweetest, mildest and tenderest flesh of all – although I have heard people say the same of sparrows. I generally grill the little chaps, it almost seems a waste to put the oven on for them, so small are they. Sometimes their fragile bones seem tender enough to crunch like the crackling on roast pork. Under a hot grill they can be cooked in 10 minutes – more or less the time it takes to cook a fish finger.

Not until recently did I think of any game as fast, midweek supper food. Yet last night I had quail grilled till crisp-skinned, with stir-fried mild white cabbage and bread to wipe my plate, on the table in 20 minutes. Followed by a slice of goats'-milk Camembert from the local cheese shop, I felt I had eaten like a king, though I had spent barely three quid. And I got to lick the cook.

A FEW GOOD THINGS TO SERVE WITH ROAST OR GRILLED GAME

Pears

Cut 4 pears into quarters and remove the cores. Melt a good 30g/1oz or more of butter in a large, shallow pan. Add the pears and sauté till the fruit is tender and the edges of the pears are slightly brown. Sprinkle with a little brown sugar, cook for a further 1 or 2 minutes to caramelise the sugar, then squeeze over a few drops of lemon. Serve hot.

10-minute Roast Pigeon

Pigeons respond to being roasted at a high temperature for a short time by retaining their moisture and adopting a crisp skin. Soaking the jointed birds in a marinade is an option which is well worth the wait. Provide lots of bread to mop up the cooking juices and a bowl of salad to accompany and a cheese, something quite wild and pungent, to follow.

2 wood pigeons
1 glass of red wine
2 tablespoons olive or nut oil
a couple of sprigs of thyme
bay leaf
1 small clove of garlic, peeled and crushed
1 teaspoon black peppercorns, roughly crushed
2 teaspoons balsamic vinegar

Cut each of the pigeons into 4 pieces, 2 breasts and 2 small legs. Put the pieces in a glass, stainless steel or china dish with the wine, oil, herbs, garlic and peppercorns. Set aside for as long as you can – an hour will just suffice, though overnight may prove more beneficial in terms of flavour.

Heat the oven to 240°C/475°F/Gas Mark 9. Place the breasts in the hot oven, on the top shelf, and cook for 5 minutes, 6 if the breasts are large. Add the legs and the marinade and cook all for a further 6 minutes or until the birds are cooked to your liking. Remove the joints to a warm plate to rest (the switched-off oven will do), then put the roasting pan over the gas and get the cooking juices really hot. Stir in the balsamic vinegar, taste for seasoning and add a little salt and pepper if you wish. Serve the roast meat, generously sprinkled with coarse salt, with the pan juices and lots of bread.
Serves 2

Arabella Boxer's Bread Sauce

Arabella Boxer's *English Food* (Penguin) is a fascinating collection of quintessentially English recipes, such as roast grouse, fish cakes and apple hat, spiked with society gossip from between the wars. A truly elegant book, it is the first place to look for a fine version of a recipe such as this. As the author comments in her book, 'It is one of those English foods which can be the best or the worst thing in the world, depending on how it is made.' Roast the birds while the milk is infusing with the spices.

360ml/12fl oz milk
½ a medium onion
2 cloves
½ a bay leaf
sea salt and black pepper
a pinch of mace or nutmeg
about 6 tablespoons soft white breadcrumbs, made
   from 1-day-old bread, crusts removed
15g/½ oz butter
2 tablespoons cream (optional)

Put the milk in a small pan with the onion stuck with the cloves, bay leaf, salt, pepper and mace or nutmeg. Bring slowly to the boil, then turn off the heat, cover the pan and let it stand for 20–30 minutes. Strain and reheat. As it approaches boiling point, shake in the crumbs gradually, stirring all the time, and stop as soon as it approaches the right consistency, remembering that it will thicken slightly on cooling. Simmer for 3 minutes, stirring often, adding more salt and pepper if required. Just before serving, stir in the butter and add a drop of cream if you have it.
Serves 4

Grapes

I can think of few good reasons to cook a grape, but I might suggest that when you are making a thin gravy to accompany the roasted birds you squash a few large black gobstopper grapes into the pan. Leave them to bubble with the pan juices for a few minutes, then season with pepper and a drizzle of honey.

Cabbage

Finely shred with a large knife, then fry till translucent in a little butter with a few lightly crushed juniper berries, a crushed clove of garlic, salt and pepper. Pour over enough double cream to come half-way up the cabbage, transfer to a medium oven and bake for 20 minutes. Serve with grilled pigeon, partridge or quail.

Onion Skirlie

An ancient Scottish accompaniment which can be made with or without the onion.

Melt 50g/2oz of dripping or butter in a shallow pan over a medium heat. Add a finely chopped onion and cook until soft, about 5 minutes. Sprinkle in 100g/4oz coarse oatmeal and season with salt and pepper. When all of the fat has been absorbed, which should take a couple of minutes, the skirlie is ready.

Mushrooms

Add a handful of mushrooms, sliced if large, to the birds as they roast. Baste occasionally with the pan juices to stop the mushrooms drying out. If I am grilling my game, then I often slide a couple of large field mushrooms under the grill too, their stalks removed and their hollows filled with nothing more than a knob of butter.

GARLIC

The strings of fat, sweet garlic I bought in the autumn have done me proud for months, dangling with the pots and pans from their butcher's hook in the kitchen, making me feel like a real pro. None of those neat, timid doll's-house specimens in boxes for me, only huge, pistachio-and-rose-tinted bulbs tied up with string.

But they have lost their magic now. Still plump and hard, but with a pungency, a crudeness, to them I don't like. Until late November they were fresh and creamy-white, with a gentle scent and a mildness that actually persuaded me to eat them raw and thinly sliced on tomatoes and to mash them to a coarse pulp with olive oil and handfuls of peppery basil for a lovely pasta sauce. Now they are full of hate. Crisp-skinned and viscous, acrid and astringent. For two pins I'd put them on the fire.

The answer perhaps, as with old birds, root vegetables and much else in the deep midwinter, is a long roasting in a slow oven. Surely a constant basting with herbs, butter and fruity olive oil will temper their anger. But it doesn't. Golden and tender they may be, but there is still a nasty bite to them.

It never occurred to me I wouldn't get through the 40-odd heads of garlic before they dried up and snarled at me. Some of them are even shooting. Perky, bright-green points bursting through papery skins. Curse the writer who suggested that those shoots are a delicacy. Maybe to the Chinese, who can appreciate the darker side to this member of the lily family. The odorous little shoots, like fat chives,

Chicken with Garlic, Cider and Cream

This sweet, creamy dish, with its soft ivory-coloured sauce, illustrates perfectly garlic's ability to sweeten and mellow once blanched and slowly cooked in butter. Accompany with green beans, properly cooked not just dunked in boiling water, or continue the pale and interesting theme with bitter chicory, split lengthways, buttered and grilled till tender.

8 fat cloves of garlic
60ml/2fl oz olive oil
30g/1oz butter
2 large chicken breasts, skin on and small bone
    attached
bay leaf (optional)
120ml/4fl oz dry cider, James White or Duskins
    Bramley for preference
90–120ml/3–4fl oz cream, single or double

Drop the garlic cloves into a small, deep pan of boiling water. Blanch them for 4 minutes, by which time they will be paler in colour and have softened a little. Scoop them out with a draining spoon and remove the cloves from their skins. They should pop out satisfyingly when gently squeezed between your fingers.

Warm the olive oil in a shallow pan and melt the butter in it. When it starts to sizzle lightly, fry the chicken breasts, skin side down first, till golden on both sides, a matter of 2 or 3 minutes. Turn the heat down as low as it will go, add the garlic, a bay leaf if there is one around, and cover the pan with a lid. Cook gently till the chicken is done right through and the cloves are very soft, about

15–20 minutes. The butter and oil mixture should be a rich golden colour; do not let it brown. Lift the chicken out and set aside. Turn the heat up, pour in the cider and bring it to the boil. Mash the garlic into the bubbling cider with a wooden spatula, scraping the tasty, crusty bits that have caught on the pan into the liquid. When the cider is almost evaporated and you have a sweet-smelling golden slush, pour in most of the cream, add a little salt and pepper from the mill, then taste, adding more cream if you wish. Return the chicken to the pan. Let the sauce bubble for 2–3 minutes, then serve.

Serves 2

gave me the mother and father of a stomach ache, and I could taste garlic for a week.

Boil them, that's what I'll do. Purge them in boiling water. Smart chefs do that to their garlic before they set the softened cloves in terrines held together with savoury jelly, or bake them with herbs and rendered poultry fat for a *confit*. After four minutes they have lost their harshness. The smell in the kitchen is soothing and mild. The water they have cooked in smells like a restoring broth, an ancient cure for flu perhaps, but still ends up going down the sink.

Sweet and white once more, I shall have another go at roasting them. A good half-hour in the oven with olive oil and thyme and they have become soft and melting, with an almost honeyed sweetness about them. Blanched and roasted, they are sweet beyond belief. Golden and soft enough to squash between thumb and forefinger, they are even more to my taste than the white and mauve bulbs you can buy during the summer. They have a warm, caramelised flavour to them that has me scooping them from their crisp skins with a teaspoon, like miniature boiled eggs.

Once rid of their sulphurous compounds, I have more uses for the mellow cloves than in the summer. With their new lease of life, they will serve as an accompaniment to cold roast meat and pickles, and as a grown-up version of garlic butter for mussels. They will be an inauthentically mild addition to a stir-fry, a smooth base for a mayonnaise and a mild spread for crisp crostini. The sweet nuggets have already been spread on toast, topped with cheese and grilled for lunch and will appear later rubbed on to lightly grilled chicken and finished in a hot oven for a few minutes.

Best of all, I can make a garlic-scented gravy for the roast. Mashed with a fork, stirred into the roasting pan with the cooking juices from the lamb and a glass of white wine, and reduced for 2 minutes, I shall have not gravy but a sweet, mellow and deeply aromatic *jus* – just like a real pro.

Roast Garlic with Goats' Cheese

A whole head of garlic, roasted with fruity olive oil and pungent thyme, is a classic partner for 1 or 2 slices of piquant goats' cheese. Alice Waters makes a rich spread of chèvre and cream to accompany her baked garlic. A simple alternative is to squash the sweet cloves on to crusty bread, sourdough would be nice, and munch with sharp, mature goats' cheese. A slice cut from one of those ash covered, fudgy-textured logs would be perfect.

4 whole heads of garlic, plump and firm
50g/2oz butter
60ml/2fl oz fruity olive oil
4 healthy sprigs of thyme
bay leaves
3 thick slices of goats' cheese per person

Bring a deep pan of water to the boil. With a small knife, pull away most of the papery skins in between the cloves without dislodging them and peel away some of the skin from each clove so that the heat and herbs can get to them. Drop the heads of garlic into the water and simmer for 7–8 minutes. Lift them out with a draining spoon. You will notice the smell has become gentler already.

Place the whole heads in a shallow dish. Cut the butter up roughly and dot it over, then pour over the olive oil. Season with salt, coarsely cracked pepper, thyme and a couple of bay leaves. Bake at 180°C/350°F/Gas Mark 4, for 40 minutes, basting once or twice with the herby juices in the dish. The garlic is done when the cloves are soft enough to crush to a pulp with finger and thumb and golden in colour.

Serve a whole head of garlic per person, with a loaf of crusty bread and the goats' cheese. Tear off hunks of bread, spread the warm, soft garlic as if it were butter and top with a lump of cheese.
Serves 4

HOW TO MAKE GARLIC PURÉE

For this smooth, mellow, versatile cream, slice 4 large heads of plump, firm garlic across their diameter, as if you were slicing an orange in half. Drop them into a deep pan of boiling water. Simmer for 4 minutes, then drain them. Tip them into a shallow dish and turn them cut-side up. Pour over a wine glass of olive oil, add sprigs of thyme, salt, pepper and 1 or 2 bay leaves, then roast at 180°C/350°F/Gas Mark 4 for 40 minutes, basting from time to time, till golden, the cut edges very lightly caramelised.

Scoop the soft cloves out from their skins with a teaspoon. Remove the tiny brown root. Mash to a purée using a pestle and mortar (easiest), a wooden spoon or, if you have done a large amount, a food processor. You will have a good heaped tablespoon of creamed garlic from each head.

You can then try the following:
- spread the neat purée thinly on toasted baguette as an appetiser;
- mix with a little cream cheese as a spread for toast;
- make a suave, rich sauce by mixing 2 tablespoons of garlic purée with a tablespoon of olive oil, a tablespoon of Marsala and 120ml/4fl oz double cream in a small pan over a low heat, cooking till thick and then season with salt – a good sauce for grilled poultry;
- add a spoonful to a casserole during cooking – it is already cooked, so can be added whenever you like;
- use as a store cupboard alternative to chopped garlic in stir-fries;
- store in an airtight jar in the fridge, with its surface covered by a thin layer of olive oil – it will keep for a week or two.

GLACÉ FRUIT

Now Christmas is over, what's left? Three dates stuck to the white paper doily in their oblong box, a handful of the silver-coated almonds that gave me an electric shock when they met my fillings, and an awful lot of nuts. Mostly almonds (because no one could crack the wretched things) and the odd brazil. There is also some candied fruit – both the expensive glacéd whole fruits from the South of France (which came as a gift; even I could not possibly spend that much money on myself) and a few pieces of the crystallised lemon and orange slices that were bought for the Christmas cake.

I have a penchant for sweet, sticky morsels to nibble with strong black coffee. No doubt my body is craving for the sugar I continually deny it. Turkish delight will do, a fudgy *marron glacé* or Elvas plum even better, but finest of all is a mouthful of sugar-encrusted crystallised fruit. I am not, just in case you are wondering, talking about those luminous red cherries (now available in fluorescent green) dripping in sweet slime or the rock-hard green and orange gravel known to cake makers the world over as candied peel. I am talking of whole fruits that have been preserved by soaking them, slowly and repeatedly, in vats of sugar syrup.

Glacé fruit is made in much the same way that it has been since the Middle Ages. The fruit is put into increasingly concentrated syrups, gently impregnating the slightly unripe flesh without damaging the fruit. Soaked slowly in sugar syrup, the traditional process can take several weeks for the

Rice Ice-cream with Rum-soaked Fruits

A somewhat indulgent ice, heavily laden with fruit, nuts and alcohol, taken from Caroline Liddell and Robin Weir's definitive and highly enjoyable book *Ices* (Grub Street). Serve in small amounts with crisp biscuits.

90g/3½oz mixed crystallised cherries, oranges,
   lemon and citron, finely diced
90ml/3fl oz dark rum
240ml/8fl oz whipping cream
100g/4oz vanilla sugar
40g/1½oz toasted almonds, chopped
435g/15oz can of creamed rice pudding

Put the finely diced fruits into a small saucepan with the rum and bring to simmering point. Cover and continue to simmer gently for 3–4 minutes, or until the peel is perfectly tender and only about 1 tablespoon of liquid remains. Leave to cool, covered. Combine with the remaining ingredients, stir well, cover and chill in the fridge.

When ready, freeze or pour into an ice-cream maker. Once the ice-cream is solid, it will need about 20 minutes in the fridge before it is soft enough to scoop.
Makes about 1l/1⅔ pints

Glacé Fruit in Vin Santo

Sweet Italian Vin Santo is similar in style to sweet Marsala, and although usually drunk after the meal with crisp biscuits, it can be used as a marinade for dried fruit or in place of sherry in a trifle. It is stocked by all licensed Italian grocery shops.

450g/1lb glacé fruit
420ml/14fl oz Vin Santo

Cut the fruit into small pieces, roughly the size of a pound coin. Place in a Kilner jar and cover with the Vin Santo. Stir well, then allow the fruit to settle. Seal and place in a cool place for at least 4 weeks, after which time the fruit will be soft and flavoured with the sweet wine.

Serve the fruit in tiny glasses and eat with a teaspoon, or better still spoon them over vanilla ice-cream along with any of the sweet wine that's left. Keep the fruit topped up with Vin Santo if you intend to keep them at all.

bigger fruits – even whole melons are given the treatment, though I have never seen one for sale outside France, where much of the process takes place.

Drained of its syrup and lightly dried, the fruit takes on an incandescent glow so that the clementines and pears shine like the baubles on a Christmas tree. The very best mandarins, probably in excess of £10 a pound, will sport a filling that is almost liquid, offering a welcome snap of bitterness to the sugary confection.

Sliced into elegant fragments and eaten with aromatic coffee or camomile tea, the greengages, pears and pineapple slices are the simplest of petits fours. Apricots are often the most juicy. Strawberries may disappoint. Yet a plateful passed around after dinner seems sometimes more appropriate than a truffle. Either way I want only a mouthful rather than a plateful.

At £14 per pound no wonder such delectable sweetmeats are sold only in the most upmarket of emporiums. The food halls of department stores are good hunting grounds, as is the glittering, red-carpeted ground floor of Fortnum and Mason's in London's Piccadilly. Produced in France, often in the Vaucluse, they are shipped all over the world, especially at Christmas. Now is a good time to splash out on a box or two; many retailers suspect that business for such luxuries will be slow after the festivities and sell them off cheaply.

The majority of fruits are made in the autumn and boxed to be sold as gifts. Some make it to the retail trade to be piled high in glowing pyramids in the world's food halls, to be dispensed by white-gloved assistants into waxed paper caskets and tied with ribbon. Lucky the recipient of such a generous gift. I would be happy to receive a moon-shaped wedge of crystallised citron, orange and lime peel that hang in plastic bags from the ceilings of Italian delicatessens. Stored in a cool place, they should keep in good condition, i.e. nearer Turkish delight than beef jerky, for three or four months.

To simply scoff them would be too decadent (and anyway I would probably feel slightly sick afterwards), but the half-dozen rattling around in their chic box are starting to get in the way now the feast is over. Such extravagant pieces need a home; fortunately they can be used in the kitchen to surprisingly good effect.

Sliced as thin as a pound coin, glacé fruits can be tossed with slices of pink and yellow grapefruit and sweet oranges for a sweet-sour dessert. Cut painstakingly into small dice, they can be scattered over vanilla ice-cream like millionaire Dolly Mixtures. Shaved wafer thin, like fragments of stained-glass windows, glacé fruits offer a fudge-like sweetness to a plate of slightly underripe pineapple. Fold them into the cream filling for a sponge cake or mix them with rich, thick mascarpone and serve them in small glasses with crisp biscuits.

Or, of course, you can always pack them away with the Christmas decorations till next year.

Candied Fruit and Mascarpone Cream

To be eaten in elegant amounts, preferably in a small wine glass, and served with crunchy biscuits. Spoon the mixture on to the biscuits as you eat.

2225g/8oz mascarpone cheese
2 teaspoons orange-flower- or rose-water
225g/8oz glacé fruit
a handful of shelled almonds

Put the mascarpone cheese into a mixing bowl and stir in the orange-flower- or rose-water. Chop the fruits into small dice and mix with the cheese. Toast the almonds till they start to smell warm and nutty, then chop them finely. Fold them into the cream cheese mixture and cover with cling film. Refrigerate for an hour or so, then place in small cups or glasses.
Serves 3–4 with biscuits

JAM

Quick Blackberry Jam

Some time ago a little book dropped through my door that contained recipes for all manner of interesting preserves. There were authentic Rillettes and Damson Relish, Tapenade and Soused Mackerel, herbed oils, flavoured mustards and even a Victorian Household Sauce for fish and chips. The basic method for this jam came from that delightful book, Simone Seker's *Quick and Easy Preserves* (BBC). Sugar-with-pectin is a commercial sugar to which has been added tartaric acid and apple pectin, which will make the fruits that traditionally have low amounts of the setting agent pectin in them set. In lieu of this special sugar, available from grocers' shops and supermarkets, I added the juice of a lemon and extended the boiling time by 2 minutes to no undue ill-effect.

450g/1lb slightly underripe blackberries
450g/1lb sugar-with-pectin

Check through the blackberries, removing any green fruit, leaves or stems. Rinse them, then drain carefully. Put them in a large, heavy-based pan with the sugar and bring to the boil. When they are bubbling and the fruit is producing lots of juice, boil hard for 3 minutes, stirring well. Settle briefly, then pot into warm, dry jars.
Makes a generous 700g/1½lb jam

Me? Make jam? Surely jam-making is for the super-efficient, the frugal and the house-proud. I am none of these. Neither am I a member of the WI. I am just not the sort of person who makes jam. But what else am I to do with a generous gift of red-, white- and blackcurrants that glare at me accusingly every time I open the fridge door?

With the exception of what I call cake-stall jams, the proper stuff made in people's home kitchens and sold at fêtes, I am not a fan of English jams and jellies. They are generally too stiff for my liking. And in the absence of a local WI stall (yes, I know the Women's Institute is no longer about swapping jam recipes and coffee mornings, but their roots lie with such things), I must make my own.

I am not sure that jam-making should be about frugality and good housekeeping. I have long suspected that the notion of squirrelling something away for winter actually appeals more than the quality of the end product. Few commercial products can compete with a good example of home-made. But it seems to me there are too many home-made jams where frugality has got the better of flavour.

Too much is made of getting 'a good set'. The British seem to prefer a stiffer jam than the rest of Europe, declaring anything with a tendency to softness 'a conserve or preserve'. I cannot see the joy in a lump of stiff jelly, dark and opaque from its long boiling, wobbling around perilously on my breakfast toast. Surely a softly set jam, thick with

Redcurrant Jelly

Eliza Acton's *Modern Cookery for Private Families* has, as perhaps you might expect from a Victorian cookery book, a comprehensive preserving chapter. The recipe that follows is virtually identical to Miss Acton's, though I have found a tiny amount of water prevents the sugar from sticking to the pot. I have ignored the writer's instructions to pull the currants from their stalks.

900g/2lb clean, dry redcurrants
900g/2lb sugar, caster or granulated

Check that the currants are free of leaves and dust. You can remove the fruit from their stalks if you wish, though I am not convinced it will make any difference. Wet the bottom of a heavy-based saucepan with a little cold water. It should be only a thin film, barely enough to see. Add the currants and the sugar to the pan and place over a low heat.

Bring slowly to the boil. Once the sugar has dissolved and the contents of the pan are bubbling fiercely, set the timer for 8 minutes exactly. Any shorter and the jelly may not set, any longer and the jelly may cloud. Remove from the heat and pour into a sieve, or colander lined with muslin, suspended over a jug. Leave for a few minutes for the juice to drain through. Do not press the fruit, or you will spoil the appearance of the jelly.

Pour the juice into clean, dry jam jars. (A rinse with boiling water and then drying with a clean tea-towel is enough, though some cooks recommend that you dry them in a low oven.) Cover with a screw-top lid or waxed-paper discs (available from kitchen shops and supermarkets) and seal tightly with cellophane. I use old jam jars with screw-top lids.
Makes a generous 1.4kg/3lb jelly

pieces of fruit, is preferable to something that sits on the plate and wobbles at you? Commercial jam-makers here could learn a thing or two by looking at the French manufacturers, whose jams ooze seductively rather than sit up and beg.

I cannot believe I am going to make jam. But if I am to make it at all then it will be in small amounts and purely for the pleasure of the result rather than as an exhibition of my good-housekeeping skills. My preserves, conserves, call them what you will, will never fill the larder (oh that I had one) and will be made in small batches. They will not be about saving a penny or two, even though I probably need to. Never will I go to the cupboard and think, 'Why on earth did I make so much rhubarb and ginger?' It will be light, contain as little sugar as I can get away with and be soft and quivering. Mine will slide unaided from spoon to scone.

I have just made a few pounds of fruit jelly. Blackcurrant, redcurrant and whitecurrant. To anyone used to commercially made redcurrant jelly with their roast lamb, this stuff will come as something of a revelation. It is softly set and glistens in the jar with jewel-like colours. The flavour is distinctly of the fruit and the result is more tart than the norm. The recipe was from Eliza Acton's *Modern Cookery for Private Families* (Southover Press), and is quite the best I have ever tasted. Miss Acton wrote her book in 1845.

The recipe comes with the following observation: 'We are told by some of our correspondents it is not generally successful in this country, as the jelly, though it keeps and is of the finest possible flavour, is scarcely firm enough for the table.' Well, it's firm enough for my table.

Breakfast for me is often a few slices of crisp baguette and some tart and slippery redcurrant jelly. I am no longer the sort of guy who can face a sausage of a Sunday morning. These jellies, as bright as a stained-glass window, will flatter everything from cold roast pork to hot roast chicken. I would be happy to swap the fashionable quince jelly eaten with cheese in Portugal and Spain for this sharper, fruitier version.

If jam-making is as easy as this, then I am hooked. I am currently making gooseberry jam. It will be strawberry next. The season for English strawberries, now extended with modern late-fruiting varieties, will last until September. For beginners to jam-making, I can recommend fruit jellies as a straightforward introduction to the genre. You can forget any special equipment, jelly bags and the like, though there are a handful of points I think worth passing on to other budding jammers before they get hooked. Me? Make jam?

Whitecurrant Jelly

You can use blackcurrants if you prefer.

900g/2lb dry, clean whitecurrants
1kg/2¼lb white sugar

Place a fine film of water in the base of a heavy saucepan. Add the currants and sugar. Bring very slowly to the boil over a low heat. When the sugar has dissolved – you can stir it just a little to help it along – and the mixture is boiling briskly, set a timer for 8 minutes.

As soon as the time is up remove from the heat. Pour the mixture into clean jars and treat as the redcurrant jelly opposite.
Makes a generous 1.4kg/3lb jelly

JAM TIPS

- Buy good-quality fruit. Second-rate fruit is bound to make second-rate jam. Anyway, it takes an age to sort through even a couple of pounds of fruit discarding all the stones, leaves and tatty berries.
- Go for something simple like a one-fruit jelly. Leave the rose and geranium jelly and rosehip and lemon verbena jam till you know what you are doing.

- Check that all jars, muslin and lids are scrupulously clean, especially if you intend to keep your jam for more than a week or so.
- Jam works perfectly well in small amounts. Even a couple of pounds of fruit is worth turning into jam.
- Once made, store the jam in a cool place; once opened, store it in the refrigerator.

LAMB

Lamb Chops with Parmesan and Parsley

Although lamb is delicious enough plainly grilled or fried, the grated Parmesan here adds an especially savoury note.

4 lamb chops, about 1cm/½ in thick, chump or
  loin
a handful of freshly grated Parmesan cheese
2 eggs, lightly beaten
50g/2oz fine breadcrumbs
a small handful of parsley, chopped
olive oil for frying
lemon to serve

Using a heavy bat or meat cleaver (or a fist if you are careful), flatten the chops a little, so they cook quite quickly. Press the chops into the grated Parmesan cheese, making certain that plenty of cheese sticks to both sides of the meat.

Dip the meat into the beaten egg, then into the breadcrumbs and chopped parsley. Heat a horizontal finger's depth of oil in a shallow pan. Fry the cutlets till golden, about 3 or 4 minutes on the first side, then a further 2 on the second. Remove and drain briefly on kitchen paper. Serve hot, with lemon on the side.
Serves 4

I love a bone to chew. The flat bone of a pork spare rib will do, or a chicken drumstick if it has been roasted for long enough, but most rewarding of all is the bone from a lamb chop. Those partial to a bone will fare better on the meat from an English butcher. That meticulously professional style of butchery practised by the French removes all the best bits, leaving the bones scraped so clean they might have been picked by vultures and parched in the desert sun. The best bones are those where a little meat still clings and roasts to gloriously crusty, chewy nuggets.

It is often said that meat cooked on the bone tastes better. I wholeheartedly go along with this notion, knowing that the results are not just juicier but also smell more tempting as they cook, the bones browning and crisping in the oven the way they do. Of course, meat roasted on its bones is less easy to cut, and I suspect many are not brave enough to do battle with a carcass at the table, with guests waiting impatiently while we carry out our pathetic attempt at amateur surgery.

The butcher will help. A thick bone, such as that on a pork or lamb rib roast, is almost impossible to cut with domestic tools, but a professional chopper will deal with it in one swoop. When the butcher asks if you want your meat chined, take him up on his offer; he will loosen the bone from the flesh without actually removing it, thus making for an easier carve-up.

My butcher tells of one customer who insists that he bashes her chicken with a cleaver, hard enough to smash the bones but not so violently as to splinter them, so convinced is she that the flavour from the bones will then more readily penetrate the meat. This makes sense. There is flavour in the bones, as we know from just how good a broth made from them tastes. Especially when the bones have been roasted.

Some bones chew better than others. Pork bones are wide and strong but often have little of interest on them as the meat comes away quite cleanly. Lamb bones are probably the most chewable, crisp and brittle with plenty of meat stuck to them; they are also small enough to gnaw at the table without making you look like Hannibal Lector. They also have lots of knobs and crevices for the best bits to hide in – the bits you really need to be alone with to get the best out of.

In one or two cases the bones seem the whole point of the dish: oxtail stew or *ossobuco* for instance, the Milanese braised shin of veal. Both dishes are enriched by the marrow contained in the bones, slowly giving up its flavour and gelatinous wealth to the sauce. Part of the fun of such food is tunnelling away with your knife and fork to extract every last bit of goodness from the bones. Bones of any sort are of value to the cook, though some more so than others; I could name a justly fêted chef who snatches grouse bones, sucked or not, from the plates in the restaurant wash-up and tosses them into the soup pot. While I applaud such culinary intelligence, I am not sure what I feel about traces of someone else's saliva in my soup.

Bones do not give up their flavour instantly. Meat takes longer to cook on the bone, demonstrated easily enough by timing the cooking of a lamb chop and a similarly thick but boneless lamb *noisette*. It is the slightly pinker meat attached to the bone which I find particularly tasty. I often wonder how anyone can leave their bones

Roast Rack of Lamb with Mustard and Peppercorn Crust

Butchers and supermarkets sell racks of lamb ready for the oven. For a fairly pink roast they need about 15 minutes per pound plus 15 minutes extra. A medium-pink roast will take about 20 minutes per pound and 20 minutes extra.

a rack of lamb with about 6 bones on it
1 tablespoon bottled green peppercorns
2 tablespoons Dijon mustard
50g/2oz butter, melted
4 tablespoons breadcrumbs

Put the prepared rack in a shallow dish or roasting tin. Crush the peppercorns slightly – easily done with a spoon against the side of a mixing bowl. Stir in the mustard, melted butter and breadcrumbs. You should have a thick paste.

Season the lamb generously with salt, then place in a hot oven, 220°C/425°F/Gas Mark 7. Roast for 15 minutes. Remove and spread the fat and cut sides of the meat with the mustard and peppercorn mixture. Return to the oven and continue roasting till it is done to your liking, probably about a further 30 minutes depending on the weight of the lamb (see timing note above) – some supermarket racks of lamb can be quite small.

Turn the oven off and leave the door ajar for 5 minutes to allow the lamb to rest. It will carve better that way, retaining its juices. Cut into cutlets and serve with any juice from the pan and a salad.
Serves 2

Braised Middle Neck with Red Wine and Garlic

4 thick-cut middle neck chops, about 225g/8oz
  each
flour for dusting
1 tablespoon olive oil
50g/2oz butter
2 large onions, peeled and sliced
6 cloves of garlic, peeled
bay leaf
a glass of red wine
2 heaped tablespoons redcurrant jelly
chopped parsley
a little grated lemon rind

Dust the chops lightly with flour. Heat the oil in a casserole and melt the butter in it. Add the chops and leave for 1 or 2 minutes to brown before turning over and colouring the other side. When they are brown and starting to smell good, add the sliced onions and garlic and cook for 4 or 5 minutes till they colour slightly. Pour over the wine, season with salt and freshly ground pepper and add the redcurrant jelly.

Bring to the boil, then turn the heat down very low, so the liquid just bubbles gently. Cover tightly with a lid and leave to cook for an hour or so. Turn the chops and cook for a further half-hour until the meat is tender and comes away from the bone without too much effort. Lift the lamb out of the pan on to warm plates.

Turn the heat up under the pan and cook for a few minutes till the sauce reduces and thickens slightly. Taste for seasoning, then spoon over the lamb. Sprinkle a little parsley, not too finely chopped, and a little grated lemon over the lamb as you serve. Offer bread and salad to mop up the juices.

Serves 4

unchewed. Why did they bother to cook a chop in the first place if they intended to leave the best bits for the dog?

Best of all cuts for the bone people such as myself is rack of lamb – the neat little joint comprising the upper ribs that form such a manageable and meaty handful. The flesh is tender and its bones are both elegant and sweet. Supermarkets now stock this joint too, making it a possibility as a weekday supper for those who do their shopping on the way home from work. Anointed with olive oil, seasoned with salt and a few herbs, this is the simplest of roasts and, with its six or eight bones, is perfect for two.

Those with a little more time will enjoy the thought of slow-cooked shanks of lamb, the knuckle end of the shoulder or middle neck chops that contain plenty of fat to moisten the meat as it cooks. Although after so long in the pot the meat may fall easily from the bones, they contain enough gelatine to remain interesting. Cooked for a couple of hours, sweetened with caramelised garlic and onions and braised in wine and its own juices, the shank and middle neck provide better eating than their low price would indicate.

Those too polite to chew a bone at table are missing something. I often wonder why, when confronted with a lamb cutlet or chop, we bother with knives and forks at all. The meat already has a handle to hold it by, so who are we to introduce man-made tools into the proceedings. It is, after all, only modern man who seems to have lost interest in chewing. We now demand foods that melt in the mouth, though if we roast our lamb carefully, we can have melting, succulent flesh – and a bone to chew.

LEFTOVERS

I am something of a larder lout. In fact, I would rather someone rifled through my dirty laundry than checked out the contents of my fridge. I know full well that they will ignore the bunch of lush green watercress, the chilled mineral water and the spanking-fresh lemon sole I have bought for supper and instead home in like radar on the minuscule scrap of cracked, sweaty Cheddar, the flattened tube of tomato purée long past its sell-by date, and the chipped cup of gravy from heaven knows when. I can almost hear the squeals of delight as they discover the lonely cooked sausage stuck to its saucer.

Open my salad drawer and their piercing eyes will cheerfully miss the ripe golden papaya, the luscious muscat grapes and the crisp, curly frisée. Instead they will pounce gleefully on the wrinkled furry tomato, the pink and grey remains of a long-forgotten tub of taramasalata and the bag of yellowing Brussels sprouts. Please God they miss the slimy black lettuce stuck to the bottom of the absurdly named salad-crisper.

Yet some of my most enjoyable meals have been made from the leftovers I found lurking in the depths of my fridge. On a cold winter's night, a rummage among the bowls, jugs and cling-wrapped saucers beats going shopping. I may not be interested in making a silk purse out of a sow's ear, but producing supper from yesterday's leftovers is quite another matter. I have eaten some of my best meals from bits found while rummaging through the fridge.

A Frugal Stew

Use the list below only as a guide to quantities – the actual choice of meat and poultry can depend on what you have around. Try to include something rich and gamy like pheasant legs, rabbit or spicy sausages. Serve with something starchy to soak up the juice and a crisp salad.

450g/1lb leftover cooked meat, game or poultry
   legs, etc.
2 sausages/black puddings
100g/4oz mushrooms
100g/4oz bacon, pancetta, etc.
a ham or prosciutto bone, as meaty as possible
1 large onion, peeled and roughly chopped
3 tablespoons olive oil
4 plump cloves of garlic, crushed
bay leaves
sprigs of thyme or rosemary or both
1 tablespoon tomato purée
600ml/1 pint water or stock

Cook the onion and garlic in the olive oil over a moderate heat until they start to soften and turn golden. If they catch a little at the edges, all to the good. Add the mushrooms, herbs and the tomato purée. Cook for 2 minutes, then add the liquid. Bring slowly to the boil, then add the meats. Season with salt and pepper, and simmer for about 30–40 minutes. Taste and correct the seasoning. Serve hot, with noodles, potatoes, lentils or rice to soak up the liquid.

Serves 2

Hotpot

Lancashire hotpot is often made with leftover roast meat. I am convinced it tastes better when slices of meat are used from yesterday's roast lamb. The result will be all the better if you include any bits of jelly, herbs and scrapings from the roasting tin, even if a note of inauthenticity creeps in.

About 450g/1lb of leftover roast lamb
2 tablespoons of dripping
450g/1lb onions, peeled and sliced
flour
600ml/1 pint water, or stock if you have it
900g/2lb potatoes, peeled
bay leaf
butter

Cut the meat into thick slices as best you can; if it comes away from the bone in lumps, then so be it. Melt the dripping in a deep, heavy pan and fry the onions till they are tender and slightly brown around the edges. Add a little flour, about a tablespoon, and stir in. Add the water or stock (I am not sure it makes that much difference in this instance) and stir to make a thin sauce. Season generously with salt and pepper.

Put the meat in a heavy casserole dish, one to which you have a lid. Pour over the onion sauce. Slice the potatoes thinly, a little thicker than a pound coin will do, then place them on top of the meat and sauce with the bay leaf. You can lay them out neatly in overlapping circles if you like. They will taste much the same if you leave them in a jumble – just so long as they are more or less level. Dot them with a bit of butter, cover with a lid and bake for about 2 hours at 120°C/275°F/Gas Mark 1. Remove the lid and leave for a further half an hour or so to brown. This is a good-natured dish, and quantities and cooking times will fit in with more or less whatever is available.

Serves 4

A find of a ham bone means soup, probably of the rich and thick variety with split peas. Some cold cooked fish needs little more than cream and breadcrumbs to make a hearty gratin, and bits of cold cooked vegetable can make a perfectly passable pottage. But we can do better than that. Cold potatoes can be sliced and sautéd in butter till crisp; cooked greens (provided they are not overcooked) can be stir-fried with garlic' and mushrooms and smothered in piping-hot gravy.

A roast chicken carcass is a positive Aladdin's cave of delights; the meat can be stripped and added to a risotto, the savoury brown jelly will add body to a casserole and the bones can be boiled up for soup. A clear broth made from the meaty carcass, strained and used for cooking *orzo*, the tiny rice-shaped pasta, makes a comforting and healthy bowl to come home to.

Gravy left from the roast is a gift from heaven. It is more than simply a way of providing employment for the cup with the broken handle and instead can be used as a sauce in which to heat things up, such as slices of cold roast meat, or as the base for a rich casserole. Yesterday's gravy can turn a lightly baked egg into that classic of the French kitchen, *les œufs en cocotte au jus*.

The best treat of all, though, must be the gravy and bits from a casserole left behind after the meat has been eaten. Can there be any greater treasure in the fridge than the thick, rich juices from *coq au vin*, *bœuf Bourguignon* or even a curry? Brought gently to the boil and served blisteringly hot over mashed potatoes, noodles or rice, this is often better than the original dish, apparently benefiting from its short sojourn in the fridge.

A night in the fridge does wonders, in terms of flavour at least, for dishes that contain a lot of sauce or juice. Flavours meld, aromas mingle and a certain magic happens while we sleep. The result is something all the more delicious for its time in cold storage. More than the sum of its parts, as they say.

Using leftovers is occasionally the point of the whole dish. Think of bubble-and-squeak, the mélange of cooked greens and mashed potatoes. Somehow the mixture needs its stay in the fridge to taste right; freshly made bubble-and-squeak never seems quite the same. This is food good enough to merit the cooking of extra vegetables for tomorrow.

Something I am particularly fond of is a rich, thick stew made from the carcasses of duck or chicken sweetened with onions and celery. The bones are used to make the stock, the meat is stripped from the bones, then the whole lot is simmered with mushrooms and bacon. Served with noodles or mashed potato, this is a comforting and frugal meal. It is also one of the few acceptable uses for that bullying ingredient, tomato purée.

Making something from yesterday's overestimations is nothing to be ashamed of and it is quite pointless to attempt to disguise the deed. You will only be discovered and declared a fraud. But I think too much is made of frugality. The point should surely be to make something good to eat rather than to amaze everyone with your resourcefulness.

It would be irresponsible of me not to mention at this point that you should use only food that is in good condition. If you are unsure of the vintage of some little morsel you have just found trapped between two saucers, then it is probably wisest to throw it into the bin rather than into the soup. But you know that already. On using leftovers from the fridge my rule of thumb is, 'If you cannot remember putting it in there, then forget it.'

Some people make an entire career out of using up the scraps in the fridge. They are the sort who suggest you should call them something other than leftovers and write entire books on the subject. What clever, resourceful, good housekeepers they

must be. I can imagine their joy at making an entire meal for six from the bits-in-bowls sulking in people's fridges. I can almost see the TV series; should it be *Celebrity Fridges*, *Through the Ice-Box* or *Fridgewatch*? Should the presenter be Loyd Grossman or Dame Edna?

Some days I dare not answer the door for the fear of the arrival of the Fridge Police. I can see the cameraman pushing through my front door to reveal to world the contents of my fridge. I can hear Dame Edna screeching, 'Madge, open the salad drawer. Oh, yuk!'

Monday Supper

Fast food from the fridge.

1 heaped tablespoon dripping or fat from the meat, plus the odd sprig of thyme, bay leaf, garlic clove, etc. from the pan
2 big handfuls of leftover pork, chicken, goose, lamb or beef
2 double handfuls of crisp fresh green cabbage
a few glugs of red wine
a wine glass of gravy

Melt the dripping, or oil if you have none, in a wok or large frying pan. Get it really hot. Chop the meat, or generally hack it about a bit. Shred the cabbage.

Throw the meat into the pan, cook for 2 minutes, then add the cabbage, which must be crisp and fresh and dark green. You can use leftover cabbage but I think you may be disappointed by its texture. Fry the cabbage and meat till the greens are vivid and then throw in the wine (3–4 tablespoons will probably be enough). Boil hard till almost evaporated, about 2 minutes, maybe less, then add the gravy. Season with salt and pepper – be generous. When all is hot – it must be really hot if it is to be good – scoop on to a plate and eat with more wine.
Serves 1

LEMONS

Moroccan Preserved Lemons

Moroccan cooks wisely exploit every bit of the lemon; but they also use it whole, preserving it in salt first, then adding both the juice and softened flesh to their cooking. A glass jar of preserved lemon is easy to prepare and will last for weeks in a cool kitchen. Nothing else quite matches their piquancy.

7 small, thin-skinned lemons
salt

Wash 6 of the lemons, but do not scrub them too hard, or you will lose some of the lemons' essential oils that lie in the skin before they get into the jar. Hold each lemon on its end and slice into quarters without cutting right through, leaving the fruit in 4 segments joined at the end. Rub sea salt into the cuts, then pile into a Kilner jar.

Add the juice of the remaining lemon and a level tablespoon of salt for the pot, then top up with boiling water. Seal and set aside for a couple of weeks.

To use:

- the liquid, which will be golden and will have thickened slightly, can be used in salad dressings, but best of all as a 'finish' to casseroles and sauces, when it will bring the dish to life;
- the peel can be cut away in strips, chopped and added to fish stews and soups;
- the pulp can be scooped out with a teaspoon and stirred into marinades, for fish, lamb or chicken;
- sliced or, more easily, quartered, add them to tagines or casseroles, or, in thin slices with a handful of chopped parsley and some black olives, to a sauté of chicken.

In my list of kitchen essentials the lemon stands equal to salt, peppercorns and garlic. Barely does a day go by without a lemon being squeezed, grated or peeled in my kitchen, and I would hate to be caught without one.

The lemon is a celebration of aromatic sourness that delights us with its fragrance, whets our appetite and accentuates the flavour of our food, offering our senses an arousing threesome. The zest, the juice and the flesh each has its part to play in the kitchen. Even the pips are used in the cosmetic business. To the cook, the lemon is a neat little bundle of joy, and one which causes most of us to salivate on sight.

The aptly named zest adds life to all it touches. Yellow and aromatic, this is the very outer rind of the lemon and is home to the fruit's essential oils. If it contains any white or bitterness, then you have gone too far and removed some of the pith, the useless (to the cook) white skin that comes between the zest and the flesh. It is the zest we want to flavour a lemon soufflé, whip into a creamy syllabub or add in long strips to an olive-oil-and-bay marinade for lamb chops.

Many recipes call for grated zest. Easier said than done – and I am not simply talking about the difficulty of removing the zest without the bitter pith. Most lemons have a thin coating of wax, not to mention a little fungicide and ammonia, none of which belongs in my pudding. Unwaxed lemons, incidentally, are still sprayed with fungicide. Organic lemons are what to choose if both wax and

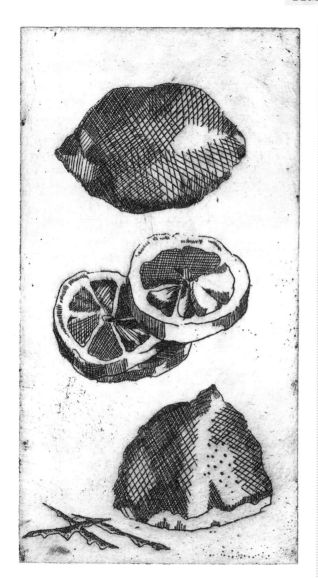

Baked Lemon Potatoes

The Greeks have a way with potatoes that is quite unforgettable to anyone who has strayed off the beaten track there. Bathed in olive oil and lemon juice, the potatoes are baked till soft, almost falling apart.

4 medium-sized potatoes, thinly sliced
1 plump clove of garlic
2 tablespoons olive oil
bay leaves
juice of 2 large lemons

Place the potatoes in an ovenproof dish. Squash the garlic clove and add it whole. Pour over the olive oil and lemon juice, and add a couple of bay leaves, a little salt and a generous grinding of black pepper. Bake, at 200°C/400°F/ Gas Mark 6, for about an hour or until soft and slightly crisp on top. Stir once or twice during cooking.
Serves 2–4

sprays offend – but in turn organic lemons keep slightly less well. It's up to you to decide your priorities.

You could wash them, of course, but I see a problem here. Rinsing them under running water

Lemon Surprise Pudding

If ever there was a dish that celebrates the clean, sharp flavour of the lemon, this is it.

100g/4oz butter
175g/6oz caster sugar
finely grated zest and juice of 3 large lemons
4 eggs, size 2, separated
50g/2oz plain flour
120ml/4fl oz milk

Butter a 19cm/7in soufflé dish and preheat the oven to 180°C/350°F/Gas Mark 4. Using an electric or hand held beater, cream the butter with the sugar until it is creamy white and fluffy. Add the lemon juice and zest. The mixture will probably curdle at this point but ignore it and beat in the egg yolks, 1 at a time, and then gently beat in the flour and the milk.

With a clean whisk, beat the egg whites till they stand in snowy peaks, then fold gently into the mixture. Pour into the buttered dish, then set the dish in a roasting pan with water half-way up its sides. Bake for about 45 minutes, until the sponge is risen and golden brown and a thick lemony custard has appeared under it. Serve with cream if you wish.

Serves 4

just seems to make them sticky, which is either the juice escaping or the wax melting. I suspect the latter. The answer is to buy unwaxed lemons and run them lightly under the tap to wash off any dust.

Removing the zest without the pith should be easy enough. I have one of those box-type graters with a handle on top. The four sides produce everything from fingernail-sized chips to slush, but little in between. On the only useful side its teeth have dulled to the point where they barely make an impression on a truly ripe lemon, although it can still manage a knuckle or two. Most new graters, although satisfying to use, are often so sharp that it is almost impossible to remove zest without the pith.

I have read instructions to remove the zest with a lump of sugar. I am not sure this works either, having never managed to extract even the smallest amount of zest with a cube of Tate and Lyle. I also have, lurking at the back of the drawer with the ravioli-cutter, a little black-handled tool with a squat blade pierced with five neat little holes. You draw it down the lemon and it scrapes off thinner strips of zest than you can get with either grater or knife. The strips are fine enough to dissolve in most things.

The flavour of the lemon's juice is quite different to that of its zest. Try it. The zest is aromatic while the juice is acid. So acid in fact, that the juice is used, often in conjunction with limes and salt, to 'cook' fish and shellfish. Thinly slice white fish or scallops and lay them in a dish with plenty of lemon juice and a generous amount of salt; their flesh will firm up and turn opaque – in other words, cook. A squeeze of juice is also invaluable to stop a cream sauce from cloying or to prevent hard fruits going brown. In my book, lemon juice also has the ability to heighten the flavour of pretty much anything it meets: fruit, vegetables, soups, casseroles, grilled fish and meats. Disaster seems to strike only when it meets tomatoes, cheese or chocolate.

Some lemons contain more juice than others. In fact some seem to contain virtually none at all. While the juice content of a lemon decreases with age, it is often the variety of fruit that really makes the difference. In my experience the rounder the fruit, the juicier it will be. Avoid at all costs the slim ones with big nipples; you'll get nothing out of them. I have no doubt that the thinner the skin, the more piquant and lip-puckering the juice that the lemon will hold. You can tell before you buy them by giving them a squeeze. A good guide is to press hard with your thumb. If you can make some sort of impression, you have got a juicy one. If the skin is hard, very glossy and covered with little white freckles, then it is certainly a thick-skinned lemon, which will offer little in terms of flesh or juice.

But here is the crux of the matter. Like most fruit, lemons are rarely ripe when you buy them. A hard lemon is no more ready to use than an unripe pear or peach. The experts insist that citrus fruit does not ripen once harvested, and I am sure that they are technically correct, but I have consistently found that they do get softer and the juice becomes more free-flowing when you have had them at home for a few days. In a week or so, their flavour changes from bitter to aromatic. If you don't believe me, try squeezing a lemon hard from the shop and one that you have had in the kitchen for a week which has softened and taken on a deep yellow natural glow. There will almost certainly be more juice in the softer lemon.

We can even improve on this if we squeeze lemons that are at room temperature rather than cold. If the oven is on for something else, pop them in for a few minutes, or pour boiling water over them before you squeeze them. Warm fruit gives more juice. And in my book, the more lemon the better. Keep one next to the salt and pepper.

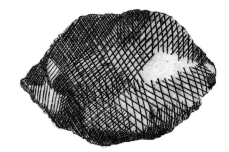

MARINADES

Baked Sea Bream with Fennel and White Wine

Bream, red snapper and sea bass are all suitable for this treatment. Ask the fishmonger to clean the fish for you.

1 bulb fennel, finely sliced
1 small red onion, finely sliced
2 cloves of garlic, lightly crushed
1 lemon, sliced
1 tablespoon fennel seed
4 small sprigs of rosemary
2 sprigs of thyme
bay leaf
2 sea bream, cleaned and scaled
4 tablespoons olive oil
3 wine glasses of white wine

Mix the fennel, onion, garlic, lemon, fennel seeds, rosemary, thyme and bay leaf together. Place the mixture in a shallow ovenproof glass or china dish large enough to take both fish – or, of course, in 2 separate dishes suitable for 1 fish. Place the fish on top of the aromatics. Pour over the olive oil and wine. Set in a cool place for at least 3 hours, turning the fish every hour.

Season with salt and black pepper, then cover with buttered or oiled greaseproof paper. Bake at 190°C/375°F/Gas Mark 5 for 20–25 minutes till the fish is tender, basting once with the cooking juices. Serve with new potatoes and green beans.

Serves 2

There is something going on in my fridge. Nothing sinister, but deeply mysterious all the same. It is something to do with the fact that I have taken to marinating things overnight in wine, oil and aromatics in the hope of making them a little more interesting. A less than flavoursome chicken, frozen prawns less exciting than the packet they came in and artichokes too tiny and tender to risk in boiling water have all been transformed overnight into things of joy.

I find the thought of all those herbs, spices and alcohol working their magic while I sleep intriguing to the say the least. I have no clue as to what chemistry goes on overnight to transform a dull old bird into a chicken really worth eating, or why a fish that has been steeping in wine, rosemary and garlic emerges as dramatically more than the sum of its parts. I only know that it does.

The very mention of marinating conjures up the thought of great joints of meat steeping in tin baths. There is still something rather outdated about the idea of soaking a joint of meat in a mixture of wine, water and herbs to render it good enough to eat. I suspect that the original purpose was to tenderise tough meat or to preserve it in prime condition till it was ready to cook. Very eighteenth century. With tough meat something of a rarity nowadays, not to mention the universal acquisition of the refrigerator, the main reason for marinating is simply one of flavour. And there is no better reason than that.

Done properly – that is with the right balance of

oil, acid and flavouring and for the optimum amount of time – food that has had a little soak in something delicious will appear more succulent and, in terms of flavour, more interesting. It is worth getting it right. Leave your chicken in its aromatic bath too long and the flesh will change in texture most disagreeably. It will turn pappy and woolly. Get it right and you will have something very special for virtually no extra work.

A simple marinade takes but a minute or two to make. Even if the method is as much chemistry as art, the ratio of ingredients is still more common sense than alchemy. You know that the chances are high that a fish swimming all night in three parts vinegar to one part brandy will not result in the exquisite morsel you are after. It is easy to guess that the wine you have written off as sour is not going to turn your prawns into a gastronomic treat just because you have thrown in a handful of chillies and some sesame oil.

Grilled Marinated Goats' Cheese

6 small semi-hard goats' cheeses, about
    75g/3oz each
3 plump cloves of garlic
4 bay leaves
1 large or 2 smaller mild chillies
4–6 sprigs of thyme
12 peppercorns
6 large basil leaves
600ml/1 pint extra virgin olive oil

Put the cheeses, garlic and herbs in a spotlessly clean Kilner jar. If you can sterilise it with boiling water first, then so much the better. Pour over the olive oil, which should cover the cheeses and leave as little air space as possible. Set aside in a cool place, not the fridge, for a fortnight.

to cook
12 slices of baguette, 6mm/¼in thick, cut at a slight
    angle
6 marinated goats' cheeses, cut in half horizontally
4 tablespoons oil from the jar

Spoon a little olive oil over each slice of baguette. Lay a half of each cheese on each slice. Cook under a hot grill till the cheese is bubbling. Serve immediately with a salad of frisée and chicory.
Serves 6 as a light snack

SOME OTHER IDEAS

Prawns

Try marinating shelled and de-veined prawns in the following mixture: 2 tablespoons of soy sauce, 3 tablespoons of rice wine (or dry sherry), 2 cloves of garlic, lightly crushed, 2 hot red chillies, the juice of 2 limes, salt and 4 lightly crushed lime leaves. Leave for at least an hour, then grill for 3 minutes on each side.

Kippers

Make a marinade with a small, finely sliced onion, 2 teaspoons of crushed coriander seeds, 1 tablespoon of grain mustard, 2 teaspoons of brown sugar, 60ml/2fl oz of cider vinegar, 10 juniper berries and 180ml/6fl oz of light olive oil. Mix the ingredients in a jug. Pour the marinade over 6 kipper fillets, then add a couple of bay leaves, four healthy sprigs of dill and 8 black peppercorns. Cover with cling film and refrigerate for 3 or 4 days. Serve with bread and butter.

I have seen sweet golden wine, thyme and orange peel transform a lacklustre farmed quail, unctuous emerald-green olive oil and a chilli breathe life into a nondescript pasteurised goats' cheese, and tangy soy sauce and lime leaves do wonders for a frozen prawn. A bath in cider vinegar and juniper berries jollied up a kipper no end. The possibilities appear to be endless.

The basic rules of the marinade are easy to absorb. Don't use an aluminium or copper pot unless you want the lemon juice, vinegar or acid to dissolve it into the sauce. Don't forget your fish is in the bath, unless you actually want it to taste like cotton wool. And don't forget to wipe the moisture from the surface of the meat before you slap it on the grill; otherwise it will steam and turn grey rather than grill crisply and turn appetisingly, gloriously golden brown.

I admit that a certain amount of forethought is required. And although I am not the type who knows what he will be eating the next day, I find the thought that tomorrow's supper is secretly being transformed in my fridge into something worth cooking faintly reassuring. It appeals to me that the ingredients can get on with some of the cooking themselves while my mind is elsewhere. Even if I don't really understand what is going on.

Grilled Quail in Muscat Wine and Thyme

If quail is not for you, chicken is just as suitable for this recipe, cut into joints. The joints may take a little longer; cooking them slightly further away from the heat will help the insides to cook before the skin burns, although a little charring is desirable.

1 carrot, finely diced
1 small onion, finely diced
1 stick of celery, finely diced
1 teaspoon coriander seeds, lightly crushed
4 cloves of garlic, lightly crushed
2 tablespoons olive or walnut oil
4 sprigs of thyme
a half-bottle of muscat wine
6 quails, split down the backbone and opened flat,
    or 6 small joints of chicken

Cook the carrot, onion, celery, coriander seeds and garlic in the oil with the thyme till soft and golden. Remove from the heat, pour in the wine and transfer to a large glass or china dish. Place the quail or chicken pieces in the marinade and set aside.

Leave the quails to marinate in the wine and herbs for at least 3 hours, turning them over from time to time – overnight would be better.

Get the grill hot. Remove the quails from the marinade and dry slightly with paper towels. Drizzle with a little olive or walnut oil and place skin side down on the grill pan. (If you are using one of those grill pans that sits on the hob you will get a crisper, juicier result than with an overhead grill.) Cook at full heat for 4–5 minutes, basting with some of the marinade from time to time. Turn over and grill the skin side for a further 4 minutes. Check for doneness. If the juices run clear when pierced with a skewer, then they are ready; if not, turn over again and cook for a little longer, moving the pan away from the heat a little, or turning down the heat. Season lightly with salt.

Serve with the pan juices, dissolved from the bottom of the pan with some of the marinade if they have stuck, salad and sautéd potatoes, or buttery mashed potatoes sprinkled with some of the pan juices. Gnawing the bones is part of the fun.
Serves 2

MAYONNAISE

A Piquant Mayonnaise

An addition of sharp-flavoured ingredients lifts the mayonnaise recipe opposite, taking away some of its richness and making it particularly suitable for serving with hot grilled lamb and chicken.

240ml/8fl oz mayonnaise
4 small gherkins, quite finely chopped
2 tablespoons capers, rinsed and chopped
a small handful of parsley, chopped
2 tablespoons tarragon, chopped
1 teaspoon grain mustard

Mix the ingredients together, adding more or less of each as you wish. Taste and season with a little white pepper.

Cucumber Mayonnaise

An aniseed-scented sauce for serving with fish.

1 cucumber, grated
300ml/10fl oz mayonnaise
150ml/5fl oz fromage frais or whipped double
  cream
2 teaspoons lemon juice
2 tablespoons fresh dill, chopped

Put the cucumber in a colander and sprinkle with a little salt. Leave to drain for 20 minutes. Mix the mayonnaise and the fromage frais or cream together carefully. Stir in the lemon juice and the chopped dill. Drain the cucumber and fold into the mayonnaise. Check the seasoning. Serve with chicken or fish (it is particularly good with cold trout or salmon) or spread on sandwiches.

Certain commercial food products are held in great esteem. Some are often cited as being better than home-made, and let's face it, sometimes they are. A world-famous ice-cream, for instance. Even a tinned tomato soup is often held up as the best of its kind. The best manufactured product is certainly better than the worst home-made version. But it is only too easy to forget that even the best factory-produced food cannot hold a candle to the best home-made. This is the case with mayonnaise.

The best commercially made mayonnaise is pretty good. Spooned from the jar, it makes a fine lubricant for a snatched sandwich, particularly one eaten late at night, when there is no one to see the generosity with which it is spread. White, creamy and mild, commercial mayo lends richness to a bacon butty, acts as a lazy dip for a raw carrot or celery stick and makes a passable dressing for a potato salad. I suggest that it is at its most useful when slathered in obscene amounts on a split baguette and stuffed with fried oysters or fish fingers, then scattered with capers and a slice or two of gherkin.

Its role in such spontaneous fare is nothing more than a rich and creamy lubricant to the crisp and the dry – which it performs admirably. But I think that this is as far as the commercial version of what Elizabeth David described as 'the beautiful, golden, shining ointment' goes. In other words, I wouldn't serve it with cold salmon. Or, for that matter, anything I was making for someone else to eat. Bottled mayonnaise is all fine and dandy for instant sustenance. But where mayonnaise is an important part of the meal, as it so often is in midsummer, I think a little more effort is called for.

Real mayonnaise, by which I mean that made at home from egg yolks, olive oil and a little seasoning, is a very different product altogether from the commercial version. For a start, the principal ingredients are different. Water, vegetable oil, sugar, antioxidant and colouring are not in my recipe. They are certainly not in Elizabeth David's. Real mayonnaise is gold in colour, it wobbles on the spoon and shines, glossy with olive oil. In the commercial alternative the water is there, of course, to make the product more manageable rather than spread the manufacturers' profits. The antioxidant is to increase its shelf life and the colouring is no doubt necessary to distinguish it from the salad cream further along the shelf. I am not sure about the sugar.

I like the taste of olive oil in my mayonnaise. Others prefer a milder flavour. If it is destined for cold salmon or, better still, cold poached or roasted cod, then the oil used should not be too powerful. Some of the deep-green, peppery extra virgin olive oils can be too big a flavour, overwhelming rather than flattering the fish. The result can be rough-tasting and greasy. A fruity oil, perhaps a Provençal one, may be more suitable. Of course, the oil is a matter of personal choice. Many like a bland groundnut or even vegetable oil for their mayonnaise. I am not sure that this is really mayonnaise, though. Its purpose can only be to add lubrication or unctuousness. The blandness of such a cream can be useful for those who make savoury mousses and the like, though it is surely too insipid as an accompaniment.

Sometimes I make my mayonnaise so thick you can cut it with a knife, though when that much oil has been beaten in, it must be a mild one if the

Basic Mayonnaise

A thick, glossy version with a fruity flavour.

2 large free-range egg yolks
300ml/10fl oz fruity extra virgin olive oil
lemon

Put the 2 egg yolks into a large round-bottomed bowl, preferably glass or china – banging a metal whisk on a steel bowl can be tiresome to listen to. Sprinkle a pinch of salt over the yolks and stir them briefly with a whisk. The salt will thicken them slightly, which makes the early stages of the thickening process easier. Add a drop of olive oil, no more than half a teaspoon at first, whisking constantly until it has disappeared. Add more oil, no more than a teaspoon at a time and whisking continually until the mixture starts to thicken.

When a quarter of the oil has been used up, you can increase the flow of oil to a steady trickle, whisking as you go. When the oil is used up, give it a final hard beating. Taste it, add salt and a squeeze of lemon juice to taste. I add the juice from a quarter of a lemon to the above quantity.
Enough for 4

TO THIN OR LIGHTEN A MAYONNAISE

- Use 1 or 2 tablespoons of warm water or milk.
- Mix in half the amount of fromage frais or softly whipped cream.
- Stir in a tablespoon of warm water and a stiffly beaten egg white.

flavour is not to be harsh. There is something about making mayonnaise that heightens the flavour of the oil used. Thick mayonnaise can be thinned down to order, making it easier to use in dressings. A little hot water for a potato salad, yoghurt for dressing vegetables or softly whipped cream for dipping asparagus or artichokes. Fromage frais will add tang without fat. A little milk, although perhaps something of an intrusion, will thin down a mayonnaise whose flavour is too strong.

Making your own is not such a trial, taking only marginally more effort than opening a jar. Don't believe anyone who tells you that making home-made mayonnaise is difficult. It's not. All you need is egg yolks, olive oil and a fairly strong arm. A little seasoning, in the form of lemon juice, salt and pepper, will not go amiss. A dollop of smooth mustard is a good idea but optional. I have made mayonnaise in a minute or two in my food processor, though the consistency is not as thick and unctuous as when I do it by hand. As it happens, I actually enjoy making mayonnaise with a hand-held whisk.

Rules for making your own are quite frightening if you care to take any notice of them. You may think that if your bowl and whisk are not the right temperature, or there is a risk of thunder or you fail to add boiling water at the end, your efforts will end in disaster. Not so. The only care you need to take is not to add too much oil to the yolk at the beginning, though I have found the 'drop by drop' rule advocated in most recipes is a little overcautious. Just don't add more than a teaspoon of oil at a time to start with.

Once your egg yolk and carefully added oil have started to thicken you can pour in the rest of the oil in a steady stream. It will not curdle so long as you whisk the oil thoroughly between beatings. Provided the oil is not actually frozen or hot, its temperature is of little importance. If your oil is very strongly flavoured, you may like to mix it half and half with a milder oil such as groundnut. The olive taste will still come through but not so loudly that it limits the use of the finished mayonnaise. I use a mildly fruity French olive oil.

It has just taken me 10 minutes to whisk up half a pint of golden, wobbling, mayonnaise. The hottest day of the year so far and I didn't even break into a sweat. Intended as an accompaniment for this evening's fish, I only meant to taste it for seasoning yet somehow the bowl found its way into the garden with a crisp baguette and a glass of wine. My 'golden, shining ointment' destined for the evening's cold salmon has suddenly become lunch for two. Imagine that, a bowl of mayonnaise for Sunday lunch. And not a famous name in sight.

MINCEMEAT

For hundreds of years Britain's food had much in common with that of the Arab world. For those who could afford it, the lemons, almonds, saffron and ground spices with which Middle Eastern food is so liberally laced were used with abandon in our kitchens. Hard to believe when we look at the way most of us use spices now – as if we were seasoning our food with gold, frankincense and myrrh itself. Even harder to believe that our only reminder of that period of culinary richness is the dear little mince pie.

That sweet, diminutive tartlet, handed round with the mulled wine after Midnight Mass, or offered in lieu of gold to the carol singers, is almost all that is left of the Arab influence on Britain's cooking. Such festive fare is the nearest we get to the vast, sweet, spiced meat pies that graced our seventeenth-century tables. How magnificent those huge tarts must have been, their pastry crusts bursting with ox tongue, veal, chicken and eggs, sweet with sugar, rose-water and raisins and sour with grape juice and lemon peel. Time, changing tastes and commercialism have whittled those glorious, extravagant centrepieces down to a spoonful of sticky black jam and a handful of dry pastry.

Yet there is a certain extravagance about even modern mincemeat. Not that you would know it from the amount some cooks put in their pies, rationing the filling as if the war was still on. Dried fruits, chopped citrus peel and brandy do much to produce a luxurious mixture. Can there be a more

Crumble-topped Mincemeat Cake

Katie Stewart is one of those people whose books I turn to when I want what I call proper home cooking: roast duck, mackerel pâté, real gravy or kedgeree. *Simply Good Food* (Macmillan), her most recent book, co-written with Caroline Young and her first in 10 years, contains recipes set to appeal to the 1990s cook: Monkfish in Green Chilli and Coconut Cream, Pear, Ham and Cabbage Stir-fry and Bacon and Apple Cassoulet. Included is this delectable mincemeat cake. I have taken the liberty of changing the authors' soft margarine for butter.

275g/10oz self-raising flour
75g/3oz chilled butter, diced
75g/3oz caster sugar
25g/1oz flaked almonds
pinch of salt
5ml/1 level teaspoon baking powder
100g/4oz softened butter
100g/4oz soft brown sugar
2 eggs
2.5ml/½ teaspoon vanilla extract
30ml/2 tablespoons milk
550g/1¼lb mincemeat
icing sugar

Heat the oven to 180°C/350°F/Gas Mark 4. Butter a 22.5cm/9in spring-release tin.

Start with the topping: sift 100g/4oz of the flour, the diced butter, and caster sugar into a processor and buzz to coarse crumbs. Tip into a bowl and stir in the almonds. Set aside.

To make the cake: sift the remaining 175g/6oz of flour, the salt and baking powder into a medium-sized bowl. Add the softened butter, soft brown sugar, eggs, vanilla and milk. Stir with a wooden spoon to blend the ingredients, then beat to a soft cake mixture. Spoon into the prepared tin and spread level. Fork the mincemeat over the batter. Sprinkle the topping over the mincemeat. Bake for 45–50 minutes till golden brown. Cool in the tin for 5 minutes before removing the sides and sprinkling the cake with icing sugar.

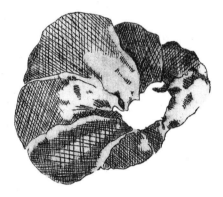

Mincemeat and Clotted-cream Croissants

The instant mince pie. Almost absurdly rich, but an alternative for those who like mince pies but don't want to make pastry. The crispness of the flaky pastry works well with the unctuousness of the mincemeat.

2 croissants
6 heaped tablespoons good mincemeat
4 tablespoons clotted cream

Split the croissants in half horizontally. Toast both halves under a hot grill until the cut edges are golden brown. Fill the bottom halves with the mincemeat, spoon on the clotted cream then place the top halves back on. Warm gently either under the grill (move the grill pan as far from the heat source as possible) or in a hot oven. Serve hot, spooning the melted cream back over the croissants. *Serves 2*

hospitable smell than that of mince pies baking, even though it must be little more than a shadow of the scent of the earlier versions?

The first mention of Christmas pies was in 1557, though they did not appear in detail until 1607, when the great hostess Elinor Fettiplace included them in her book of receipts. In Hilary Spurling's 1987 (Penguin) edition of Lady Fettiplace's book, mincemeat appears a much more savoury affair, full of beef and its suet and flavoured in Middle Eastern style with rose-water, cinnamon and orange peel. The texture would have been drier and the flavour considerably spicier than the gungy preserve we know today.

Robert May's mid-seventeenth-century recipe (in *The Accomplisht Cook*, Prospect Books) contained a leg of veal and 6 pounds of beef suet, the sweetness coming from dates, peel and currants. Spiced with nutmeg, cinnamon, ginger and pepper, the mixture is given a sour note by crab apples and preserved oranges and fragrance by no less than 1 pint of rose-water. A beef pie of the period was likely to be sweetened with currants and raisins and spiced with nutmeg and mace, while mutton gets its dose of sugar and spice from prunes and caraway.

By the time Lady Clark of Tillypronie recorded three recipes for mincemeat in the late 1800s meat was no longer part of the recipe. In the welcome new facsimile of her practical 1909 book, *The Cookery Book of Lady Clark of Tillypronie* (Southover Press), two of her mincemeat recipes had replaced the traditional beef with large quantities of port and brandy, while another contains lemon juice and both fresh and candied lemon peel.

Even suet, all that remains of what was originally a savoury pie, is losing favour. In commercial products suet is added more as a token than for its original purpose, which was to help preserve the mixture. I have been told countless times that home-shredded suet is better than the packet variety, enabling the mincemeat to keep longer. Not that I will ever know. I seriously doubt the sanity of anyone prepared to grate several pounds of hard white fat into their spiced currants. Even Elizabeth David, hardly a sloven in the kitchen, was too idle to do it. 'Shredding suet is a terrible task. I cannot make myself spend so much time and effort on it,' she writes in her *Spices, Salt and Aromatics in the English Kitchen* (Penguin).

Modern mincemeat relies on sugar as its preservative. And don't we know it. So sweet has commercial mincemeat become that it is in danger of turning into Christmas jam, losing the underlying tartness that stops its tendency to cloy. Originally the flavour was sharpened with verjuice, the juice of unripe grapes, or, more likely in Britain, crab apples. Gooseberries and redcurrants were added to the meat sometimes, a mixture I would dearly like to taste. Nowadays I add a slug of brandy and lemon juice to commercial mincemeat. It cuts through the sweetness no end.

In the eighteenth century the vast, pompous pies were reduced in size to something nearer the little tarts we have today. They were coffin-shaped, to represent the Christ child's cradle. The spices were considered to represent the gifts of the three kings. Such flagrantly papist pies were banned by Cromwell. The mince pie has been round ever since. Perhaps this also explains the lack of spice in commercial versions. Or is it simply manufacturers once again underestimating the sophistication of the British palate?

Ancient recipes were generous with the nutmeg, saffron, cinnamon and ginger in a way we cannot begin to imagine. Even scaled down for modern use, the quantity of spice is gargantuan in comparison with today's tastes, though the pies may well have been somewhat staler than ours, and therefore weaker in flavour. Certainly few contemporary cooks would suggest pepper as one of the essential mincemeat spices.

Mincemeat made to an old recipe will naturally be more opaque than a modern, fatless recipe, the fat turning the mixture cloudy as it cools. The more shiny and transparent the goo around the fruit, the less traditional it will taste. But do I really want bits of fat and meat in my mincemeat? I am not sure I do.

There are signs, though, that our interest in simultaneous sweetness and spice in meat dishes is returning. North African and Arab food, with its long, slow cooking and flavourings of cinnamon, chilli, honey and raisins, is growing enormously in popularity in this country. A typical cous-cous recipe contains lamb in a stew spiced with chilli and saffron and sweetened with raisins. A mixture not at all dissimiliar to the original filling in our dear little mince pie.

Pan-fried Panettone and Mincemeat Sandwich

A crisp and buttery snack that somehow tastes and smells like the very essence of Christmas. The recipe is taken from *Nigel Slater's Real Fast Puddings* (Penguin).

for each person
1 slice of panettone, 10mm/⅓in thick
2 tablespoons good mincemeat
30g/1oz butter

Cut the panettone into semicircles and spread 1 half with mincemeat. Press the other half gently on top. Melt the butter in a small frying pan over a moderate heat and when it bubbles add the sandwich. Fry till golden brown on both sides. Remove with a palette knife, cut in half and eat while hot and crisp.

MUSSELS

Tender, sweet and tantalisingly salty, the humble mussel comes into season in September. A fat bag of shiny black mussels is the cheapest fish supper you can buy, barely more than pence per person. Like oysters, red mullet and sea urchins, mussels offer the very essence of the sea. For landlubbers like me, a bowl of tangy *moules marinières*, or *mouclade* with cream and saffron, is the nearest I get to a dip in the ocean.

I have just bought a bag of the tiniest mussels. Their flesh is sweet and the texture of jelly. It cost £2 from a city fishmonger too close to directors' dining rooms to care about overcharging, but it will feed two with bread and wine. Like spaghetti, mussels play heavily on the fact they are awkward to eat. You think you have eaten more than you actually have. But they should satisfy with a sufficiently stodgy pudding afterwards.

Of course, not everyone likes mussels. I have heard many refuse to eat them, convinced they will be poisoned. A little care is needed in their preparation. Dump the mussels in a sink of cold water and leave them for 10 minutes. Tap them firmly on the side of the sink and if they fail to close, then throw them away. Likewise any that are suspiciously heavy or whose shell is chipped or shattered.

With the cold-water tap running, pick up each shell and pull away the fuzzy beard. It will probably have bits of shell and seaweed in it. One good tug should do it. You can chip away at any barnacles too, though there is no need to be too fussy. If the mussels are young, there will be only one or two anyway. Leave the plump, clean little shells in a fresh change of water while you prepare the rest of the supper. Do not feed them with oatmeal or whatever else you have been told about; mussels do not eat porridge.

I hesitate to eat my mussels raw. They are harvested from relatively shallow waters around the British coastline and if I am to eat something that has grown fat on sewage, then I would prefer it to have been cooked at least a little before it gets to my mouth. But overcooking is the death of these wobbly, beige and gold molluscs. Once the heat has prised open their shells, they are ready. Much more cooking and their jelly-like flesh will turn to rubber.

Methods of cooking the mussel are limited to those which do the task as quickly as possible: deep-frying, grilling and sautéing will give a better result than slow stewing or baking. Slow cooking does nothing for a mussel. Steaming – high temperature, moist heat – is by far the most successful if the flesh is to wobble seductively on the half shell rather than bounce around like a school rubber.

If you have never tried mussels grilled with butter and breadcrumbs, then you are in for a treat. Such classical treatment is often overlooked by those in search of a quick supper – yet a plate of stuffed mussels can be yours in under an hour, quicker with a little help prising the top shell off each mussel. If scrupulously cleaned raw mussels were available from a source you could trust, in other words Marks and Sparks, it would make a mussel supper much less daunting.

Cider and white wine make good bed-fellows for the mussel, as does parsley, tarragon, butter and cream. I am less convinced by the addition of garlic, which is often used with too little discretion in mussel dishes. The flesh has a delicate flavour that can easily be lost in the pungent haze of too many

Warm Mussel and Potato Salad

I am pleased that *Cooking for Occasions* by restaurant critic Fay Maschler and novelist Elizabeth Jane Howard has recently been republished (Macmillan). Its original approach of menus for specific occasions, including Foolproof Dinner, Late-night Shopping, Funeral Tea and Impressing People, makes good reading. The introduction to Weekend Entertaining, 'It is deeply depressing for guests to open wardrobes and find them full of clothes you haven't yet sent to Oxfam,' alone is worth the price of admission. This recipe is from the Budget Dinner Party chapter.

1kg/2lb waxy potatoes
1.5kg/3lb mussels
1 glass of white wine
6 shallots or spring onions, cleaned and chopped
parsley, some chopped and some in sprigs
black pepper
180ml/6fl oz well-seasoned vinaigrette

Boil the potatoes in their skins. When cooked, peel and slice them. While they are cooking, scrub the mussels thoroughly, remove any barnacles with a sharp knife and pull away the beard that protrudes from one side. Discard any cracked or open mussels or any that fail to close when tapped.

Put the cleaned mussels, wine, shallots, some parsley sprigs and some black pepper into a large pan, put over a high heat, cover and bring the liquid to the boil. Remove the mussels as soon as they open, discarding the shells.

Put the mussels in a dish to cool and strain the hot cooking liquid over the potatoes. Drain the potato slices when they are not quite cold, mix them with mussels and trickle on enough vinaigrette to moisten well. Arrange in a shallow dish and garnish with the chopped parsley.
Serves 6

Mussels with Cider and Bacon

Use white wine instead of the cider and add finely chopped garlic if you wish.

4 rashers of smoked bacon, diced (or 2 large
   handfuls of prepared lardons)
550g/1¼lb cleaned mussels
a wine glass of dry cider
5 or 6 black peppercorns
a handful of parsley, chopped

Fry the diced bacon or lardons in a large pan till the fat has turned golden. If your bacon is particularly lean, you may need to add a little fat to the pan. Add the cider and peppercorns and bring to the boil. Throw in the cleaned mussels and parsley and cover with a lid.

As soon as the shells open, lift the mussels out into bowls and pour the broth over them. Serve with crusty bread and large napkins.
Serves 2

Fried Mussels

If you have the time and patience (a good friend will also do) cook the mussels briefly with a little white wine, then quickly remove from the heat as soon as they have opened and remove the mussels from their shells. This is easy: just push the fat little mussels out with your thumb. The most important point here is not to overcook them. Toss the mussels in flour, which you have seasoned with a little finely ground black pepper, then shallow-fry them in very hot groundnut oil for less than a minute. Eat the golden plump and crisp morsels with a squeeze of lemon or better still stuffed into crisp rolls which you have spread generously with garlic mayonnaise.

crushed cloves. Despite its inherent saltiness, bacon renders a mussel even more succulent, as does a squeeze of fresh lemon juice.

There are sadly few British mussel recipes. Mrs Beeton is devoid of ideas. Later writers use French recipes to fill their mussel chapter. Yet our plump blue-black bivalves are as good as anyone else's. Bigger does not necessarily mean better. The small ones, barely 2 inches in length, can be particularly sweet.

Cheap though they are, a big bowl of mussels shrouded in steam is something of a feast. I suspect it is partly the sheer generosity of a huge bowl piled so high with the shining shells that some always seem to fall off on to the table. But it is the prising apart of the shells and the sucking out of the juicy morsel within that give the greatest pleasure, while the salty, sticky liquor runs down your fingers. The ubiquitous accompaniment of crusty bread is essential here. No soft, floury ciabatta or limp and doughy sandwich loaf will work. A lump of crusty bread will absorb the cooking juices effectively just in time before the crust goes soggy.

Mussels are available pretty much all year, although supplies dip in the summer. The unofficial season is from September to April, and I am happy to respect that, even though I do occasionally buy a bag for a summer lunch in the garden.

Finger bowls, dishes of warm water with a slice of lemon, are the traditional accessory to a mussel supper, but there is something rather precious about such things for everyday dining. I would rather have a large napkin instead, though I have been known to use a tea-towel. Paper serviettes will not do. Neither will the kitchen roll. I am not being grand; it is simply that the paper sticks in little squares to your fingers, leaving your hands looking as if you cut yourself shaving. And make sure the napkins are big enough, you can get into a right old mess scoffing a bowl of hot mussels.

Stuffed Mussels

A classic mussel dish which is too often forgotten in favour of the easier *moules marinières*. I think it deserves to be remembered.

approximately 32 large mussels, cleaned
1 plump clove of garlic, peeled
1 shallot, peeled and halved
2 tablespoons parsley, chopped
1 tablespoon fresh tarragon, chopped
100g/4oz unsalted butter, diced
juice of ½ a lemon
a handful of fresh, white breadcrumbs

Get a large frying pan hot. Add the mussels and cover with a lid. Peep every few seconds and remove each mussel as it opens. Break the top shell from each mussel, leaving the flesh sitting in the bottom half. Arrange them snugly in an ovenproof dish.

Mix all the remaining ingredients except the breadcrumbs together. You can do this in seconds in a food processor or in minutes with a wooden spoon. Season with a little ground black pepper and a very little salt. Place a dollop of the herbed butter in each shell, then place under a hot grill to melt. As soon as the butter has melted, scatter over the breadcrumbs and grill till golden. Serve hot and bubbling.

Serves 4

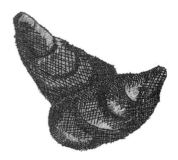

MUSTARD

Haddock with Mustard, Parsley and Garlic

Mustard works well with most herbs, but particularly parsley. I suspect that dill or tarragon might be interesting substitutes here. Serve in deep plates to hold the thin yet tasty juice, with plenty of bread for mopping it up, with perhaps some lightly cooked French beans and boiled new potatoes.

5 large sprigs of fresh parsley
3 plump cloves of garlic, peeled
4 thick pieces haddock fillet, about 175g/6oz each
3 tablespoons grain mustard
1 wine glass of white wine
3 tablespoons double cream
1 teaspoon lemon juice

Remove the leaves from the parsley and chop them finely with the garlic. Brush the fish fillets with the mustard, then roll them in the chopped parsley and garlic.

Put the fillets in a shallow ovenproof dish and pour the wine around them. Cover with a piece of buttered foil and bake in a preheated oven, 200°C/400°F/Gas Mark 6, for 15–20 minutes. Check for doneness, then carefully remove the fish with a fish slice and keep warm. Place the wine over a high heat for a couple of minutes until it has reduced by half, then add the cream. Simmer for a minute, then add the lemon juice.

Serves 4

It is probably true to say that as much mustard has been thrown away as has ever been eaten. Quite why we help ourselves to so much of this stimulating, aromatic ointment, only to leave most of it on the side of the plate is something of a mystery. The vivid yellow condiment which seasons the country's washing-up water every Sunday deserves a better end.

With the exception of a ham sandwich, which the French seem somehow better at than us, I prefer mustard in my food rather than on my plate. The forkful of roast beef with its compulsory spreading of the hot ochre balm known as English mustard is less attractive to me than the warm, deep flavours that mustard can offer to a dish where it has been used as an integral ingredient. In other words, I like my mustard stirred in rather than spread on.

Made from mustardseed ground with water, vinegar, salt and sometimes herbs or wine, mustard makes as good a kitchen seasoning as it does table condiment, some would say better. Its warm spice notes do much to flatter everything from a pork casserole to a dish of boiled haricot beans. Cooking with mustard, though, is very much a matter of timing: at least 10 minutes should elapse between mixing English mustard powder and (cold) water in order for the flavour to develop; its flavour will all but disappear if it is added to a cooked dish too early, yet adding hot mustard to a sauce too late can leave an unwanted harshness and, most annoying of all, the essential oils contained in the black, brown or white seeds are infuriatingly volatile once mixed with liquid. In other words, don't forget to screw the lid back on properly.

Like lemon or yoghurt, mustard can lift the flavour of any dish it is stirred into, especially when this is done shortly before the end of cooking. A murky, cluttered casserole can take on a clearer, fresher flavour if a tablespoon of mild mustard is added prior to serving. The spice's heat soon disappears, leaving behind a deep, rich flavour that is hard to pin down. A favourite of mine is to spike the cream sauce that accompanies a sauté of chicken with a crunchy grain mustard, making it less likely to cloy.

I have wheedled my way out of sauceless situations more than once with an instant sauce made from butter, heated till it froths, then thickened with the same amount of double cream, a little lemon juice and a generous blob of grain mustard. Mackerel is fond of such spontaneous saucery, as are pork steaks and grilled mushrooms.

Although my fridge collects opened jars of mustard like a teenager collects spots, I am not overly fussy about particular makes. Generally I opt for a couple of traditional French brands and a tin of powdered English rather than doing battle with the array of new-wave mustards that are, to my mind, interesting but more of a relish. The regular occupants of the middle shelf on the fridge door are usually a grainy French version, particularly useful for sauces and dressings, a smooth and slightly hotter version for sandwiches and a slightly darker French tarragon mustard of which I am unfashionably fond.

I have long given up trying to break the red wax seal of one well-known French variety without the little bits of shrapnel finding their way into the condiment and now tend to stick to small glass jars. I have become somewhat attached to a deep-purple variety, Moutade Violette, which is mixed with

Pork and Mustard Casserole

A rich, aromatic and unctuous casserole for a cold night. No trouble to make, but it takes a good few hours to cook. You may like to reserve a fingerful of the chopped dill to scatter over at the table. Accompany with a crisp salad involving raw cabbage or chicory and plenty of bread.

4 medium-sized onions, peeled and roughly
  chopped
3 cloves of garlic, peeled and sliced
50g/2oz butter
a teaspoon of fennel seed
bay leaf
450g/1lb strips of belly pork
2 medium-sized potatoes, cut into rough cubes
flour
a handful of fresh dill fronds and stalks, chopped
scant tablespoon of drained and rinsed capers
2 tablespoons grain mustard
juice of ½ a lemon

Cook the onions and garlic slowly in the butter in a deep, heavy ovenproof pan, one to which you have lid. They are best cooked over a low heat for about 20 minutes, until the onions are soft but not particularly coloured. Add the fennel seeds and bay leaf.

Remove the onions, turn up the heat and add the belly pork, cut into large lumps, and let it cook for a few minutes till the fat is coloured. Mix the cooked onions in with the pork, add the cubed potatoes and grind over a little salt. Add a sprinkling of flour, then cover with a butter paper. Cover tightly with the lid, then place in a low oven at 150°C/300°F/Gas Mark 2 for about 2 hours.

Remove from the oven and stir in the chopped dill, capers, mustard and lemon. Cover again and return to the oven for an hour. Eat with a crisp salad to mop up the savoury juices.
Serves 2 with second helpings

grape juice, though it is far from easy to locate. And I use too little of the satisfyingly hot, turmeric-yellow English mustard to keep a jar of ready-made around. When I use it, I invariably make it from the powder, mixing it with cold water. Hot water quells its flavour.

It is for mustard's aromatic quality, rather than its heat, that I find this yellow paste so useful. If I have developed a tendency to buy French rather than English mustard, it is because I find even the milder English varieties a little on the hot side. But

Cabbage with Mustard and Cream

Slow-cooked cabbage, spiced with caraway and coated with cream and mustard, is a fine accompaniment to cold roast pork, sausages or black pudding.

1 small, hard white cabbage
100g/4oz butter
1 teaspoon caraway seeds
120ml/4fl oz double cream
1 tablespoon grain mustard
a squeeze of lemon juice

Shred the cabbage finely, discarding the tough core, and wash thoroughly. Melt the butter in a heavy casserole and add the caraway seeds and the cabbage. Cook very gently, covered with a lid, over a low heat until the cabbage is soft. This may take up to an hour. Pour off any excess butter.

Season with a little salt and stir in the cream and the mustard. Bring slowly to the boil, then add a squeeze of lemon juice and serve.
Serves 4 as an accompaniment

that extra heat soon cools in a casserole and the flavour creeps up slowly. In a slow-cooked dish, they are quite interchangeable.

Mustard has the ability to make the most mundane snack sing. Cheese on toast, the lazy cook's answer to Welsh rabbit, becomes more of a treat if a layer of hot, crunchy mustard is spread on the toast before the cheese is added. A spoonful stirred into a bowl of oxtail or chicken soup will perk up even the tinned variety. Try spreading a layer of smooth, hot mustard on to ham before you shred it and toss it into an omelette.

Until recently I had never thought to try a dollop of mustard in the gravy for roast lamb, or in the mayonnaise to accompany cold salmon, even though I have enjoyed mustard sauce with gravadlax, the cured salmon, for years. I have just taken to tossing lightly cooked French beans in an equal mixture of olive oil and grain mustard to accompany roast cod fillet and have become hooked on the leggy purple-tipped broccoli dressed with a similar mix of mustard and lemon juice.

Lapin moutade is a classic of the French kitchen where young rabbit meets cream, mustard and bacon, the mustard giving interest to a bland meat. But stronger meats, such as pheasant and venison, also benefit from a dose of the piquant paste, which can be dissolved into the cooking juices to make a spicy sauce. A small whisk will ease the process.

Mustard's ability to speed up blood circulation and ease rheumatic pain has led to a life beyond the bounds of the kitchen. But traditionalists who only ever spread the heart-warming yellow paste on their plates or their feet may actually find the stuff more interesting stirred into a casserole, used as a savoury crust on a rack of lamb or shaken into a dressing for crisp leaves of chicory or frisée. There is a lot more to mustard than roast beef and chilblains.

NOODLES

Watching an experienced noodle-maker stretching and twisting a dough so elastic that it can bounce from his head to his feet without breaking, it is easy to forget a noodle is nothing more than a bit of flour and water. Better theatre than an Italian pulling pizza dough, a noodle-master can take up to two years to learn to produce over 200 threads from one lump of dough in 15 minutes. After a recent display and to a round of applause, I heard the exhausted chef apologise that he was a little rusty. Everyone, he said, buys their noodles nowadays.

The noodle is being hailed as the food of the 1990s. It has got the lot: it is easy to buy, cooks in minutes, is low in fat, exotic, comforting and as cheap as can be. It is also seriously fashionable. Suddenly the noodle is chic. Quite why it has taken so long is anyone's guess.

The British took to pasta like a nation possessed. Hands up who didn't eat pasta at least once last week. Yet noodles have only recently been given our seal of approval. They have, of course, been part of our late-night take-away food for years, but most of us were too drunk to notice. The Eastern names too are easier to pronounce. *Udon* and *soba*, the two oldest Japanese noodles, roll off the tongue a lot more easily than tagliatelle and fettuccine.

I once suggested doing a piece on noodles to the editor of a women's magazine. The idea was killed on the grounds that noodles were too downmarket. So I wrote about pasta instead, which went down a treat. It is the noodle's entrenchment as the food of

Chicken Noodle Soup

A classic noodle soup with slices of sweet chicken and silky oyster mushrooms that makes a light lunch or supper.

2 small chicken breasts
60ml/2fl oz dark soy sauce
2 tablespoons *mirin*
1 clove of garlic, crushed
1 teaspoon sugar
60ml/2fl oz groundnut oil
100g/4oz fresh oyster mushrooms
175/6oz dried noodles, any sort (or 200g/7oz fresh)
600ml/1 pint good chicken stock
2 spring onions, finely chopped

Place the chicken breasts in a glass or china dish. Mix the soy, *mirin*, garlic and sugar with the oil and pour over the chicken. Leave for about 45 minutes to marinate.

Place the chicken breasts under a hot grill and cook until the juices run clear when they are pierced with a skewer, about 6 minutes, basting from time to time with the marinating liquid. Add the mushrooms for the last 2 minutes' cooking time, tossing them gently in the cooking juices.

Bring the stock to the boil and add the noodles, cooking for 2 minutes if the noodles are fresh, 4–5 minutes if you are using dried. Slice the chicken. Tip the noodles and soup into 2 large bowls. Place the sliced chicken and mushrooms in the broth, scatter over the chopped spring onion and serve.

Serves 2

A Simple Noodle Soup

If you are using fresh noodles, double the weight and cook for 1 or 2 minutes only.

225g/8oz dried egg noodles
600ml/1 pint good vegetable or chicken stock
2 tablespoons dark soy sauce
1 teaspoon sugar
1 tablespoon rice wine or medium-dry sherry
1 tablespoon coriander leaves

Cook the noodles in boiling water till tender, about 4 or 5 minutes, depending on their thickness. Drain and drop into cold water.

Mix the stock, soy, sugar and wine or sherry. Bring gently to the boil in a saucepan. Season with pepper. Add the noodles and heat for 2 minutes. Pour into bowls, add the coriander leaves and eat while hot.
Serves 2

Chinese Noodles with Chicken and Mushrooms

Similar ingredients here but a different method, resulting in a very different dish. This makes a substantial supper.

225g/8oz dried egg noodles
1 red onion
1 tablespoon groundnut oil
4cm/1½in knob of fresh root ginger, peeled
2 cloves of garlic
350g/12oz boned chicken breast cut into 2.5cm/
   1in strips
225g/8oz large brown mushrooms
2 tablespoons dark soy sauce
2 tablespoons *mirin* or dry sherry
2 teaspoons cornflour dissolved in 2 tablespoons
   cold water
coriander leaves

the poor that may hold the clue to its currently smart status. Over the last few years we have munched our way through mountains of pasta, gallons of polenta, and tonnes of French lentils. Smart restaurants have rediscovered the delights of fish cakes, faggots and chips. As the fashionable gobble their way round the foods of the world's poor it is only natural that they should eventually come to the noodle.

There is not a fat lot of difference between a bowl of pasta in *brodo* and one of *ramen* in *dashi*. Both are made with egg noodles. Both are starch floating in a seasoned broth. The difference between pasta and noodles is mostly the flour from which they are made. Japanese, and Chinese, wheat flour is usually softer than the hard durum wheats used in Italian pasta. Asian noodles can also be made with flour made from rice, mung beans, peas, buckwheat and potato starch. But the principle of extending a meagre quantity of expensive ingredients (the meat sauce of spaghetti Bolognaise or the slices of chicken in a *ramen* soup) with a pile of cheap, warm, filling starch remains the same.

Cooking noodles at home is a game anyone can play. You need lots of boiling water, about 10 times the quantity of water to noodles. You need a big, deep pan. Once the water is at a fierce boil, drop in the fresh noodles gradually. When the water comes back to the boil, turn down the heat and let the noodles cook at a light boil for about a minute, then drain. Dried noodles will take about 4–5 minutes.

Once you have cooked your noodles, they can be put into hot broth with sliced meat or fish and chopped green vegetables. You can use a Japanese *dashi*, the ubiquitous seaweed and dried fish stock, or a light chicken stock. (A vegetable stock cube, diluted to half its usual strength, makes a surprisingly soothing medium.) They can be tossed with finely sliced onion, beansprouts, chicken and soy sauce, sprinkled with *mirin* (sweet rice wine) or dry sherry and a little sesame oil, then tossed in a hot frying pan. Or fry them Chinese style with pork you have marinated in soy and rice wine and serve them with a hot chilli sauce.

Smooth, silky, fresh egg noodles can be bought in Chinese food shops. Fresh Japanese *soba* and *udon*, and elegantly packaged dried noodles, are available from Japanese stores. You can buy little cakes of dried noodles in most supermarkets and all oriental grocers. Fresh noodles will keep for two or three days in the fridge; dried will keep for months. The ultimate convenience food. The ultimate fast food. Look out, fettuccine, the noodle is here.

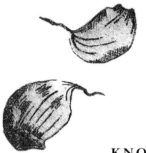

Cook the noodles in boiling, salted water for 4 minutes. Drain and run cold water over them to stop them cooking. Peel and slice the onion into thin rings. Heat the oil in a wok or frying pan and when it is hot add the onion rings, stirring till they start to soften. The heat should be quite high, though not so high that you cannot control the cooking. Add the ginger and garlic. Continue frying and stirring till the garlic colours – it should be pale brown rather than the usual pale gold. Throw in the chicken, which should splutter a little if the oil is hot enough. Stir the mixture only when the chicken is gold on one side. Leave to cook, then stir again.

Meanwhile, slice the mushrooms and add them. Continue cooking till the mushrooms are tender, about 4 minutes, adding more oil if they soak it all up. When all is tender and sizzling, sprinkle over the soy sauce and *mirin* or sherry. You will get a cloud of steam. Stir and add the cornflour mixture. Stir quickly and then, as the mixture starts to thicken, drop the drained noodles into the pan. Toss the mixture around for a few seconds, then scoop out on to warm plates or bowls. Scatter over a few coriander leaves and eat while all is hot.
Serves 2

KNOW YOUR NOODLES

Egg Noodles The common, all-purpose Chinese noodle. Made from wheat flour, egg and water, available fresh or dried, in thin threads or wider flat ribbons.

Sha He Chinese noodles made from rice flour, very popular in southern China, where they are sold as street food in broth or thin sauce. Deep-fried till they puff up, these white noodles can be used as a crispy base for a stir-fry.

Cellophane or beanthread Made from ground mung beans, salt and water. Fine, white and very long, sold in bundles like balls of wool, they become transparent when cooked. Soak in warm water rather than boil them, then add to soups or fry them straight from the packet in very hot oil.

Soba Thin, brown noodles made with buckwheat flour, a grain belonging to the sorrel family, which survives the harsh northern conditions around Tokyo, where it is particularly popular.

Cha Soba Expensive buckwheat noodle flavoured with powdered green tea.

Udon Cream-coloured, wheat noodle popular in southern Japan. Thicker than *soba*, made from flour, salt and water, typically served in broth.

Ramen Most popular Japanese noodle, thin, yellow Chinese style, made from wheat flour and egg.

Somen Fine, white, delicate noodles resembling vermicelli, made from wheat flour.

NUTS

Nut Brittle

Any nuts are suitable here, provided that they have not been salted. Almonds, hazelnuts, pistachios and peanuts are perhaps the most usual. For a deeper flavour, skin the nuts first; almonds skin most easily after being soaked in boiling water for 15 minutes, hazelnuts after being grilled till they flake and then rubbed gently to remove the papery skins. Then toast again till pale gold in colour.

100g/4oz shelled almonds, hazelnuts and pistachios
100g/4oz caster sugar
4 tablespoons water

Put the nuts in a deep pan with the sugar and water. Choose a pan with a thick bottom so that the sugar caramelises slowly and evenly. Don't stir. Cook over a medium heat till the sugar melts and turns a light golden-brown colour.

Now watch carefully, else all will end in tears, until the caramel is a rich golden brown. Depending on the heat and size of the pan this may take anything from 10 to 15 minutes, maybe a little less or more. When the caramel is more or less the colour of sweet sherry it is ready. Pour the whole mixture on to a lightly oiled baking sheet. A pliable one will be easy to remove the cool brittle from.

Leave to cool and harden. Remember that the tin will get very hot and should be on a heatproof surface. When quite cool, twist diagonal corners of the tin and the brittle should come effortlessly off the tray. Failing that, prise a spatula between brittle and tin. Snap into pieces and store in an airtight tin or jar.

The smell of roasting nuts, sweet bubbling caramel and burning leaves from next door's garden has filled my kitchen all week. I wish I could trap the homely, welcoming atmosphere in a Kilner jar, for sniffing in the dead of winter, when the trees are bare and the nuts have lost their joy. But I shall make do instead with those new-season's nuts, toasted and encased in crisp caramel, to be kept in a jar for seasonal nibbling.

Known as *croccante* to the Italians, praline to the French and *turrón* to the Spanish, such a golden, nutty sweetmeat is better known here in Britain as brittle or, occasionally, cracknel. Although methods and results differ slightly from country to country, the marriage of warm, freshly roasted nuts and glistening caramel lives up to its name. The nuts are cracked, then snap and spit in the caramel. The brittle will crackle as it cools and then shatter as you break it into shards for crunching between the teeth.

Some commercial versions, though tempting, are rarely as good to eat as they are to look at. Made at home in 30 minutes, the results will be instantly superior. The trick is to toast the nuts before tipping them into the molten sugar. Toast them in a frying pan, roast them in a hot oven or leave them under a blazing grill to intensify their flavour.

In the heat, the papery skins between the shell and the meat of the nut start to blister and flake. They will annoy in the mouth and need to be removed. A good rub with a tea-towel removes most of the skin. It also leaves you with a tea-towel

Praline

Prepare the above mixture. Almonds or hazelnuts are the usual nuts to use. When cold, break into small pieces and smash to a coarse powder either in a food processor, a matter of seconds, or with a pestle and mortar, which will take considerably longer.

Brown-sugar Pecans

There is something about the flavour of the stronger brown sugars which brings out the best in pecans, which may explain why they are so good in dark fruit cakes. Store these little nuts for nibbling on, though their flavour and texture are at their best when sizzling hot from the oven.

225g/8oz shelled pecan nuts
100g/4oz soft dark-brown sugar, Billingtons for
    preference
2 tablespoons water

Scatter the pecans in a single layer on a baking sheet and grill till warm and fragrant. Turn them once to cook on both sides. They may brown a little, but take care not to burn them, which would end in bitterness.

Melt the sugar with the water in a heavy-based pan. When it starts to bubble, add the toasted pecans. Cook over a medium heat for 1 or 2 minutes, until the sugar turns to dark caramel and starts to stick to the nuts. It is ready when quite viscous and bubbling. Take care not to overcook; the sugar burns easily.

Tip the sugar-coated nuts out on to an oiled sheet. Serve warm or cold. They can be stored in an airtight jar, but are best eaten as soon as possible.

full of papery flakes that refuse to brush off. A better bet is to leave the nuts till cool enough to handle, then rub them together in your hands over a tray.

White and naked, the nuts are then returned to the heat source to tan to a soft golden brown. Cooked too little and they will keep some of their flavour to themselves. Cooked too long and they will darken, their volatile oils turning unspeakably bitter. They should be a pale golden brown.

OTHER GOOD IDEAS WITH NUTS

Praline Cream

Fold the crushed praline into softly whipped cream. Leave for 15 minutes before using as a nutty accompaniment to apple tart.

Croccante

Italian cooks keep jars of caramelised nuts for nibbling with coffee. Their method is a little more time-consuming, but the result is quite different. Toast the nuts under the grill to loosen their skins. Peel away the flaky skins and chop the nuts into tiny pieces. Add to the sugar only when it has melted and turned a rich golden brown. Turn out and cool as above.

Chocolate Dipped

As with any nut or caramel mixture, nut brittle is well suited to being coated in chocolate. Break off pieces of the brittle or *croccante* and partially submerge them into warm, melted chocolate. Leave them on non-stick baking parchment to cool.

Ice-cream

The crunchy nuggets of finely smashed praline make a startling contrast to ice-cream. Scatter coarse praline over vanilla, coffee or chocolate ice-cream.

The sugar is important too. It must be absolutely clean, with no lumps from (someone else's) wet coffee spoon, and it must be either caster or granulated, not a mixture. The crystals should be allowed to melt in water, which gives a little more control, over a medium heat. A heavy-based pan is pretty well essential. Thin pans with pitted bases will cause uneven cooking, with some patches burning before others are even dissolved, looking like smoke signals in the snow.

Tossed into the blisteringly hot caramel, the nuts crackle and snap. Cooked with the sugar from the start they can sometimes soften in the cooking process. Lazy praline can be made by throwing the unskinned nuts in with the sugar and cooking till golden, though the flavour tends to be more sweet than nutty. Once all is a deep, rich golden brown the mixture can be pushed out of the pan on to a lightly oiled baking tray to harden. As it starts to cool, it can be stretched with the back of an oiled spoon or hand to the desired thickness. I prefer a thicker sweetmeat, others may like it paper thin, with the nuts standing proud.

Then comes the best bit. The brittle must be broken – it will not cut – into bite-sized pieces. I have tried several methods over the last week, including shattering the golden sheet with a rolling pin (which left me with thousands of fine splinters) and snapping it with my fingers, which left enough prints for the fraud squad. Slamming the tray on the table sent sweet missiles hurtling through the air.

It took several goes to hit on the winning method. Twisting the large metal cooling tray slowly at diagonal corners resulted in a huge, perfect, golden, nut-spiked window popping cleanly from the tray. It was quite irresistible. It was time to get the hammer out.

ORANGES

Nothing quite lifts the spirits on a cold, grey January afternoon like a sharp, juicy orange. Better still, a plate of them, sliced into rounds and dripping with their own juice, a sprinkling of orange-flower-water and perfumed with a slug of glowing orange liqueur. A fine grating of zest from the oranges' skin and the whole thing will really start to sing.

But they could be so much better. Heading south, it is difficult to travel far without the temptation to scrump oranges straight from the tree. Those fruits are a different thing altogether from the ones I have just picked up in a red cotton net at the supermarket. Something happens to an orange between grove and supermarket checkout that robs this ubiquitous winter fruit of so much of its charm. Highly polished and gassed to increase their brightness and thus the chances of them catching my eye, the softly shaded, pitted fruit has now emerged as a brassy, glitzy globe robbed of its charm and magical fragrance. The highly perfumed and pleasantly piquant fruits I have picked from the bough are a world away from the vicious, bright-orange globes screaming at me in the greengrocer's like edible Belisha beacons.

Sweeter than nature intended, and waxed and polished to ensure our attention, the orange is still a most welcome addition to the fruit bowl at this time of year. If the meddling of commerce particularly bothers me (and it does), there are always unsprayed and unwaxed fruits in my local supermarket. These organically grown and untreated

Orange Tart

I rarely embark on long recipes, let alone suggest them to anyone else, but I feel the end result here is worth it. The contrast between the buttery orange pastry, the tart apple filling and the sweet and syrupy orange slices makes this worth the trouble. You will need a 23 x 30cm/9 x 12in tart tin, preferably with a removable base, and a large, sharp knife to cut it with.

3 small to medium-sized oranges
275g/10oz sugar
900g/2lb dessert apples, peeled, cored and chopped
juice of an orange
for the pastry
275g/10oz plain flour
175g/6oz butter, in chunks
2 teaspoons finely grated orange zest
2 egg yolks

Slice the 3 oranges horizontally into approximately 10 pieces each. Put them with the sugar and enough water to cover in a stainless-steel pan. Cook over low heat – once the sugar has dissolved, the syrup should barely simmer – until the white pith around the orange slices has turned translucent and the fruit looks candied, about 45 minutes.

Rub the butter into the flour with your fingertips. It would be quicker in the food processor but is hardly worth the bother. The mixture should resemble coarse breadcrumbs and there should be no lumps of butter left. Mix in the zest and egg yolks with a fork and bring to a firm dough with a little water, maybe a tablespoon or so.

Bring the dough together to form a ball, then roll out on a floured surface to a rectangle a little larger than the tart tin. Line the tin with the pastry, taking care to push the dough well into the corners. Lay a piece of greaseproof paper or tin foil on the pastry to cover the bottom and the sides, then pour in some baking beans to hold the pastry down. (I use old white haricot beans.) Chill in the fridge while you make the filling.

Put the apples, peeled, cored and chopped, into a stainless-steel or enamel saucepan with the juice of the oranges. Cook over a medium to low heat until they have softened. Stir occasionally so that they do not burn. You should have a thick purée. Reduce on a high heat if there is too much liquid and set aside. Bake the pastry case in a preheated oven at 200°C/400°F/Gas Mark 6, for 10 minutes. Remove the paper and beans carefully and return the pastry to the oven till crisp but not brown, a further 5 minutes or so.

Fill the pastry case with the apple mixture. Remove the orange slices from their syrup with a draining spoon and place in rows on top of the apples. Bake for 15 minutes, till the oranges have coloured a little and the pastry is golden. Serve warm, with a little of the orange syrup, spiked, if you wish, with a little orange liqueur.

Serves 6, at least

fruits, sold in trays of four and wrapped in cling film, have at least some of the sharpness now bred out of the average fruit, and often more of the orange's uplifting fragrance. But they do lack the extravagant juice of the big boys on the shelf below, and the natty string bag for carrying them home.

While I enjoy its juice for breakfast, the segments of plump flesh in a salad and occasionally the dried rind used to perk up a pork casserole, for me the real joy of an orange is its zest. This is not the rind, which usually includes at least some of the bitter white pith, but just the very, very outside of the skin, where the aromatic essential oils lurk. Sadly, this is also where those unwelcome trappings, the waxes, fungicides and pesticides, hide too. In washing the fruit, which almost every cookbook tells you to do, you risk loosing the best of the zest if you scrub too hard. Insufficient rinsing may result in more froth to your orange mousse than you expected.

Better still are the Seville oranges which we squander on marmalade. These bitter fruits, pale-fleshed and tinged with green, have a kick to them which I gather is nearer the oranges referred to in ancient recipes – thus explaining why they now seem such pointless additions in the instructions for sweet, dark fruit cakes, icings and gingerbread.

Carefully removed with the fine teeth of a stainless-steel grater, or one of those little gadgets called, appropriately enough, a zester, the zest is the very spirit of the orange. It is easy to overlook it in preference for the more obvious flesh and juice, yet to do so is to miss the real point of the fruit.

A spoonful will lift a buttery pastry for a fruit tart, add interest to a dish of bananas and mingle fragrantly with orange-flower-water and sections of its juicy flesh for a fruit salad to end a meal. Half a teaspoon of orange zest stirred into your morning fruit juice will wake you up like nothing else.

An Orange Salad

All aspects of the orange are exploited here: the spicy zest, the copious juice, refreshing flesh and the perfumed water made from its flowers. The best orange-flower-water seems to come from Turkish or Middle Eastern food shops.

6 juicy oranges, Navel or Valencia
2 tablespoons orange-flower-water

Grate the zest carefully from 1 of the oranges using the fine side of the grater. Scoop it into a small china or glass bowl. Peel this and the remaining oranges with a knife to remove all the peel (this can be dried in a sieve over a radiator and used to flavour stews) and carefully cut away all the bitter white pith, leaving 6 clean oranges. Slice them, over the basin containing the zest, approximately as thick as pound coins, collecting the escaping juice in the basin. Stir the orange-flower-water into the juice and zest.

Lay the orange slices on a large plate with a rim. Spoon the scented juice over the slices and leave in a cool place for an hour or so, basting from time to time with the juices. If there were any leaves attached to your oranges – if, in other words, you bought them from a food shop that was neither a supermarket nor a greengrocer's – use them to good effect around the edges of the plate.
Serves 4

Sad that its invigorating essence isn't enough to shake those who assume we want only what is on the inside, and that they can poison the rest for the sake of commerce.

To remove orange zest, wash the orange thoroughly under running water, but do not scrub, as some books suggest, as you will graze the skin and thus lose the essential oils. Ideally, use a zester. This short-handled blade has five little holes punched in it which shave off thin curls of zest and it costs pence rather than pounds. Draw it firmly across the skin of the fruit. Alternatively, use the fine side of a grater, very gently removing the first layer of skin, but without cutting through to the white pith beneath. Let the zest fall on to a plate rather than a wooden chopping board, which will absorb the essential oils. Use immediately, before the volatile essence evaporates.

Bananas with Orange Zest and Almonds

A simple dessert that shows the effect of orange zest to the full.

3 juicy oranges, Navel or Valencia
4 slightly underripe bananas
a handful of flaked almonds

Remove the zest from 1 of the oranges using the fine side of the grater and scrape into a china bowl. Squeeze the juice from the grated orange, plus the 2 others. Skin the bananas and slice into rounds almost 1cm/½in thick. Marinate them in the juice and zest for 15 minutes, though no longer, lest they become soft. Toast the almonds, either in a dry frying pan or under a hot grill, till they are light brown in colour. Seconds before you plan to eat the bananas, scatter the almonds over and eat while the nuts are still crisp.
Serves 2

PARSNIPS

Can there be a vegetable rack in the land without its token shrivelled parsnip? This plump, sweet root, dismissed by the snooty French – who feed it to their pigs – and misunderstood by the British – who boil it like a potato – deserves better than to end its days wrinkled and forgotten, beckoning the cook from its dark corner like a witch's finger.

The parsnip has more uses in the kitchen than its sweeter sister the carrot. It makes a fine roast round the Sunday joint, its edges caramelising delectably and sticking enticingly to the tin. It produces the most sustaining of soups, the most reassuring of purées and surprisingly good chips. Yet the parsnip is passed over time and again, only just making it above the swede in the popularity stakes.

We have to thank Jane Grigson, who wrote for the *Observer* for over 20 years, for restoring our faith in this outwardly uninteresting vegetable. It was Mrs Grigson who thought to match the parsnip's sweet subtlety with the warmth of Indian spicing. Her parsnip soup with curry powder, garlic and cream has become a classic of the British kitchen, and probably her most famous recipe.

Parsnips and spices had met before, notably in John Evelyn's *Acetaria* (now published in an exquisite cloth-bound facsimile by Prospect Books). In 1699, Evelyn wrote: 'Take the large roots, boil them and strip the skin: then split them long-ways into pretty thin slices; flower and fry them in fresh butter till they look brown. Some throw sugar and

Mashed Parsnips with Spiced Onion Butter

A warming accompaniment to cold roast chicken or pork. Hedonists may add more butter or drizzle a spoonful of cream over at the table.

2 large, fat parsnips
1 large onion, peeled
75g/3oz butter
1 tablespoon garam masala

Scrub the parsnips or peel them if their skin is coarse and thick. Chop them into pieces roughly the size of a champagne cork. Cover them with salted water and bring to the boil. Simmer for 15–20 minutes, until you can squash them to a pulp against the side of the saucepan.

Meanwhile, slice the onion thinly into rings and stew it slowly in a good half of the butter. Let the onion turn soft, golden and dark brown at the edges, but without burning the butter.

Drain the parsnips and mash them with the remaining butter using a potato masher or a fork. When they are light and fluffy, spoon them into a warm dish. Stir the garam masala into the onions and cook for a minute until the fragrance rises. Take care the spices do not burn. Pour the spiced onion butter over the mashed parsnips.
Serves 2 as an accompaniment

Parsnips Roasted with Fat Bacon and Thyme

Adding further sweetening to parsnips is not as redundant as it might seem. A little brown sugar or a spoonful of honey brings out the vegetable's natural sweetness. Serve alongside a roast or cold cuts.

4 medium parsnips, peeled
1 tablespoon vegetable oil or butter
150g/6oz piece fat bacon (such as Italian pancetta), cut into large dice
1 tablespoon honey
a healthy sprig of thyme

Chop the parsnips into large chunks, the same size you would normally cut for a roast potato. Put the oil or butter in a roasting tin and melt over a moderate heat. Add the bacon and cook until the fat is golden. Add the parsnips and cook until golden brown, turning them gently to colour on both sides.

Roast them at the top of a preheated oven, 220°C/425°F/Gas Mark 7, for 30 minutes, stirring them once or twice. Remove, add the honey and leaves from the sprig of thyme, and a little salt and coarsely ground pepper, and return to the oven. Roast for a further 15 minutes, tossing the parsnips in the cooking juices once or twice. When golden brown and sticky, they are done.
Serves 2 as an accompaniment

cinnamon up on them.' He also cites a mash seasoned with lemon, cream and currants.

Many argue that the parsnip's flavour is better for being caught by frost. It is said that the starch in the parsnip is turned into sugar by the cold snap, rendering the vegetable sweeter and deeper in flavour. They are considered by some gardeners to be at their best, in terms of flavour, shortly after Christmas. I will not argue with that, but I would like to know what the insipid baby versions, barely longer than a finger, which the supermarkets seem to have taken something of a fancy to, have in their favour. There seems little point in such an effete version of such a robust root. Perhaps it is that they are easy to pack into those neat blue punnets.

A parsnip is gnarled and knobbly by nature, and it is worth rooting around for the best, by which I mean hard, sweet and fresh-looking. My local organic supply – at the health-food shop, wouldn't you know – were wizened and pliable and long out of the ground. The greengrocer had some fine specimens still sporting a green stem and covered with soil, while the supermarket had an abundance at a good price that I could rummage through to my heart's content.

These roots are awkward, pointed things. They poke through my shopping bag, telling the world what I am having for supper and reminding me that once men used to wear them around their necks to reduce swollen testicles. I hurry home to turn them into mash.

I am not sure the parsnip benefits from being dunked in water. Its rock-hard texture suddenly opens up like a sponge, becoming too waterlogged to be of interest on the plate. To my mind it is far better cooked in butter or dripping. Best of all is when the vegetable turns golden brown and slightly sticky, as it will if cooked next to the Sunday roast or sautéd slowly in butter.

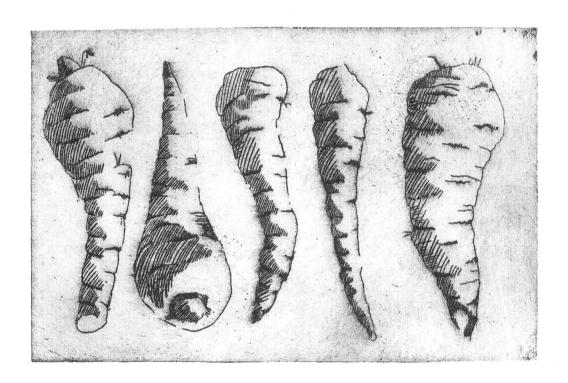

Parsnip Soup with Mustard and Cheese

A thick, rich and spicy soup for a cold night. Use any cheese you happen to have around; a sharp farmhouse Cheddar is ideal, but a milder cheese will do too.

2 large parsnips, peeled and roughly chopped
2 plump cloves of garlic, peeled and chopped
1 medium onion, peeled and roughly chopped
50g/2oz butter
a little flour
1 teaspoon chilli flakes
1 teaspoon ground turmeric
1.2l/2 pints vegetable stock
120ml/4fl oz single cream
2 tablespoons mild, grainy mustard
100g/4oz cheese, any sort will do, diced

Put the parsnips, garlic and onion in a large, heavy pan with the butter. Cook over a moderate heat, lid on, until the vegetables have begun to soften and the edges of the parsnips have turned golden. Resist disturbing the vegetables too much as they cook. The slight browning of the parsnips is important for the flavour of the soup.

Sprinkle a dusting of flour over the vegetables, add the chilli flakes and the ground turmeric, then stir and cook for 1 or 2 minutes to remove the taste of the raw flour. Add the stock and stir. Bring to the boil, then lower the heat to a light boil and cook until the vegetables are soft, about 20 minutes.

Pour into a blender or food processor and whiz to a thick purée. Add salt and fresh coarsely ground pepper, and the cream. Taste, then add more seasoning if you wish. (If you have the time, cool, then refrigerate and reheat the next day.) Pour back into the cooking pot, stir in the mustard and bring to the boil. As soon as the soup is really hot, drop in the cubes of cheese and serve immediately.

Serves 4–6

Of course, a parsnip will bring sweetness to a stew or braise, though the flavour can sometimes bully. This is I suspect why the carrot seems to be many cooks' first choice as a sweetener. Whether you remove the core or not depends, I think, on what you intend to do with them. For soups and braises I see little point in discarding the hard central core. If you are steaming them and tossing them in, say, a vinaigrette dressing, perhaps with a few toasted pine kernels, then you may prefer to remove the woody core. Most modern varieties do not appear to be as inpenetrable as of old.

I have found few more enjoyable ways of eating this vegetable than roasting it with fatty bacon. The essence of the dish is to roast the roughly chopped parsnip in sweet bacon fat until it has formed a sticky, golden-brown crust. It is only the sides touching the roasting tin that will do this. An occasional shake will ensure an even coating of this delectable goo.

Parsnips may be sliced thinly and baked with cream, garlic and a little brown sugar, or roughly chopped and poached in milk, then drained and mashed with a little of the cooking liquor and lots of black pepper. They are mustard when sliced and fried in butter, then sprinkled lightly with a mild garam masala and coarse salt, and perfectly soothing when boiled and mashed with butter and a little hot cream and freshly grated nutmeg.

Now tell me, just what is that long, brown shrivelled thing doing poking out of the vegetable rack?

PEARS

I have just finished the last of the blushed, yellow Williams pears that I have been cosseting for the last couple of weeks. Every day, I have dutifully checked each fruit, monitoring its steady climb from the rock-hard to the lusciously ripe.

It may come as no surprise to those who frequent the major supermarkets that those pears, bought a fortnight ago, bore the legend 'Ripe and Ready to Eat' – a thoroughly inappropriate claim that has led me to suspect that such stickers are actually applied to anything fast approaching its sell-by date.

I suppose it is unrealistic of me to expect all but the most exclusive of emporiums to offer fruit at the perfect point of ripeness. The ensuing mess as busy shoppers rummaged through the shelves of fruit would soon turn supermarket fruit displays into swamps. The growing mania for one-stop shopping means that a tender, juicy and perfectly ripe pear stands little more than a snowball in hell's chance of arriving home in one piece.

To lump apples and pears together is, I think, rather missing the point. The crisp crunchiness we look for in an apple is quite inappropriate in a pear, though I occasionally buy hard, glassy, grainy pears for munching with a hard and savoury cheese such as Parmesan. What I am looking for in a pear is sweet juice and melting flesh. The pear I have just eaten had soft, thin yellow skin and white flesh almost as melting as a water-ice. But it was only patience and a watchful eye on my part that got it there.

Pears should never touch one another. They

Pears with Beaujolais and Spices

Juniper berries, cloves and coriander seeds add warm spicy, orangy notes to this classic French bistro dessert. Don't be tempted to roast or crush the spices – their presence should be discreet. If using ripe pears, take care not to overcook them.

8 small, hard pears
100g/4oz sugar
1 bottle of red wine
4 tablespoons Crème de Cassis
juice of ½ a lemon
8 whole cloves
12 juniper berries, lightly squashed
1 teaspoon coriander seeds
2 small bay leaves
cinnamon stick

Cut the pears in half from stalk to base. You can peel them if you wish, but I rarely do if the skins are thin and tender. Combine all the ingredients in a suitable-sized deep saucepan, stainless steel or enamel for preference (aluminium will taint the cooking liquor).

Bring the wine and aromatics to the boil, then turn down the heat to a simmer. Add the pears and cook till tender to the point of a knife, about 30 minutes depending on the ripeness and variety of the pears. They must be thoroughly tender, though not squashy.

Turn the pears from time to time. Switch off the heat and allow to cool. Serve at cool room temperature, straining the juice over the pears to remove the majority of the whole spices.

Serves 4

A Plate of Pears

Choose ripe, juicy pears, Williams or Comice perhaps. They should be firm enough to be picked up easily when sliced but ripe enough to dribble a little when you peel them – except you are not going to peel them. Cut the pears in half and in half again, then remove the cores. Place the pear pieces on a white plate; they can be arranged prettily or piled hugger-mugger, but they should have their fleshy side up, skin side down.

Get out the eau-de-vie bottle. Poire William would be wonderful, but Framboise, which is the very essence of crushed raspberries, is surprisingly good here too. Covering most of the open bottle neck with your thumb, sprinkle a little of the heavenly scented liquor over the fruit. Serve slightly chilled.

Honeyed Pears with Vanilla Ice-cream

Hot, sweet pears with cold vanilla ice-cream follows my favourite combination of the freezing cold and the blisteringly hot. Use a good-quality ice-cream.

3 ripe pears
75g/3oz unsalted butter
2 tablespoons runny honey, such as thyme,
**   chestnut or orange blossom**

Cut the pears in half and remove their cores. Chop the fruit into chunks, roughly 2.5cm/1in cubes, but don't be too precise about this – the uneven size of the pear pieces is part of the pudding's charm.

Melt the butter in a pan, add the pears and cook for 7–8 minutes over a medium heat, tossing gently without breaking the fruit to a mush. When the chunks are golden, dribble over the honey and serve hot with balls of vanilla ice, hard and cold from the fridge.

Serves 4

bruise as easily as peaches, though often conceal their dark scars under a perfect skin. Check that they are unblemished in the shop as best you can, then bring them home carefully. They ripen best slowly in a cool place, rather than quickly in a warm room. Kept too hot, they are likely to rot from the inside out, giving the appearance of perfection while hiding a brown and mushy interior. I usually reckon on a week to 10 days in a cool place to take an impregnable pear to buttery, honey-fleshed ripeness.

My local greengrocer is currently offering two varieties of pear: a hard, thin and bland Conference and a plumper though equally unexciting Comice. My local supermarket has both, plus an anonymous red-skinned variety, as hard as nails and as boring a fruit as it is possible to imagine.

While happy to celebrate the large food retailers' success in fostering supplies of our old-fashioned varieties of apple, I have to bemoan their seeming lack of interest in the pear. The appeal of the pale-green fruits they offer from hotter climes can be only their long shelf-life (they take weeks to wrinkle) and their low price. And why only three varieties when there are 300?

French Doyenné du Comice, their stalks sometimes sealed with red wax, are for many the finest-tasting pear. Commonly known as Comice, they are easily recognised, sitting blushed and squat, their freckling becoming more apparent as they ripen. Aromatic in the extreme, they are a true dessert pear, losing much of their joy when used in cooking.

Good though the Comice is, I long to taste some of the lost fruits so popular in seventeenth-century France: the obscenely plump Marguerite Marillat, the rare, round Duchesse de Bordeaux and the hyacinth-perfumed Joséphine de Malines. Am I to believe that the diminutive, rock-hard, brown-red

Warm Pears and Melted Mascarpone

Mascarpone, that sweet, voluptuous Italian cream cheese, is available in tubs from supermarkets and good grocers' shops. This is one occasion when the fruit should be drippingly ripe.

2 ripe pears
100g/4oz mascarpone cheese

Quarter the pears and core them. Place the fruit, skin side down, in a shallow, heatproof dish. Spoon a dollop of mascarpone cheese over each quarter, then place under a medium-hot grill till it melts. Serve while the cheese is still soft and runny.
Serves 2

pears in the supermarket can be as delectable as the ancient Cuisse-madame or the rich and winy Triomphe de Vienne? Though the buttery russet and yellow Bosc pear will be here soon, it is the bland Conference, easily detected by its elongated snout, that will see us through the winter. Or at least until the ubiquitous yellow-green New Zealand pears, masquerading as the honey-fleshed and musky Williams' Bon Chrétien, land here.

Even with tender loving care, pears are the most unpredictable of fruit. I have had them sulk on the fruit plate, selfishly keeping their sweetness to themselves. Worse still, many never seem to ripen at all. The only answer is to cook them. Red wine, white wine, almonds, juniper and lemon all draw out the fruit's elusive flavour. Ginger will help too. Spike a rich syrup with slices of fresh ginger and strands of lemon rind and you have a warming winter dessert difficult to better. Honey does the trick too, somehow lifting a bland fruit's flavour. If the pears are sweet but have little flavour, a little acidity will not go amiss. A good slug of lemon or lime juice will perk up even the dullest fruit, as well as preserving their delicate colour.

Perhaps the partnering of apples and pears in everything from Cockney rhyming slang to nursery rhymes has not worked in the pear's favour. Perhaps the shops actually believe that a ripe pear should have the crisp and crunchy attributes of a ripe apple. Despite their romantic and fanciful names, Williams' Bon Chrétien and Doyenné du Comice are actually our most common varieties of pear, and more often than not the only varieties on offer. Perfectly ripe, I expect them to be luscious enough to dribble juice down my chin, their flesh melting on the tongue like a water-ice. Apparently a different thing altogether from 'Ripe and Ready to Eat'.

PEAS

I have just had lunch in the country. My host, a passionate vegetable gardener, kindly pointed out the four-legged brown and white things at the roadside and the green stuff they were lazily munching as if I had arrived by spaceship rather than the 10.40 from Marylebone. In turn I pointed out that I had spent the first 25 years of my life in the country (two buses a week and a mobile shop on Thursdays) and could just about remember the basics.

Lunch, bowls of fresh vegetables from the garden and a huge, glorious pot of glowing garlic mayonnaise, was one of those blissful events that sow seeds of restlessness through even the most committed townie's soul. A few minutes' drive away from one of the most celebrated restaurants in the land and I am sure there was nothing on that menu I would have swapped for the garden-grown vegetables and home-made nasturtium bread on my plate.

I barely worked for my lunch, picking from the most prolific vegetable garden I have ever encountered. A garden lush with rows of broad beans, baby beets, waving carrot fronds, chicory, chard and corn. There were aubergines and peppers under glass and, of course, tomatoes. But best of all there were peas. Peas which the gardener plunged straight into boiling water and cooked for just three minutes. Peas which took my taste buds back 20 years.

I guess it takes a gardener to understand the pea. Those who have been brought up on the frozen

Sugar Snap Peas with Mint

Whether picked from the garden or bought from the supermarket, the sugar snap pea cooks quickly. About 3 minutes in boiling water should do it. I am not sure salting the water is a necessity. The peas are cooked when their pods turn the brightest, almost translucent green. Mint leaves, a handful per pound of peas, are an unbeatable inclusion, as are sprigs of savoury. You can rub a little butter over the cooked peas if you wish, though it takes the edge off their fresh, green flavour. 450g/1lb of peas will serve about 6.

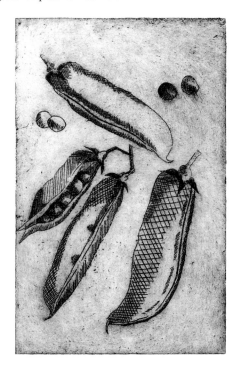

Peas with Lemon and Mint

225g/8oz shelled peas
4 tablespoons olive oil
2 sprigs of mint
juice of ½ a lemon

Put the peas in a medium-sized saucepan with the olive oil, a little salt and 2 tablespoons of water. Bring slowly to the boil, then add the mint. Turn the heat down to a simmer. Give them 10 minutes, then add most of the lemon juice, taste and add more if you think they need it. Serve hot.
Serves 2

Peas with Parsley and Artichoke Hearts

A light lunch, to be eaten with crusty bread or served as an accompaniment to fish or chicken.

120ml/4fl oz olive oil
4 large cloves of young garlic, sliced
450g/1lb tinned artichoke hearts
juice of ½ a lemon
350g/12oz shelled peas
1 tablespoon thyme, chopped
2 tablespoons parsley, chopped

Warm the olive oil in a large pot, then add the garlic. Cook over a medium heat for 1 minute till fragrant – the garlic should not colour at all. Meanwhile, drain the artichokes and cut them into quarters. Add them to the pot with the lemon and the peas. Throw in the thyme and cook for 10 minutes over a medium heat. Season with salt and pepper and stir in half of the parsley. Cook for a further 3 minutes. Stir in the last of the parsley and serve in bowls with open-textured crusty bread.
Serves 2

version of our most popular green vegetable must think that there is nothing more to peas than sweetness. They could not be more wrong. The frozen pea is nothing but a sweet shadow of the real thing. The gardener explained that it was all a question of timing – not so much of cooking, but of picking. Peas turn from the pointlessly sweet to the disappointingly tough in a matter of hours. Picking at the right time will catch both the pea's sweetness and enough of its starch to give the vegetable some point. Picked too soon, like those sent to the freezer in their billions, there is nothing but sugar; picked too late and you will have a starchy little bullet.

Shop-bought fresh peas can sometimes let you down, lacking the true pea sweetness and flavour of those eaten straight from the vine. Even modern transport systems barely get the pods to the shop in time before the sugar turns to starch and dullness sets in. Peas can lose almost half of their sugar within a few hours of picking. A spell in the fridge will slow, though not halt, the process. Garden-grown peas freeze successfully enough, and offer more interest than the commercial 'sweet nothings'.

The Italian gardeners of the sixteenth century would be saddened by what for most of us has become the only pea we know. They worked hard to develop varieties that outshone the grey, dried peas that had previously provided store-cupboard sustenance in winter but were rarely eaten fresh. The sweet, cheerful green vegetables that they produced turned this most humble of vegetables into a thing of joy, interesting enough to be wolfed straight from the pod. So interesting, in fact, that a century later the new varieties became the darlings of the court of Louis XIV, eaten in secret by the ladies of Versailles.

Those who have neither the time nor the inclination to grow their own may fare better with the shelled fresh peas sold in plastic trays in the supermarket or with the very flavoursome bottled peas sold under French labels in posh delicatessens. The fresh-tasting sugar snap might be an answer too: a small, plump variety with sweet peas and juicy pods. You eat the whole thing, pod and all. They have the sweetness and flavour of the traditional pea varieties and the bonus of a sweet edible pod. Their season is long and they are less prone to going tough overnight. Best of all, they are crisp and properly juicy – which is more than you can say for the ubiquitous mangetout that seems to have superseded the true garden pea.

I have a loathing of the mangetout, that flaccid, gutless impostor on the pea scene. Even more so when restaurants serve them up with equally tasteless and sweet mini-corns to compensate for the mangetout's impotence. It doesn't. Mange-non as far as I am concerned.

The pea-picking season starts in June and, depending on the weather and the variety planted, may last through till mid-September. Sugar snaps may last even longer. I have never been one to get excited by the first peas, or for that matter the first strawberries or asparagus, in the market, usually showing more interest when quality and quantity go up and prices come down.

While I wallowed in the nostalgia of sitting in the garden shelling traditional peas, eating twice as many as went into the cooking pot, I nevertheless marvelled at the waste-not-want-not bonus of the sugar snap. Its balance of sugar, starch and flavour is reminiscent of old-fashioned garden peas at their best, but its long season and superior keeping qualities make it a better bet for those who buy their vegetables rather than grow them.

As I left, the gardener pushed a care-package of greens and a little book into my hand. The book was called *Vegetables for Small Gardens*, by Lynda Brown (BBC). It was full of all manner of things I can grow in town. Tomatoes in containers, spinach in pots and beans that climb up canes. It tells me what to sow and when to sow it. It tells me of clubroot and caterpillars, of coir, crop rotation and compost. And best of all, it tells me all about peas.

Sugar Snap Salad with Bacon and Feta

A salad that is both refreshing and savoury. The juicy peas and their pods are a perfect foil for the salty cheese. Young mint leaves, the smaller the better, are more appropriate for eating raw than the coarse, older ones.

350g/12oz feta cheese
225g/8oz sugar snap peas
4 rashers smoked streaky bacon, diced
1 tablespoon olive oil
1 tablespoon young mint leaves, finely chopped

Break the feta into bite-sized chunks and place in a large serving dish. Put a pot of water on to boil. Slice the peas diagonally, as if you were slicing runner beans, and discard the short stem. Plunge the peas into the boiling water for 1 minute. Remove and cool under running cold water. Drain and add them to the cheese.

Grill or fry the bacon till crisp, adding a little oil if necessary. Tip the hot bacon over the feta, then toss gently with the chopped mint. Serve immediately.
Serves 2

THE PESTLE AND MORTAR

Classic Basil Pesto

All manner of herbs and nuts are ground up nowadays in the name of pesto. Although coriander and walnut or parsley and brazil nut may have their place, no mixture is ever quite as fragrant or useful as the classic basil and pine nut.

a handful of pine nuts (about 30g/1oz)
a large cup, loosely packed, of basil leaves
(about 50g/2oz)
a little sea salt
2 cloves of young garlic
90ml/3fl oz extra virgin olive oil
4 tablespoons Parmesan cheese, finely grated

If you wish, you can toast the pine nuts; it will bring out their flavour a little but it is not absolutely necessary. You can either bake them in a hot oven for a few minutes or toss them in a frying pan over a medium flame.

Tear the basil leaves slightly and put them in a mortar. Add the salt, garlic and pine nuts and pound until the ingredients have formed a rough paste. It should not be too smooth. Pour the oil in gradually, then stir in the grated cheese.

Use pesto as a sauce for pasta, stirred into soups, particularly bean soups, and as a flavouring for gnocchi. Try 1 or 2 spoonfuls folded into a dish of risotto.

I am beginning to hate my food processor. Yes, it can whiz a pan of summer tomatoes and basil to soup in seconds, reduce a bowl of strawberries to sauce at the click of a switch and turn a colander full of lightly boiled summer carrots into a smooth purée in the time it takes to say baby food. But somehow the whole effortless process leaves me wanting.

The modern food processor is a cumbersome beast. It takes up valuable space in my small kitchen, is a hassle to put together and a nightmare to clean. Even upside-down in the dishwasher the bowl and lid collect water, which I invariable tip over the clean cutlery. But worst of all, it cannot make pesto.

Of course, the staggeringly sharp blade can reduce fat cloves of new garlic, pots of basil leaves and a handful of pine nuts to a pleasant enough glop with which to lubricate a bowl of pasta. But it's not real pesto. There is something too smooth, too sophisticated, too . . . well . . . processed about the result.

Pesto is traditionally made by pounding. Its name actually comes from the Italian verb *pestare*, meaning 'to pound'. A food processor chops, whizzes, purées and creams. But it cannot pound. There is something about the action of pushing down while applying pressure that achieves a result far more interesting than a quick whiz from the food-processor blade.

There is something boringly consistent about machine-made pesto – or machine-made anything for that matter. I would also argue that the taste is different. I have made sauces in the machine from basil leaves, grated Parmesan, olive oil and pine nuts that were bitter. This has never happened with the pestle and mortar.

It amazes me that so few homes seem to have a working pestle and mortar. It breaks my heart to see this most ancient and efficient of kitchen implements end its working life as a place to store the dog's lead or the keys to the shed. Few kitchen utensils are such a pleasure to use. Crush a handful of basil leaves and the peppery green scent wafts up. Put a little pressure on a spoonful of dark-purple juniper berries and the unmistakable smell of a freshly poured gin and tonic will fill the kitchen. Even if you stick your nose down the funnel of a food processor, the aroma will just not be the same as basil leaves you have pounded with a pestle.

Enormous pleasure can be had from using a pestle and mortar. There is something about the way the pounding action releases the herbs' essential oils that is therapeutic and relaxing. After a hard day I find the scent of freshly crushed garlic and basil lifts the spirits.

Even the most automated of homes will find a stone pestle and mortar of use for the little jobs that are too small to warrant the use of the food processor. Crushing crystals of sea salt, for instance, or grinding a small quantity of spice. A well-made pair will last you a lifetime. I can recommend the plain stoneware variety for pretty much everything. It is especially good for crushing olives, anchovies and garlic, three strong flavours that would impregnate a wooden mortar. Less successful, I think, are the polished marble mortars. Whole spices are inclined to slide round the bowl and the pestle can barely get a grip. Ideally I would like a second one with a ridged bowl or rough

Tapenade

A deeply savoury paste from Provence, too often reduced to a smooth purée in a processor, is much more interesting when made in the traditional way.

2 tablespoons capers, rinsed
4 anchovy fillets, rinsed
a good pinch of thyme leaves
1 plump clove of garlic, peeled
225g/8oz black olives, stoned
1 tablespoon extra virgin olive oil
1 teaspoon brandy

Put the capers in the mortar and crush them with the anchovy fillets and thyme. Add the garlic and pound it till it is finely crushed. Now add the olives, a few at a time, pounding with the pestle until thoroughly crushed, but stop before the mixture becomes slushy. Stir in the olive oil and brandy and season with a little black pepper.

Tapenade makes a wonderfully savoury dip for raw vegetables, in particular fennel and celery stalks. But it can also be used as a spread for crisp French-bread toasts. When not reduced to a purée, this rough olive paste makes a good light lunch with crusty bread.

Aïoli

This is the classic, thick Provençal aïoli, rich with garlic and oil. You cannot achieve a proper version with a machine. Only the steady action of a pestle and mortar will achieve the right consistency. Essential to this recipe is new, plump garlic. Wizened old cloves will give a bitter finish. The amount below is for a large pestle and mortar, though it will work well in half-quantities.

4 large, juicy young cloves of garlic
a little sea salt
2 egg yolks
500ml/17fl oz extra virgin olive oil
a little lemon juice

Crush the garlic cloves, their thin skins peeled off, in a mortar with a little sea salt. The mixture should resemble a thick lumpy paste. Add a drop of water then an egg yolk. Stir until it is blended with the garlic, then add the second yolk. Slowly pour in the oil, drop by drop at first, then in a steady stream, working it in with the pestle. When it is rich and golden and has the consistency of mayonnaise, it is ready.

Serves 6 as a dip

Aïoli is traditionally used as a dip for crisp raw vegetables, but it is a richer alternative to mayonnaise in a sandwich and is particularly good spooned on to round toasts of French bread and dunked into fish soup.

surface, like the Japanese or Indian versions, for crushing chillies and oily seeds such as sesame.

If you have only one mortar, let it be a medium-sized one. Smaller ones are fine for tiny amounts of spice, but impractical for pesto or aïoli, the golden garlic mayonnaise. It can be just as infuriating, though, chasing a teaspoonful of coriander seeds around an oversized bowl.

The pestle and mortar must surely have been invented for pesto. There is really no excuse for not making your own in high summer, with good basil so plentiful now. I get more fragrant results from the larger, tougher leaves of my pot-grown basil out of doors than I do from the fleshy fragile plants in the supermarkets. If we have a hot summer, the blazing sun seems to concentrate the herb's essential oils. A lack of water seems to produce a more potent leaf. Even shop-bought specimens harden up when replanted in real soil instead of the brown cotton wool they were grown in. Watered from underneath rather than on top, a trick recently learned from a friend, they keep going for weeks.

A pestle and mortar get more fragrance from the basil leaf than a knife or a processor. As the leaves turn from lush bright green to a darker, deeper colour, their oils are released. You can hold their flavour in suspension with olive oil, where they will keep in a screw-top jar in the fridge for a few weeks. Or better still get out the pestle and mortar, add the new season's garlic, pine nuts and cheese and make a real version of pesto. A hundred times better than that from a bottle, and head and shoulders more interesting than a Magimix version, I suspect pesto is what your right arm is really for.

A FEW POINTS

- Wipe the pestle and mortar out every time you use them. Some smells, particularly garlic, anchovy and capers, can linger on the pestle no matter how many times you scrub it.
- If the pestle is made partially of wood, as many are, do not put it in the dishwasher.
- You may find it easier to place the mortar in your lap rather than on a work surface.
- Wooden versions are unsuitable for mashing salt cod, making mayonnaise or crushing anchovies, whose smells they will absorb.
- Don't be tempted to overfill the mortar. It is easier to use when it is about a quarter full.
- If the food starts to slide around, add a little sugar or salt, whichever the recipe calls for, to enable it to get a grip.

PINEAPPLE

Hot Buttered Pineapple

50g/2oz butter
4 thick slices of ripe, peeled pineapple
3 tablespoons caster sugar

Melt the butter in a shallow pan. Add the pineapple slices and sugar and cook very gently until the fruit starts to colour around the edges and a loose caramel forms. Serve the fruit hot, with the caramel spooned over and a jug of thick cream.
Serves 4

Baked Pineapple with Honey and Kirsch

1 medium pineapple
butter
2 tablespoons Kirsch
3 tablespoons honey

Peel the pineapple and remove its crown of leaves. Cut into 6 wedges from stalk to crown and place them in a generously buttered baking dish. Sprinkle with Kirsch and the sugar, and any juice saved, and bake at 180°C/350°F/Gas Mark 4 for 25 minutes till all is rich and bubbling. Serve with cream.
Serves 3

The point of the pineapple is its copious, sweet juice – juice that is both sugary and slightly tart, sticky and refreshing. This is what makes the pineapple the most welcome of winter visitors.

It is not a fruit to be picked up casually, like a winter apple or late summer peach, and munched from the hand. The grandest of fruits, its crown of pointed leaves ensuring its position of king of the fruit bowl, the pineapple requires a little forethought on the part of the eater.

At around £1 for a large fruit, the pineapple is no longer the special-occasion fruit it was in my childhood. (If there is a pineapple in the fruit bowl, then it must be Christmas.) More recently, in the lush, tropical heat of Goa, the fruit became a daily ritual during a beach-bum holiday. Armed with a plump pineapple, chosen for its ripeness and stripped of its inedible skin by the stallholder's fearsome machete, we would wander far along the deserted beach to make the most of the fruit and its sticky juice.

Six months later, in the frost-covered gardens of Versailles, the statues and urns wrapped up for winter, such a fruit seemed even more welcome, cheering us up as our teeth chattered and we dripped juice into the snow as we walked. It is this fruit's impeccable timing, turning up sweet and gold in the depths of winter, that probably makes it so popular.

From November to May they appear in good condition, at an affordable price. Come the dark evenings, only the lowliest of fruit shops will not boast a pineapple or two, hung like lanterns from a meat hook above the nuts. Only in high summer do they lose their real magic. But who cares then, when a glut of scarlet clothes the fruit stall?

Ripeness is paramount. Cut too soon, when its etched skin is still green and the flesh inside pale, you might as well eat an apple. Time your cut right and you will need a bath afterwards, or at any rate a clean shirt. A ripe pineapple is heavy. It will be deeply fragrant. If it does not smell, do not cut it. The skin will be deep mustard gold and tender to touch. Its grenade-like appearance is its worst enemy – at its peak of ripeness, it will bruise as easily as a peach.

It is tempting to believe the tale that the fruit is ripe when its leaves can be removed with a light tug. Do not. Many a fruit's leaves will remain unbudgeable till the flesh is long overdue, by which time the fruit will be brown and winy. And you will have missed it. Smell and tenderness are far more reliable guides.

Too much is made of the rights and wrongs of cutting a pineapple. The Indians slice off its skin and leave the flesh whole. The Thais, when they are not carving it into a chrysanthemum, will slice the fruit in spiral fashion, removing the eyes, and hand it too you to eat like a giant lollipop. In Britain we tend to quarter it from leaf to stalk and slice it into chunks, the way they do a slice of melon in seaside hotels. I am not sure it matters either way. The point is not to lose the juice.

I find the easiest method is to treat the fruit like a small whole cheese, cutting off its plume and a little of the flesh to act as a lid and then taking a horizontal slice as and when I fancy. It will last a few days in the fridge if you keep it away from the fish. A soup plate underneath will keep any stray juice from being wasted. A thick slice, eaten digestive-biscuit style, makes a refreshing start to the day.

Ananas au Kirsch

1 medium-ripe, sweet pineapple
2 tablespoons Kirsch

Peel the pineapple if you wish, though the skin is easy enough to remove as you eat. Cut the pineapple into thick slices, almost 2.5cm/1in thick. Put 2 slices, a large and a small one, on each plate. Upend the Kirsch over the fruit and leave for 10 minutes or so before serving.
Serves 4

Pineapple with Mint

1 medium-ripe pineapple
1 heaped tablespoon mint leaves, chopped
1 tablespoon Cointreau or Grand Marnier

Cut a lid from the pineapple, and cut and scoop out the flesh to leave a shell. Chop the fruit quite small, saving the precious juice. Stir in the chopped mint leaves and pile back into the shell. Pour over Cointreau or Grand Marnier and chill very thoroughly. When the fruit is deeply chilled, then serve at once.
Serves 4

Cinnamon Pineapple

Peel a large, chilled ripe pineapple and cut it into slices. Place 2 slices on each plate and dust lightly with powdered cinnamon. Serve immediately.

Only in Britain has pineapple with Kirsch disappeared from the menu, along with profiteroles with chocolate sauce. It deservedly went out of fashion here when it was invariably served underripe and with a spirit not dissimilar to paraffin. Yet it is offered unapologetically in every decent Paris bistro. The best I have tasted was at a bistro just down from the dazzling, majestic Institut du Monde Arabe, though sadly it was only a taster from a friend's plate. I was meanwhile embarrassing myself with a huge bowl of poached meringue floating in a vanilla custard.

Although they once flourished in the heated greenhouses of eighteenth-century England, the pineapples on our shelves now tend to come from the Ivory Coast. Sad that they no longer amuse both gardeners (who once grew them by the thousand) and architects (who perched them on gateposts). Oh for a pineapple-shaped folly at the foot of my garden or a pineapple turret for a rooftop den. Now they come with user-friendly labels round their necks telling you how to cut them.

You can cook a pineapple. It is a good fruit to cut into slices and top with sponge or to add in chunks to a chicken curry. The popular pairing of pineapple and green pepper in salads and stir-fries is a great worry. A more wretched mismatch I can hardly think of. I lose interest in the fruit when it is added to savoury dishes and have never been convinced of its merits with meat. But that bastion of 1960s steak houses, the gammon steak with its sad, tinned pineapple garnish, is not so bad when made with good, not too salty ham and a slice of fresh fruit served hot rather than lukewarm.

The pineapple's affinity with cheese goes beyond the supporting role it still occasionally plays for cocktail sticks of Cheddar and silverskin onions. Such a piece was *de rigueur* at my parents' Christmas buffet. It was always there, next to the Twiglets. But it is the creamier cheeses that are right with the sweet tartness of pineapple, not Edam. Thick, sweet mascarpone, the Italian cream cheese, is a pleasant enough partner for a slice of the dribbling pine, as is clotted cream. I recently surprised myself with a slice of the ripe fruit, a dollop of mascarpone and a scattering of crushed digestive biscuits. A far more pleasant mouthful than one might think.

A friend went one better, hollowing out the fruit, then chopping the flesh and returning it to the skin with chopped fresh mint and a slash of Kirsch. Served seriously cold it was a most welcome end to a rich meal. Though the fruit's natural sweetness intensifies on cooking, it loses much of the appeal of the fresh fruit, with rivulets of juice running down as you pare away its thorny skin. And don't be tempted to throw away the core. If the fruit is ripe, the central core will be sweet enough to eat, and only slightly less tender than the body of the fruit. How to capture the juice as it drips from the ripe pineapple is something I shall leave to your own ingenuity.

PLUMS

There were plum trees in the garden when I was young, gnarled and bent and covered in sage-green lichen. Come September their fruits would glow like candles. There were gold oval plums flushed with red, virtually transparent and dripping with juice, and little round greengages which turned a rich golden yellow as they ripened. We picked crates of them for pies, crumbles and jam, and the rest we left for the wasps.

Plum pie, plum jam and plum crumble mark the end of the summer fruit. The scarlet berries and currants must now move over for purple, gold and crimson plums that herald the onset of autumn. If they strike one sour note with me, it is that they were a reminder that the return to school was imminent.

The plum receives none of the respect that we reserve for the peach and the apricot. It is rarely used as a commercial flavouring for sweets or ices. More than any other fruit, it is likely to turn up in farm shops, village fêtes and cake stalls. The plum is a country girl rarely understood by city folk. It is one of my very favourite fruits.

I wish some whiz-kid chef would do for them what he did for the kiwi or the passion fruit. Then perhaps the imported ones we suffer from for the rest of the year might improve. Imported plums are only good for cooking, never making it high enough in the flavour stakes to qualify as a dessert fruit. Like out-of-season peaches, most never ripen satisfactorily.

In the late summer the Victoria plum is the one

Pork with Plums

Pork with prunes is about as classic as you can get. Using fresh plums instead is slightly more unusual but works well with the mild Chinese spicing of this dish. Here, the plums dissolve into the cooking liquor.

1 tablespoon groundnut oil
450g/1lb/2 large spare-rib pork chops
salt
1 tablespoon Muscavado sugar
2 tablespoons light soy sauce
4 tablespoons white wine
2 tablespoons Amontillado sherry
8 slightly underripe red plums, halved and stoned
300ml/10fl oz water
a little fresh parsley, chopped

Heat the oil in a casserole dish and fry the chops for a minute or so on each side until they have coloured slightly. Add a good pinch of salt, the sugar, soy and alcohol. Bring slowly to the boil, add the plums and cover with a lid, then reduce the heat and leave to simmer very gently for 50 minutes.

Check the pork for tenderness. It should come away from the bone with only a little pressure from a knife. Lift out the meat and transfer to a warm plate. Add the water to the pan, turn up the heat and let the sauce bubble rapidly, until it has reduced by half and has started to shine. Mash the plums into the sauce with a fork, then return the pork to the sauce. Continue cooking for a minute then serve, scattered with the chopped parsley.

Serves 2

most commonly offered by the shops. Really ripe Victoria plums can be sweet and juicy, almost honeyed, and they make a fine cooking plum. But there are, I think, more interesting varieties, although you will have to look hard. Commerce has not been kind to the plum family, or perhaps it is the other way round.

Size is rarely any guide to flavour. The small golden plums, the Pershore Yellow Egg and the luscious little Mirabelle of France, often have the richest flavour of all, though this year I have tasted some very fine maroon Marjorie Seedling with honey-coloured flesh from my local greengrocer. But this is a far cry from the 60 or so varieties that were recorded in the sixteenth century. Without access to a specialist orchard, what chance have I to even taste all the others?

Where can I get my hands on a Warwickshire Drooper or Coe's Golden Drop? Why has no shop ever offered me a Golden Esperen, the tiny golden fruit raised by one of Napoleon's generals? And what about the golden Jefferson, Count Althann and Oullins Gage, all recorded as worth eating in their day but now apparently forgotten. All I seem to see is the ubiquitous Victoria and the dry old Stanley.

It appears that difficult or poor-cropping varieties of plum have been tolerated less than their equivalent in the apple world. The six weeks of the English plum season, from the end of August to the middle of October, longer if we are lucky, is our lot. Plums will freeze (and will dry famously as the prune) but are rarely worth eating out of season. We have secured reasonable out-of-season supplies of strawberries, raspberries and cherries, but we have never managed an imported plum worth eating. It is one of our truly seasonal fruits, whose season cannot be extended.

Of all plums it is the tiny golden ones that interest me most. They are as welcome on the table as they are in the kitchen. And they make heavenly jam. Britain is the only country to separate the plum from the 'gage'. This hails from Sir Thomas Gage, who, on receiving an unlabelled sapling of the small and delectable Reine Claude plum from his brother in France, called it after himself. Surely these are the most delicious plums of all. But only if they are allowed to ripen properly.

Plum Tart

A simple, juicy plum tart in the French style.

100g/4oz cold unsalted butter, cut into chunks
225g/8oz plain flour
2 tablespoons caster sugar
1 egg yolk
700g/1½lb small, ripe plums

Rub the butter into the flour with your fingertips until it resembles fine breadcrumbs. Add the sugar. Use a fork to stir in the egg yolk with enough water (probably about a tablespoon) to bind the mixture together into a ball. Roll the pastry into a rectangle roughly 20 x 30cm/12 x 8in. Transfer it carefully on to a baking sheet. Pinch the edges deeply with your thumb and forefinger to give a shallow rim. Prick lightly with a fork to stop it rising in the oven. Set aside to rest in the fridge for at least 20 minutes.

Remove from the fridge, bake in a preheated oven for 10 minutes at 200°C/400°F/Gas Mark 6. Slice or halve the plums, depending on their size, and place them over the pastry. Bake for 20 minutes until the fruit is tender. Sprinkle the fruit and pastry with sugar and return to the oven for 10 minutes. Serve warm with cream.
Serves 6

It is easy to criticise the greengrocer or supermarket for selling unripe plums, but we are talking about a fragile fruit whose point of perfect ripeness lasts only a day or two. A wooden crate of ripe golden plums can turn to slush in hours, as anyone who has left a bag in the salad drawer of the fridge for too long will know. Unless we have access to a tree of ripe fruit, we must buy them barely ripe and bring them to ripeness ourselves. The flavour will not be as magnificent as when picked straight from the tree, but you can say that about anything.

A small greenish plum will turn to rich, glowing ripeness in a couple of days in a brown-paper bag. A ripe one added to the hard green fruit will speed up the process. As soon as the fruit is golden and transparent it is ready. If the skin has wrinkles around the stalk it may be quite superb. A droplet of sticky juice on the skin like a tiny golden bead means the fruit is begging to be eaten.

As with many short-season foods, I tend to get carried away and overbuy. A glut of plums can wreak havoc on the gut, though, like prunes, I find their reputation somewhat exaggerated. Juicy sweetmeats though they are when plucked straight from the bag, any variety of plum can be cooked. The golden varieties make sensational tarts, while the darker, larger varieties are good in pies. The Victoria is the traditional crumble plum. They all work in a savoury context too. The slight acidity in a plum flatters pork and game, particularly chops and bony cuts. The partridge that has just come into season is a happy partner for plums. At this early point in their life simply add the whole plums to the roasting dish as if they were tiny baked apples; they will take about 15 minutes to cook. Their slight tartness is a good foil to the game's rich flesh.

In the last few years we have seen old-fashioned apple varieties returning to the supermarket shelves. We are buying as many Michaelmas Reds and D'arcy Spice as the growers can produce. So why not give us some old-fashioned plums too? I for one long to taste the Maître Claude and the Myrobalan, the Blue Perdrigon and the Jefferson. And which inquisitive shopper could resist the perfumed Drap-d'or or a handful of Warwickshire Droopers?

Grilled Plums and Blackberries with Hot Mascarpone and Sugar

A simple mélange of dark fruits, molten cream cheese and sugar. The plums must be ripe, otherwise the dish loses its point.

4 ripe plums
a few blackberries
2 teaspoons brandy or Kirsch
8 heaped teaspoons mascarpone cheese
4 tablespoons caster sugar

Cut the plums in half and remove the stones. Put them, snuggled up together, in an ovenproof dish. Scatter over the blackberries and trickle over the booze. Place a teaspoon of mascarpone in each hollow and sprinkle over the sugar.

Place under a hot grill till the sugar melts and the cream cheese runs, about 5–8 minutes. Eat warm from the grill.
Serves 2

POTATOES

Baked Anchovy and Dolcelatte Potatoes

6 fat cloves of garlic
4 tablespoons olive oil
4 large baking potatoes
sea salt
8 anchovy fillets
1 tablespoons flat-leaf parsley, chopped
100g/4oz dolcelatte, Cashel Blue or Gorgonzola

Place the garlic cloves in a small dish. Pour over the olive oil and bake in a preheated oven at 200°C/400°F/Gas Mark 6.

Wash the potatoes, insert a metal skewer into each of them, shake off most of the water and roll them in sea salt. Bake until the skewers come out easily. This will, of course, depend on the size of the potato, but most large ones take about an hour.

When the garlic is soft, squeeze the insides out of the skins and mash the flesh with a fork. Take the cooked potatoes out of the oven. Slice a lid off each potato and scoop out the filling with a teaspoon into a bowl. Mash with a potato masher or fork. Chop the anchovy fillets and add them to the potato, stir in the garlic, parsley, half the cheese and a little freshly ground pepper. Spoon the mixture into the potato shells.

Divide the remaining cheese into 4, and place a piece on top of each potato. Return to the oven and cook for 7–10 minutes until golden and bubbling, and replace the lids.

Serves 4

Some foods are made for each other, some to such an extent that the one becomes pointless without the other. Think of thick slices cut from a white farmhouse loaf, toasted and spread generously with cold, salty butter; fat, golden chips fried till hot and crisp in proper dripping; pasta glistening with olive oil and Parmesan cheese. Just three examples of the most perfect gastronomic partnership: the marriage of starch and fat.

Potatoes lose all point without a lubrication of fat. What is a new potato without its thin coat of melted butter, a fat, crisp-skinned baked potato without grated cheese or a sliced boiled potato without a slathering of rich mayonnaise? Where is the point in *pommes dauphinoise* without the garlic and cream it is slowly baked with, or the roast potato without its skin made crisp and golden brown with the fat from the roast?

Despite Britain's recent adoption of rice and our new-found passion for pasta, potatoes are still our national starch. Some would say they are the heart and soul of our cooking. The good news is that health experts feel most of our energy should be coming from such carbohydrate-based foods. But surely such experts cannot expect us to eat our starch without at least one of its more voluptuous natural partners.

Baked Potatoes

Butter and grated Cheddar are still the favourite gilding for a baked potato – the simplest combination and almost impossible to beat, though far from the only one suitable. Goats'-milk cheeses, grilled fatty bacon, soured cream and thick, peppery olive oil are all possibilities for a luxurious lubricant.

All potatoes, new, old, waxy or floury-fleshed, red- or white-skinned, can be baked successfully. There is no rule that says they must be King Edwards or they should be the biggest in the shop. The results will differ according to variety. I quite like the solid texture of a baked waxy potato such as Pink Fir Apple or Belle de Fontenay. New potatoes bake to delectable little morsels, especially if you throw a couple of squashed garlic cloves and a sprig of rosemary in too. Good though they can be, however, it is always the oversized, floury potato which gets the most votes. It certainly gets mine.

The quintessential baked potato has a crisp shell and fluffy flesh. There are few who would disagree with that. A fat, creamy accompaniment marries more successfully with a floury potato than a waxy one. King Edwards are fine, as are Golden Wonder and Maris Piper. The most popular supermarket potato, Record, is no better for baking than it is for anything else. Its only fans are the growers who applaud its resistance to disease. Pity it is so unexciting when cooked.

The simplest things are often the hardest to get right and I would include baking a potato in that. You will not get a crisp skin by wrapping the thing in foil, as I see so many people do. Inside its metal jacket, the potato will steam instead of bake. Washed and dried, then rubbed lightly with sea salt

Salt-crust Baked Potato

Preheat the oven to 220°C/425°F/Gas Mark 7. Scrub the potatoes, but not so hard that you graze the skin. While the potatoes are still wet, roll them in crushed sea salt. Pierce with a steel skewer, then bake for about an hour, maybe longer. Remove from the oven and retrieve the skewer. It should come out easily if the potatoes are cooked. Crack the potatoes open instantly, as overleaf, and serve with cold butter and grated cheese or any of the following:

- a spoonful of tapenade, the French anchovy and olive dip;
- crumbled goats' cheese and a trickle of very green, peppery olive oil;
- chicken livers, sautéd in butter and sprinkled with balsamic vinegar;
- a large, sweet onion, sliced into rings rather than chopped, cooked till golden, and lightly caught in a little butter;
- cold unsalted butter, straight from the fridge, and a grinding of gritty sea salt;
- a dollop of crème fraîche with spoonfuls of caviare;
- sliced sun-dried oil-packed tomatoes and coarsely chopped flat-leaf parsley;
- home-made garlic mayonnaise;
- streaky bacon (it must be streaky, back bacon isn't fatty enough), grilled till the fat is golden then scissored into strips and poured over the potato with the fat from the pan.

Baked Potatoes with Kidneys in Their Fat

A recipe from Lindsey Bareham's *In Praise of the Potato*, to fill 4 potatoes.

4 lambs' kidneys encased in their own fat

Dijon mustard

salt

pepper

Place the encased kidneys on a baking tray and bake alongside the potatoes. After 1 hour, remove the kidneys and trim off any remaining fat. Remove the potatoes and cut off a lid. Scoop out the flesh, mix with 1 tablespoon mustard per potato, season and pile back into the potato. Add a dribble of the delicious kidney fat and pepper and serve. This is remarkably rich and filling.

Serves 4

Parmesan Potatoes

per person

4 new potatoes

1 tablespoon olive oil

1 tablespoon grated Parmesan cheese

Wipe the potatoes, or wash them if they are very dirty. Slice them thickly, about 4 slices from each potato. Put them into a shallow ovenproof dish, in a single layer. Pour over the olive oil, then bake in a preheated oven, 200°C/400°F/Gas Mark 6, for 20 minutes. Remove the potatoes from the oven, turn them over and scatter with the grated Parmesan cheese. Return to the oven and bake for a further 5 or 6 minutes till the Parmesan is golden. Serve hot.

while still slightly damp, a naked potato will crisp nicely in a hot oven. To speed its cooking, you can spear it with a metal skewer. Cooked on the bars of the oven rather than on a baking sheet, the skin is more likely to go crisp. The skin will remain crisp only if it is eaten straight away. Keeping a spud warm will ensure it develops the hide of a rhinoceros.

The texture of a baked potato varies according to how you break into it. I know this sounds absurd, but I promise it is true. The texture of a baked potato sliced with a sharp knife and one opened by force is as different as chalk and cheese. Lindsey Bareham, in her celebrated book *In Praise of the Potato* (Michael Joseph), gives cookery writer Rosie Stark's brilliant karate-chop method as the best way to ensure a floury potato. 'When the potato flesh feels soft to the touch (on no account pierce the skin) remove and place on a wooden board. Cover the potato with a folded cloth and crack it open with a swift karate-style chop with the side of your hand. This alarming method lets the steam out quickly and the potato is wonderfully floury.' This trick is invaluable to those who take their baked potatoes seriously.

There are those who prefer to stuff their baked spuds. I can see the merit in this method: the top is removed, boiled-egg style, then the potato flesh scooped out and mashed with butter. Whipped to a light and airy mash, the seasoned filling is then stuffed back into the jacket and returned to the oven to crisp. A bit of a fiddle, but sublime. The filling can be padded with grated cheese that will melt into the hot mash, or butter and chopped herbs.

I am less of a fan of the baked potato as an accompaniment; it is too filling to sit alongside a roast or grill. Anointing it with copious amounts of cholesterol seems less of a joy when there is meat alongside. A really fine baked potato, the most welcoming of smells on a cold night, should be served in all its majesty as the main part of the meal. We can go to town on the fillings or keep them simple. It is probably best to err on the side of simplicity, so as not to kill the flavour of the potato itself, which deserves to be treated as more than a vehicle for the filling.

Few people would dream of putting anything on a baked potato that is not creamy, cheesy or buttery. Only the most miserable of cooks would offer anything 'healthy' or lacking in the pure unctuousness of melting butter and oozing cheese. After all, isn't that what starch is for?

New Potatoes

I find nothing so easy to recall as the taste of childhood meals eaten out of doors. Strawberries with tinned Nestlé cream, sandwiches of cucumber and Kraft cheese slices, 'cress', tinned ham (I hated the jelly it came in and would spend hours methodically removing it) and salads stained purple with beetroot. There was Neapolitan ice-cream (with wafers for the grown-ups) and dandelion and burdock to drink and something called cream soda. There were also tinned new potatoes.

I don't know why we ate tinned new potatoes at the height of summer, I just know that we did. It was only when my father retired and started to grow his own that I tasted freshly dug new potatoes. I remember eating the first he grew with the sort of solemnity usually reserved for a restaurant meal that you know is costing too much money. I don't think we ever ate tinned ones again.

New potatoes are a treat. They are also unreliable. Sometimes they look the part, small and flaky skinned, but fail to deliver. To come across an

New Potatoes rolled in Pancetta

Pancetta is available in Italian delicatessens and some supermarkets. Use thinly sliced streaky bacon if pancetta evades you. A stock cube, on this occasion, will do if there is no fresh stock.

50g/2oz butter
16 new potatoes
16 thin slices of smoked pancetta or streaky bacon
300ml/10fl oz vegetable stock

Preheat the oven to 200°C/400°F/Gas Mark 6. Butter an ovenproof dish with half of the butter. Scrub the potatoes well. Wrap each potato in a slice of bacon and place in the buttered dish. Dot the remaining butter over the potatoes and pour on the hot stock. Bake for 30–40 minutes till the potatoes are tender and most of the stock has evaporated.
Serves 4

New Potatoes with Olive Oil and Mint

750g/1⅔lb new potatoes
75ml/2½fl oz extra virgin olive oil
4 cloves of garlic, very finely chopped
1 small handful of parsley, chopped
1 small handful of mint, chopped

Wipe the potatoes and thinly slice them. They should be about as thick as pound coins. In a large frying pan, heat the oil over a medium flame. Add the potatoes, cooking them for about 20 minutes. Shake the pan from time to time. When they are golden, soft in the centre and crusty on the outside, then sprinkle them with salt and pepper, the garlic and chopped parsley and mint. Serve immediately.
Serves 4

Roast New Potatoes with Mushrooms and Breadcrumbs

450g/1lb tiny new potatoes
juice of ½ a lemon
2 teaspoons chopped thyme leaves
1 tablespoon olive oil
100g/4oz small mushrooms, wiped and halved
4 tablespoons dry breadcrumbs

Put the new potatoes, wiped thoroughly, into a roasting tin. Squeeze over the lemon juice and scatter on the thyme leaves. Pour in the oil and place over a moderate heat for 4 minutes, shaking the pan from time to time.

Add the mushrooms and toss them with the potatoes, then season with salt and pepper. Roast in a preheated hot oven, 200°C/400°F/Gas Mark 6, scattering over the crumbs after 10 minutes. Toss gently and continue to roast. All should be tender and golden after about 25–30 minutes.

earthy, nutty, buttery batch of new potatoes is a joy, but unless they are really good I would rather eat old ones – or maincrop, as they are called now. But they are a bit funny in late summer, breaking up in the water and collapsing in the pan.

In terms of flavour, new potatoes often let you down. Jersey, Cornwall, Egypt and Cyprus can send some exquisitely flavoured potatoes, but much of the market is often lacklustre to say the least. I am rarely one to gild the lily, but hopefully the first to recognise that something not up to scratch may benefit from a little adornment. With new potatoes coming down in price as the season wears on, it may be time to take a break from the mint and melted butter that traditionally anoints the early-season new crop.

Once the new potato season is on its way and the price (and quality) drops, I am happy enough to break with tradition. In the last couple of weeks I have rolled them in bacon and cooked them in stock, baked them in a hot oven and smothered them with cream and herbs. I have eaten the tiniest cooked slowly in butter and olive oil and the largest, which only just make it into the category, sliced, deep-fried and then dunked into garlic mayonnaise.

New potatoes can take loud savoury flavours more readily than I had imagined. Their flavour is deeper than one is led to believe. Anchovies, chopped and stirred into a potato salad with lots of chopped parsley, garlic in any form, and sea salt, the crystals so large you can crunch them between your teeth, are all possible partners for the not-so-diminutive new potato. Though I wouldn't do any of it to a Jersey Royal, the nuttiest, earthiest tasting of them all.

Bacon, or better still Italian smoked pancetta, with its sweet and plentiful fat makes a good wrapper for baby potatoes, basting the spuds as they cook. Even Parmesan cheese, the most savoury of mouthfuls, does not mask a new potato's flavour – only heightens it.

And then there are the new potato salads. When warm, their waxy flesh soaks up the dressing to give a luxurious velvety texture. A bold vinaigrette, with a little more vinegar than usual, makes a lively change from the ubiquitous glop of mayonnaise. Be generous with the herbs, and not just parsley – try basil or coriander too.

Try scraping their skins and roasting them in the traditional way. The result will be an elegant, pale gold version of the genre. You can pierce them with a skewer and bake them till crisp in a hot oven. Slide them from the skewer and dip them in crème fraîche, a forkful at a time. Or try them steamed and sliced, and dressed with creamy yoghurt and chopped dill.

I am not sure why I have encountered so many dull spuds this summer. Only the best will be gently brushed with soft butter and rolled in chopped herbs. Any little charmers which don't come up to scratch can expect a little rough treatment. Like sizzling oil, robust herbs and dousing in loud dressings. They will be sprinkled with Parmesan, scattered with coriander and deep-fried in hot fat. I shall show them no mercy.

French Potato Salad with Mustard and Parsley

A gutsy dressing for not-so-young potatoes.

450g/1lb new, waxy-fleshed potatoes
3 tablespoons white wine
5 tablespoons mild olive oil
1 tablespoon red wine vinegar
1 heaped tablespoon grain mustard
2 spring onions, finely chopped
a small handful of parsley, chopped

Boil the potatoes in salted water till tender. Drain them and slice thickly. Sprinkle the hot potatoes with the wine. Mix the olive oil, vinegar and mustard and season generously with salt and pepper. You can whisk it a little but it really should be a loose mixture rather than a thick dressing. Stir in the chopped spring onions and parsley. Pour the dressing over the warm potatoes and serve at room temperature.

Serves 2–4

PUMPKINS

Grilled Pumpkin with Butter and Parmesan

Butter and cheese have something of an affinity for pumpkin. Grilled slices of pumpkin can be served as a light supper with a salad or as an accompaniment to grilled chicken or game. Best of all, serve with slices of thickly cut Parma ham.

a large wedge of pumpkin, about 450g/1lb in weight

butter

4 tablespoons grated Parmesan cheese

Remove the fibres and seeds from the pumpkin. Cut into crescents no more than 2.5cm/1in at their thickest part. Place the slices flat side down on a baking sheet, one with a small lip so that the butter doesn't run off. Spread with butter. Be generous. Sprinkle with salt and grind over some pepper.

Place the buttered and seasoned pumpkin under a preheated grill. It should be about 20cm/8in from the elements if the flesh is to cook through without burning. Cook for 10 minutes. Turn the pumpkin over and spread more butter and seasoning on each piece. Grill till tender and golden brown.

Remove from the heat, sprinkle each piece of pumpkin with Parmesan cheese and return to the grill for a couple of minutes till the cheese turns golden. Remove carefully with a palette knife and eat while hot and buttery.

Only the luckiest of pumpkins ever make it on to a plate. Used as haunting lanterns or makeshift cauldrons for steaming party punch, the fate of most of these plump, golden squashes is to lie in the garden, collapsed and burnt out, while their scooped out flesh sits in a plastic bag in the fridge till someone turfs it out in disgust.

It is easy enough to dismiss this rock-hard, dry-fleshed vegetable as fit only for fun. The tell-tale signs that something might be good to eat – fragrance, juice and a certain sensuality – are all missing here. Yet there can be magic in a pumpkin. It needs fierce heat to soften its fibrous flesh, spices to perk up its delicate flavour and butter in generous amounts to enrich its watery flesh.

There was something warm, jolly, yet curiously sinister about the row of plump, smiling pumpkins at the greengrocer's this week. I often buy a pumpkin at this time of year to slice in half and bake with butter and pepper for supper. I usually go for the smallest in the shop. It is no more tender, just easier to cart home. I suspect their absence from the supermarkets has more to do with making your basket too heavy to fill with the lightweight pre-packed suppers further down the aisle than with customer demand.

Once home my pumpkin sat, as it always does, on the kitchen counter, as smug and squat as a Cheshire cat. I was half tempted to turn it into a glowing Hallowe'en lantern, if only to frighten the local children, or keep it for a Bonfire Night party, but it would be more interesting when cooked.

Pumpkin marries well with other golden things; its ochre flesh brightens up immeasurably when matched with butter, cheese, walnut oil and spices. Orange, in the form of juice or zest stirred into a soup of its flesh, will also lift its spirits.

A pumpkin needs little more attention than anointing with butter, sprinkling with cumin, coriander and coarsely ground black pepper and roasting till its flesh is soft and melting. Some cooks use its flesh in risotto or as a stuffing for pasta. Chillies will help, as will a light sprinkling of sugar and a dusting of very finely ground cinnamon bark. But little else. Like its slimmer, less interesting sisters, marrows, courgettes and cucumbers, you get very little flavour per pound.

But pumpkins make perhaps the most comforting soup of all – a golden, glowing glop known by the French as *soupe à la citrouille*, after its glorious citrus colour. Add crisp bacon or grated cheese, golden croûtons or a pat of spiced butter, and supply crackling, crusty white bread for a deeply sustaining supper. For me, it is soup, rich, thick and immensely heart-warming, that is the whole point of the pumpkin. Add a lump or two of cheese to the hot purée, Gruyère, Fontina or our own deep-orange Cheshire. The cheese will melt under the hot liquid into long, satisfying, savoury strings.

Forget the fairy-tale stagecoaches and magic lanterns and get the great golden globe into the kitchen. It is there that the real magic begins.

Roast Pumpkin

A medium pumpkin weighing about 1.5kg/3lb will serve about 10 as an accompaniment to a roast.

Cut the pumpkin into wedges, just as you might slice a melon in summer. Scoop away all the stringy fibre and the seeds. Be thorough; the fibres are annoying and unpleasant in your mouth. Place the slices in a roasting tin and spread each slice with a little soft butter or dripping. Season with salt and pepper. Roast in a moderate oven for 40 minutes or so. The pumpkin is ready when the flesh is golden brown and slightly blackened at the edges. It should be tender to the point of a knife.

Hard to beat as a side dish for roast pork or chicken, roast pumpkin is also a pleasant alternative to a baked potato. Smother with butter to which you have added a little ground cinnamon or nutmeg or both. A substantial enough supper when preceded by a hearty soup such as mushroom.

Spiced Pumpkin Soup with Bacon

A warming soup for a cold day. Cooking the pumpkin till golden brown at the edges will give a deeper flavour. Any soup left over till the next day will taste even better.

1 medium onion, peeled
50g/2oz butter
2 plump cloves of garlic, peeled and squashed
900g/2lb pumpkin – about ½ medium size
1 tablespoon coriander seeds
2 teaspoons cumin seeds
2 small dried chillies
1 teaspoon ground turmeric
1.2l/2 pints vegetable or chicken stock
4 rashers of smoked bacon
120ml/4fl oz single cream

Roughly chop the onion. Melt the butter in a large, heavy-based pan and cook the onion and garlic in it till soft and translucent. Meanwhile, peel the pumpkin, remove the stringy bits and seeds and discard them with the peel. You will probably have about 650g/1½lb of orangy-yellow flesh. Chop into rough cubes and add to the softened onions. Cook till the pumpkin is golden brown at the edges.

Roast the coriander and cumin seeds in a small frying pan over a low heat until they start to smell warm and nutty, about 2 minutes (keep this pan to one side). Grind the roasted spices in either a spice or a coffee mill, or, if you have time, with a pestle and mortar. Add them and the chillies and turmeric to the onions and pumpkin. Cook for a few minutes over a medium heat. Pour over the hot stock and stir. Cook for 20 minutes or so, till the pumpkin is tender.

Fry the bacon in the pan in which you roasted the spices, till crisp. Cool a little, then cut up with scissors into small pieces. Whiz the soup in a blender or food processor to a smooth, golden purée. Pour in the cream and taste for seasoning, adding salt and pepper if necessary. Return to the pan, bring almost to the boil and then serve, piping hot, with the bacon bits scattered on top.

Serves 4 generously

RABBIT

It's Beatrix Potter's fault. I am sure my 30-year boycott on eating one of the tastiest, most delectable of meats was because I was brought up on her delightful *Tale of Peter Rabbit*. That and the fact that I kept a huge, fluffy bunny as a pet, for most of my childhood. Like most children's pets, it was kept in too small a cage, spent too little time on the lawn and met a violent death. It would have been better off in the pot.

Rabbit is good to eat. Of course it depends how you put it. 'We are having rabbit for supper' sounds better than 'We are having *a* rabbit for supper'. No doubt the reason for referring to beef instead of cow, pork instead of pig and veal instead of calf is to divorce the furry, doe-eyed, smiling animals of childhood literature from the steak on your plate. Supermarkets, with their beautifully packaged cuts of meat, have got this down to a fine art.

Simon Hopkinson, co-author with Lindsey Bareham of *Roast Chicken and Other Stories* (Ebury Press), is not one to be concerned by such things. He wilfully flies in the face of the squeamish, with fan-letters to calves' liver, brains (sautéd with chillies and ginger), tripe (deep fried with coconut and coriander) and sweetbreads. He is one of the few professional chefs whose words are worth reading and whose recipes actually work for non-professionals. In fact, his book is a joy from beginning to end.

With only a handful of exceptions, chefs' cookbooks have little to say to the home cook and seem to be written to satisfy the chef's ego or to be

Roast Rabbit with Mushrooms and Herbs

A straightforward roast, the meat kept moist by oil and wine.

10 juniper berries
50g/2oz butter
2 cloves of garlic, crushed
6 cloves
6 rabbit joints (unless they are very large, in which case 4 will do)
350g/12oz wild mushrooms
2 glasses of red wine
6 tablespoons olive oil
75g/3oz prosciutto or pancetta, diced
bay leaf
2 healthy sprigs of thyme

Lightly crush the juniper berries and mix them into the butter with the garlic, cloves and some salt and freshly ground black pepper. Smear the seasoned butter over the rabbit joints. Put them in a roasting tin with the wild mushrooms, which you can chop slightly if they are very large, then drizzle with the wine and oil. Add the prosciutto, bay leaf and thyme.

Roast in a hot oven, 220°C/425°F/Gas Mark 7, for 30 minutes, basting twice with the cooking juices, or until the meat is tender and cooked through. Serve with mashed potatoes to soak up the juices from the roasting tin.
Serves 2

Rabbit Stew with Raisins and Pine Kernels

650g/1½lb rabbit meat, off the bone
flour
2 tablespoons olive oil
2 medium onions, peeled and sliced
1 stick of celery, chopped
2 tablespoons balsamic vinegar
150ml/5fl oz game or chicken stock
150ml/5fl oz red wine
a handful of seedless raisins
2 tablespoons pine kernels

Cut the rabbit meat into large chunks and dust with flour. The easiest way to do this is to put the meat in a plastic bag, add the flour and shake. Heat the oil in a pan and fry quickly, over high heat, till golden at the edges. Transfer to a deep, ovenproof casserole.

Add the onions to the frying pan, with a little more oil if needed, and fry till soft and golden. Add the celery and continue to cook for 2 minutes, then add the vinegar, stock and wine. Bring to the boil, add the fruit and nuts and scrape the bottom of the pan to dislodge any delicious crusty bits into the sauce. Season with salt and black pepper and pour over the rabbit.

Place in a preheated oven at 180°C/350°F/Gas Mark 4 and cook for 30–40 minutes till the sauce has reduced a little. Serve with mashed potatoes and peas or wide noodles such as pappardelle.

Serves 2

drooled over by wannabe kitchen apprentices. Not so this one. Mr Hopkinson's treatment of pigeon, kidney, custard and cod has already earned the book a place by my cooker. The man has even got me to eat rabbit.

Hopkinson likes the farmed variety – 'They can happily be gently braised, resulting in a melting pot of goodness.' He braises them with rosemary and cream, stews them with balsamic vinegar and parsnips, and roasts them with bacon and mustard sauce. Farmed rabbits are rarely as tough as those shot in the wild, who spend much of their time hopping clear of the guns. You can grill them too, but marinate them first in wine, olive oil, garlic, thyme and rosemary.

I was relieved to find jointed rabbit, as divorced from Peter as you could get, packed in neat little trays in the supermarket. I was even given a choice of legs, saddle or fillets, though the fillets lacked the bones which I regard as particularly important in a meat inclined to be dry. I was eyed suspiciously by my fellow queuers at the checkout, although I admit I had bought rather a lot of rabbit, as one does for testing and photography. Even skinned and primped they did look slightly more gruesome than a neat row of chicken breasts.

Still, it tasted good. It was tender but had more bite to it than chicken. It stayed moist and juicy when I casseroled it, and roasted well too. The bones were small and suited to picking up and sucking, like those of chicken or chops. The only blots on the landscape are the rabbit's lack of natural fat (though this is soon remedied by the addition of a rasher of bacon) and, of course, Beatrix Potter.

Roasted Leg of Rabbit with Bacon and a Mustard Sauce

Simon Hopkinson's recipe. The rabbit that you use for this dish should be the French farmed variety. They are large, tender and succulent. If you find it impossible to obtain one and make do with a smaller variety, then you may have to serve 2 legs per person. A wild rabbit will not do. If you have an enterprising butcher, then hopefully you can buy just the rabbit legs. If not, then buy 2 rabbits and use the remaining parts for another dish.

4 rabbit legs
100g/4oz unsalted butter, softened
1 clove of garlic, peeled and chopped
1 tablespoon fresh tarragon, chopped
1 tablespoon fresh parsley, chopped
grated rind of 1 lemon
salt and pepper
20 thin smoked streaky bacon rashers, de-rinded
for the mustard sauce
450ml/15fl oz whipping cream
2 heaped tablespoons smooth Dijon mustard
salt and pepper

Preheat the oven to 220°C/425°F/Gas Mark 7. With a small knife, remove the thighbone from the rabbit leg by forming a little tunnel around the bone rather than coming through from the side. This is only slightly tricky and just takes a little time and trouble. Mix together the butter, garlic, tarragon, parsley, lemon and seasoning. Divide this between the 4 cavities, wrap each leg with 5 rashers of bacon and then place on a lightly buttered baking tray. Make sure that the ends of each rasher meet on the underside.

Roast the legs in the oven for about 10 minutes until crisp and golden brown. Remove from the oven and leave to rest for a further 10 minutes in a warm place (back in the oven with the door ajar, for instance).

Meanwhile, make the sauce. Simply heat the cream with 1 tablespoon of the mustard and a little salt and pepper. Simmer for 5 minutes or so until slightly thickened. Keep warm. To serve, cut 3 slices from the bulbous end of each leg and, being careful to collect the herby juices, arrange neatly on 4 plates. Sit the bony part upright alongside the slices. Add the second spoonful of mustard to the sauce, whisk, reheat and serve separately in a sauce-boat.
Serves 4

GOOD THINGS TO SERVE WITH RABBIT

- parsnip purée
- red cabbage
- pears poached in cider
- mashed potato
- buttered noodles
- sautéd mushrooms

RICOTTA

Ricotta with Chocolate and Cognac

This cream for biscuits could, by leaving out the fromage frais, be used as a cake filling.

4 tablespoons golden raisins
1 tablespoon cognac or Marsala
100g/4oz ricotta
4 tablespoons fromage frais or Petit Suisse
2 tablespoons caster sugar
2 tablespoons good-quality cocoa powder
biscotti to serve

Sprinkle the raisins with the cognac and set aside for 20 minutes for the fruit to absorb the spirit. Sieve the ricotta into a pudding basin and stir in the fromage frais. Fold in the sugar, cocoa powder and lastly the soaked raisins. Chill for 15 minutes or longer. Serve in tiny pots or glasses with the *biscotti*.
Serves 2

'Would you consider writing about ricotta?' asks Gabriella Ashtiani, apparently home-sick for the 'large, dewy white mounds of ricotta *freschissima* displayed next to the mascarpone' in delicatessens all over Italy. Such a request comes as no surprise. I have watched these charming, bland, granular curds slowly gaining in popularity over the last few years – I hope because of their versatility rather than their relatively low fat content. I would hate to be tricked into beating the drum for low-fat food.

Interesting though it is, ricotta is not a cheese to be served alone with bread. Boredom would set in after a mouthful or two. Its mild, cool, milky flavour is best exploited as a base for more strident things: herbs with pepper or aniseed notes such as basil or tarragon, salty olives, smoked ham or sweet, candied citrus fruits. This is not to say that the cheese is without charm. Those who find Greek feta overly salty, mascarpone too unctuous or Petits Suisses a little bland may enjoy the uncomplicated freshness of Italian ricotta. Piled on to soft, floury Italian ciabatta bread with ripe sliced apricots, it makes a pleasant mid-morning snack, or even a light lunch with a handful of olives and the mildest of cured ham. But this is not its forte.

Ricotta performs best in a supporting role. It needs salt, sugar or spice to give point to its milky curds. Like its creamier sister mascarpone, ricotta swings both ways, happily taking to sugar or salt as the mood grabs it. This is part of the young cheese's charm.

Mix it with finely chopped, flat-leaf parsley, black olives and a little thick yoghurt to provide a pleasantly salty accompaniment for a salad of sweet ripe tomatoes. Sweeten it with a dusting of sugar and a trickle of strawberry purée and you have a quick, light and uncomplicated dessert. The only demand it makes is to be used at the peak of freshness. Ricotta ages badly.

As with other white, mild fresh cheeses, freshness is all. With ricotta it is the whole point. Wrapped in wet greaseproof if you are lucky, corseted in sealed plastic if not, these white, crumbly domes are sold everywhere from dark, cool Italian grocery shops to mesmerising, panic-inducing supermarkets. Unless you are being palmed off with a sealed and sell-by-dated pot, you will need to know its age. But you don't have to ask.

The freshest ricotta is white, a soft chalky white. It has a faint tang of soured milk and its texture should be granular and slightly crumbly, but it should not be dry, or yellow, not even at the edges. Buy only that which is wet and white. This is one cheese that waits for no one, turning sour and yellow in a couple of days. For once, 'use on day of purchase' means exactly that. In Italy, where it is displayed in large pudding-shaped domes on the delicatessen counter, it is rarely made in high summer – it cannot take the heat – though you will see it here pretty much all year round.

Ricotta can be made from both sheep's and cows' milk. That made from sheep's milk is considered the finest: that from cows' milk is looked down upon. Its name means recooked, a reference to the fact that the whey from which the curds of ricotta are lifted has been heated twice, first to produce curds that are scooped off to make cheese, any cheese, and secondly to produce the grainy flakes that become ricotta.

Spinach and Ricotta Dumplings with Cream and Parmesan

Italian gnocchi vary from the featherlight and inconsequential to the seriously rib-sticking. This rich cheesy version has some of the lightness of the former while managing to keep the comforting qualities of the latter.

300g/10oz ricotta
350g/12oz spinach leaves, washed and chopped
1 egg, lightly beaten
6 tablespoons plain flour
3 tablespoons grated Parmesan cheese, plus a little extra
8 tablespoons double cream

Put 225g/8oz of the ricotta into a food processor with the spinach leaves and blend till thick and creamy. Scoop out into a basin. Stir in the egg, flour and the 3 tablespoons of Parmesan cheese, and season generously with salt and freshly ground pepper. Set aside in the fridge for 30 minutes to firm.

Bring a deep pan of water to the boil, and add salt. Turn the oven to 200°C/400°F/Gas Mark 6. Drop dessert-spoons of the dumpling mixture into the boiling water, then turn down to a simmer. Cook, in batches about 8 at a time, until each dumpling rises to the surface. Let them simmer there for 1 minute, then lift out with a draining spoon and place in a shallow, ovenproof dish.

When all the dumplings are cooked pour the cream over – it will come about half-way up the sides – and sprinkle generously with more grated Parmesan. Bake for 10–15 minutes till the cream is bubbling and the cheese is golden brown.

Serves 4

The curds are then scooped into either a wicker basket or, more likely nowadays, a ridged, sterile plastic container. Progress in the food business is so unromantic. It is a cheese relatively low in fat and mild of flavour, for which read versatile. Its open texture becomes a happy host to Italy's fat raisins and jewel-like candied fruits, its almonds, pine kernels and walnuts, and the zest of its ubiquitous citrus fruits, the orange and lemon. But there are surprises. Coffee and bitter chocolate have an affinity with this light cheese, as do vanilla and the berry fruits, ripe scarlet strawberries in particular.

But it is with spinach, the lush bright-green bunches piled high in market-places throughout the region, that ricotta is most famously paired. A time-honoured filling for navel-like tortelloni and cushion-shaped ravioli, spinach and ricotta was until recently the only vegetable option for pasta stuffings available here.

Ricotta is also a gentle partner for mild, fragile herbs. Creamed with a little thick yoghurt and freshened with chopped peppery basil, flat-leaf parsley or the aniseed notes of chervil, it gives a light spread for crusty French bread. It can be seasoned lightly with pepper and feathery dill, then rolled up in thin slices of smoked salmon or tangy prosciutto, mashed with thick yoghurt, finely shredded mint leaves and chopped walnuts as a creamy dressing for earthy new potatoes.

Beaten with whole eggs, double cream and a dusting of nutmeg, ricotta makes a soothing filling for a savoury tart. Season the mixture with chopped herbs – peppery basil, aniseed-scented chervil and tarragon or lemony sorrel – and bake inside a short pastry case. Served warm, with a salad of tiny spinach leaves in a mustardy dressing, the result makes an interesting garden lunch.

In Italy, it is used as a filling for fritters, both savoury and sweet. No bigger than apricots,

Ricotta and Chocolate Tart

A light cheesecake baked in a sweet-pastry crust. The ricotta lends a light texture, giving a cheesecake less cloying than is often the case. Use raisins instead of the candied peel if you prefer, add a handful of pine kernels or chopped walnuts, or miss out the chocolate altogether. You will need a 23cm/9in tart tin with a loose bottom.

50g/2oz candied orange and citron peel, finely
    chopped
3 tablespoons Marsala or sherry
300g/10oz (total weight) shortcrust pastry
350g/12oz ricotta
150ml/5fl oz double cream
125g/5oz caster sugar
1 teaspoon vanilla extract
grated zest of 1 small orange
75g/3oz ground almonds
4 eggs
50g/2oz bitter chocolate, finely chopped
a little icing sugar

varcocchini are nothing more than flour, sugar and eggs flavoured with ricotta and vanilla which puff up into fluffy spheres when fried in deep golden fat. On Saint Joseph's Day only, *sfinci*, the light doughnuts dipped in honey, are filled first with a ricotta cream. Sweetened with cinnamon, cocoa and Marsala, they also turn up as *cannoli*, deep-fried crisp cylinders with a stuffing of ricotta, cream and candied peel.

A lump of ricotta, fresh and white, with authentic basket-weave indentations on its side, is a supremely useful thing to bring home. It is gentle and mild, milky and sweet, discreet and un-demanding. Just make sure it isn't the only thing in your shopping basket.

OTHER WAYS OF USING RICOTTA

- Ricotta can also be roughly crumbled and stirred into cooked pasta with shredded basil, ripe tomatoes and olives.
- Mix into a classic tomato sauce before it hits the pasta.
- Try it crumbled and stirred into scrambled eggs with dill.
- Perhaps the most charming way of all with ricotta is this:

Stir the crumbled cheese with half the quantity of thick yoghurt and leave in a stainless-steel colander or sieve lined with muslin on a plate for 4 hours in a cold place. Remove from the muslin, sweeten to taste with caster sugar, then serve it in small mounds on dessert plates. Spoon a small quantity of very softly whipped cream over each mound and surround with ripe raspberries, strawberries or slices of peach.

Set the oven to 200°C/400°C/Gas Mark 6. Soak the orange and citron peel in the Marsala for 30 minutes. It will soften slightly. Use the pastry to line the tart tin. Cover with greaseproof paper and fill with rice or beans, then bake for 20 minutes in the preheated oven. Remove the paper and beans and return the tart case to the oven for 5 minutes until it is lightly cooked, but not coloured. Remove and set aside.

Mix the ricotta, cream and sugar together, using an electric beater if you wish. Add the vanilla, orange zest and ground almonds, then beat in the eggs 1 at a time. Fold in the chopped chocolate, peel and its soaking liquid. Scoop the mixture into the baked pastry case, turn the oven down to 190°C/375°F/Gas Mark 5, and bake for 30 minutes till the filling is risen and golden and the pastry crisp.

Cool slightly, then carefully remove the tart tin. Dust with sieved icing sugar and serve warm or cool.
Serves 6

Gingered Ricotta

A smooth thick cream in which to dip crisp biscuits such as brandy snaps or *biscotti*.

100g/4oz ricotta
4 tablespoons crème fraîche or fromage frais
1 tablespoon caster sugar
2 tablespoons ground almonds
2 lumps of ginger in syrup
2 tablespoons syrup from the ginger jar

Sieve the ricotta and stir in the cream or fromage frais. Add the caster sugar and the ground almonds. Cut the ginger into small dice and stir in with the syrup.

Chill for at least 20 minutes for the flavours to blend, and serve in tiny pots or in a small bowl with the *biscotti* alongside.
Serves 2

SALSAS

Salsa Cruda

This is the standard chilli-tomato accompaniment found throughout Latin America. Almost as much a part of any meal as salt and pepper is in Europe. Peel and seed the tomatoes if you wish. I am not sure that it is necessary. Certainly the salsas I have eaten on their home ground contained skins, seeds and all, and were none the worse for it.

1 small red onion, peeled
2 jalapeño chillies, fresh or tinned
450g/1lb ripe tomatoes
2 tablespoons coarsely chopped coriander leaves
a little sugar

Dice the onion finely. Split the chillies in half, scrape out their seeds with the point of the knife and chop the flesh finely. Add them to the onions. Cut the tomatoes in half, then chop them finely. Toss gently with the coriander and the rest of the ingredients. Season with salt and a little sugar if you wish, and serve immediately.

Serves 2

I had my first salsa in Cartagena. It appeared, unasked for, on a corn cake I was buying from one of the tiny stalls that set up of an evening outside the smart hotels of this Caribbean resort. Its vivid heat and fruity freshness startled me at first, but helped the dull maize patty down against a background of riotous music.

A salsa is as lively as its name. Hot, light and sparkling, this Latin American invention is also the sauce of the moment. I have been finding such pools of finely chopped vegetables, heavily laced with chilli, on London restaurant plates for months. With chicken, particularly grilled, with fish, especially squid, and with pretty much everything else too.

Salsa means little more than sauce, be it cheese or chocolate, to the average South American. In Europe the word salsa is used exclusively to define a spicy, finely chopped relish of raw ingredients. Unless you are a fan of *Come Dancing*. Yet relish isn't quite right, as it implies that only a little is taken. I can get through a whole plateful if the cook hasn't gone overboard with the chillies. The texture lies somewhere between a sauce and a salad. It must be at once crunchy and soft. Tomato is essential. So is onion. Coriander is pretty much obligatory too, though not as much as chillies.

I like this new addition to our cooking. It remains refreshing, with its finely chopped, juicy tomatoes, while its wild side can make your eyes water and your nose run. Unlike the more gentle Italian tomato salads, with their torn basil leaves and rich, green olive oil, a salsa can be made with tomatoes that, although ripe, need not be at the very point of perfection. They just need to be juicy and firm. Too ripe and they turn to slush under your knife.

Although simple to make, a little care is required. The mixture should be a finely chopped, though absolutely not smooth, purée. It should stop just short of slush. I am not a fan of liquidiser salsa. There is something about a quick whiz in the food processor that makes the sauce fizz on the plate as well as the palate. The consistency can be messy too, jagged little cubes floating in a froth. I am convinced a knife does a better job.

Unless you are making salsa for one, you will need a decent knife. Which knife is a matter of taste. Use the one you feel most comfortable with. I invariably go for the easy option, which in this case is a stout cook's knife with an 8-inch blade. It is the best knife for the job. You can't actually chop with a serrated knife. The entire blade of the knife must touch the board. With a serrated knife only the highest points of the teeth touch the board. My favourite little knife, a 4-inch blade and as light as a feather, is one that I bought at a professional catering supply shop in Paris. I use it for pretty much everything, though it is useless for salsa.

All my knives have stainless-steel blades. Don't let anyone fool you into buying carbon-steel knives by telling you they are the only type that can be sharpened properly. They are living in the dark ages. Stainless steel has come a long way and is perfectly sharp enough for anything you are likely to do in the kitchen. Unless you plan on major surgery.

Go for something solid, generally speaking the heavier the better. Friends have accused me of being a touch neurotic about my knives. I am not. As it happens. I just like them clean and sharp. Very

Avocado Salsa

One of my favourite salsas. This is one that I keep fairly coarse, handling the avocado as little as possible to keep it from becoming mushy. Serve beside grilled meats and fish or stuff into a tortilla or pitta bread for a snack.

1 medium-sized avocado, ripe but firm
3 medium-sized tomatoes
½ a small onion, peeled
1 mild green chilli
2 teaspoons lime juice
2 tablespoons coriander leaves, coarsely chopped

Peel, stone and cut the avocado into small dice. Halve and chop the tomatoes and the onion. Split the chilli in half, scrape out the seeds and chop the green flesh finely. Toss gently with the other ingredients and a little salt. Serve straight away.
Serves 2

Roasted Tomato Pepper Salsa

It would be wrong to give the impression that all salsas are made from raw ingredients, even in our use of the term. In the recipe below the ingredients are grilled before chopping, giving a rich, smoky flavour to the sauce. This is one that can be made quite smooth, perfect for dipping forkfuls of grilled chicken into.

1 medium-sized red pepper
450g/1lb tomatoes
2 or more hot chillies
1 small red onion
2 tablespoons parsley, chopped

Place the pepper, cut in half lengthways, skin side up on a grill pan and cook under a hot grill till the skin has charred. Remove from the pan, then put the tomato and chillies in its place. They will take much less time to grill.

Meanwhile, peel the skin from the pepper and discard. Chop the flesh finely – it will be really quite soft – and scrape it into a bowl. Skin the tomato and the chillies (as best you can) and chop finely. Stir into the pepper. Chop the onion very finely and stir into the rest of the ingredients, seasoning the mixture with a little salt. Drain off some of the juice if it appears excessive.

Serves 2

sharp. I get ruffled only when I find them in the washing-up water, lurking perilously under the suds, or it turns out they have been used to prise the lid off the treacle. Then it is better not to be around.

Making a salsa without a large sharp knife can be tedious in the extreme. You might as well not bother, unless you want to spend all day making the salad. The ingredients must be chopped small. Smaller than Dolly Mixtures but larger than sugar – about the size of a baby's fingernails. Smaller than that and the mixture becomes impossibly wet. Larger and you cannot use the salsa as a dip, as the lumps fall off your food.

The more chilli you put in, the less salsa you will need to make. I like mine somewhere between a

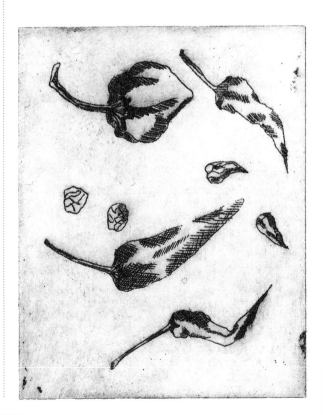

salad and a relish, slightly coarser than in its traditional home. (Commercial salsa is always smoother than home-made.) I find the most useful is one that can be used as a sauce, an accompaniment or a dip, depending on everyone's taste. There are no rules. Eat it as you wish.

The same *laissez-faire* applies to what goes in. Tomatoes, chillies, onions and coriander will give you *salsa cruda*. Onion, tomatoes, pineapple, lime and chillies will give you *salsa fria*. Fresh red chillies, garlic, vinegar and olive oil will give you Colombian *salsa de aji*. It will also dissolve your tastebuds. The only immovable factor seems to be the chilli, fresh, red or green and very finely chopped. After that it is up to you.

Papaya and mango, finely chopped and stirred in with the tomatoes and coriander, are both bizarre and successful. *Salsa cruda* with avocado, lime and coriander is my current favourite stuffing for pitta bread, though a tortilla would be more orthodox. But I am rarely that. I find a good handful of chopped flat-leaf parsley in with the coriander is good for calming the mixture down if I have got carried away with the chillies. Watermelon is my favourite addition of all.

A doddle to make, this will be my sauce for the summer. With tomatoes, with avocado, with melon, with mango, with herbs. With salty feta cheese stirred into it, spooned into halved avocados, drizzled over grilled fish or served with extra chilli or Tabasco as a dip for barbecued chicken. Lively, bright, hot and versatile, this is the original all singing, all dancing spring-summer sauce. And one that tastes just as it sounds.

Mango Salsa

A wonderfully refreshing accompaniment to grilled meats, particularly pork or beef. Substitute papaya for the mango if you prefer. The fruit should be ripe and juicy. Add a couple of tomatoes if you wish.

1 large red pepper
1 large, ripe mango
juice of ½ a lime
1 small red onion
1 teaspoon sugar
1cm/½in knob of ginger, peeled
1 small red chilli
1 tablespoon coriander leaves, chopped

Cut the pepper in half and grill it, skin side up, till the skin chars. Remove from the heat, then peel away the blackened skin. Chop the soft flesh finely.

Peel the mango and slice the flesh away from the stone. Cut the flesh into very small dice. Place in a bowl with the lime juice. Peel and chop the onion very finely. Toss gently with the mango. Sprinkle with the sugar. Grate the ginger and stir in. Chop the chilli, removing the seeds if you wish, and stir. Set aside for 15 minutes before serving. Stir in the coriander leaves just before you serve.
Serves 2

SAUSAGES

Sausages with Apples and Cider

6 plump butcher's sausages
75g/3oz butter
450g/1lb juicy dessert apples, such as Cox's
120ml/4fl oz dry cider or apple juice
6 juniper berries, lightly squashed
120ml/4fl oz double cream

Over a low heat, fry the sausages in half of the butter. Quarter and core the apples, then slice them into segments. Fry them in the remaining butter till they have softened a little and the edges are turning golden. Lift the apples on to a warm serving dish.

Add the cider to the pan with the juniper berries. Turn the heat up slightly and let the cider bubble down until nearly half has disappeared. Pour in the cream, season with salt and pepper and leave to simmer for a few minutes.

Place the sausages on the apples and pour the sauce over both.

Serves 2

A local butcher stands or falls by the sausage he makes. A good recipe for a generously seasoned and juicy pork sausage will get the punters in the shop, hopefully taking with them some of the chops, steaks and roasting joints we are buying less of nowadays. It is a foolish butcher who forgets how passionate the British are about their bangers.

The sausage has had its ups and downs. Right now things are looking up, with plump, herby sausages appearing in the supermarkets, often made to old regional recipes. There is a sausage appreciation society and the *Guardian* holds an annual quest for the finest sausage in the country. What is more, butchers' shops recently seem to have brought the sausage up front, giving it pride of place in their displays rather than tucking it away at the back with the pigs' liver.

Small local butchers' shops are essential to the survival of the sausage. Unlike pork pies and pâté, sausages are invariably made on the premises. The sausage is the butcher's equivalent of a top chef's 'signature dish'. A good recipe will ensure something of a following and if there is more than one local butcher's shop the customers loyalties may well be divided by the sausage recipe.

There are still horrid sausages around, but they are easy to spot. A tray of cut-price skinless sausages must be one of the most depressing sights for shoppers who loves their bangers. The meat will have a slight glow to it, no doubt from the added colouring, and the poor little things will be devoid of the tell-tale freckles of chopped herbs and coarsely crushed pepper of a good sausage. Worst of all, they will have no skin. The very antipathy of the fat, jolly butcher's sausage, sizzling and popping in the pan.

Seasoning is crucial. A classic English recipe will contain little more than salt, pepper, parsley and sage, though exact measurements vary. Once established, a butcher diverges from his recipe at his peril. Most people go for a judicious quantity of pepper, but nineteenth-century recipes also include nutmeg and often ground mace, the nutmeg's yellow outer case, though we have lost our taste for mace. Feelings run high about garlic. I think a little added to the basic recipe is in order, but brave is the butcher who fails to tell his customers. A stronger-flavoured sausage is in favour at present. The interest in spicier fillings comes from Spain and North Africa, where even the lowliest sausage is rife with powdered red chilli, coarse black pepper and milder paprika. A banger to blow your head off.

I can see no reason not to make my own. A sausage is nothing more than herbed minced pork held in shape by a tight skin. A faggot in tights, someone once said. My butcher has sausage skins, though you have to ask for them. I had forgotten the true nature of a sausage's skin until I opened the little plastic bag handed to me by the assistant. She had asked how much I wanted and I had stretched my arms to show her. Quite why I now have about 50 feet of slimy pigs' intestine in my sink is best known to her.

'Rinse the casings in cold running water,' says the recipe. The long, shimmering white skin narrowly misses slithering down the plughole and putting an end to my supper. I am somewhat relieved at the suggestion that a little lemon juice or vinegar will 'remove any odour' and add far more than I should. I leave them to soak.

Quick Sausage and Bean Hotpot

An everyday version of the classic spiced bean and sausage hotpots eaten throughout Europe and America. Using tinned flageolet or haricot beans, it is possible to make this dish in just over half an hour.

6 plump sausages, the spicier the better
2 x 400g/14oz tins of haricot or flageolet beans
1 x 400g/14oz tin of butter beans
1 x 540g/19oz jar of tomato passata
2 teaspoons chilli paste such as harissa or 3 hot chilli peppers
2 tablespoons grain mustard
1 teaspoon made English mustard
3 tomatoes, halved
chopped flat-leaf parsley

Fry the sausages, if necessary in a little oil, till golden but not brown on each side. Mix the beans, drained and rinsed, the tomatoes and all the seasonings except the parsley and spoon into an ovenproof casserole.

Add the cooked sausages and bake in a preheated oven, 230°C/450°F/Gas Mark 8, for 20–25 minutes till the mixture is bubbling. Scatter with parsley and serve. *Serves 3*

Sausage with Lentils and Balsamic Vinegar

This is one of the most satisfying of dishes, yet it has a frugal simplicity about it and is not overly rich.

4 plump butcher's sausages
100g/4oz small brown or green lentils, such as those from Le Puy
75g/3oz pancetta or smoked bacon
1 small onion, finely chopped
100g/4oz brown mushrooms, chopped
1 large clove of garlic, thinly sliced
2 tablespoons parsley, chopped
a little balsamic vinegar, about a teaspoon

Fry the sausages, in a little fat, over a slow heat. They will take anything up to 40 minutes. Rinse the lentils in a sieve under running cold water. Cut the pancetta or bacon into small cubes and fry in a deep pan till the fat runs. If it fails to do so – in other words, if your bacon was too lean – then add a tablespoon of oil. Fry the onion in the fat for 4–5 minutes till it starts to soften and then add the mushrooms and the garlic. Stir, cover with a lid and cook for 5 minutes.

Add the lentils and enough boiling water to cover them by about 2.5cm/1in (roughly 1 pint). Cook over a moderate heat for 20 minutes, then test for doneness. They will probably need another 5 minutes but should not be too soft. Season with salt and pepper and stir in the chopped parsley.

When the sausages are done, turn the heat up under the lentils to evaporate most, but not all, of the liquid. Stir in a few drops of balsamic vinegar, tasting as you go. The flavour should be rich and mellow. Slice the sausage thickly. Serve the lentils on warm plates, with the slices of sausage on top.

Serves 2

Making my own filling is reassuring. A good 50 per cent of the meat content should be fat – hard white fat from the back of the animal. It is what makes the sausage juicy. The lean can be from the neck or shoulder. Salt is essential. The rest is up to you. A teaspoon of fennel seed will add an Italian touch. Coarsely chopped meat and a whiff of garlic will give it a Gallic note. Paprika, the sweetest of the ground chilli peppers, is redolent of East European recipes, while a spoonful of marc, the grape spirit, will give you *saucisson de Bourgogne*.

But my intestines are still in the sink. I hold one end on the cold tap and let the water run through for almost 10 minutes. At this point the whole thing comes alive and takes some holding. The few holes hiding along its length ensure that everything within 6 feet is soaked, and that includes the cook. I have no sausage-filling attachment on my mincer. The neat step-by-step photographs in my manual assure me that I can fill the casings with either a piping bag or a funnel. The page is headed 'The Simple Art of Sausage-making'.

I am not sure it is possible to stuff a slippery length of sausage casing with minced pork without musing, as anyone who has made their own will surely testify, on the origin of the condom. Though that was apparently the smaller sheep's intestine. Strange, then, that the butcher had told me they were suitable only for chipolatas. I roll the open end of the casing over the nozzle of my piping bag and squeeze.

The first signs are impressive. The soggy tangle of intestines is becoming unmistakably sausage-shaped, though to be honest the skin is a bit loose. The trick seems to be to squeeze with one hand and tease the filling along with the other. If it wasn't for the occasional hole, my efforts would resemble the continuous coils of herby Cumberland sausage a friend brings down from Carlisle.

'To form links, twist lengths of the sausage through one complete turn, to prevent them unwinding again, twist successive links in alternate directions,' says my manual. I can knit, I can lace up my mountain boots, I can even untangle the Christmas tree lights, but I cannot secure a sausage in its skin. Especially when that skin has holes. There are some things best left to the professionals. Anything involving pigs' intestines is one of them.

I shall stick to cooking. I don't know why I thought I could do better than the butcher anyway. When it comes to cooking the sausage, I have found no better tool than the frying pan. I agree wholeheartedly with Matthew Fort, writing in *The Sausage Directory* (Fourth Estate), when he recommends a pan 'blackened with heat and with age, gleaming genially with layers of accumulated grease that have fused into a natural non-stick surface'. Slow cooking, 20 minutes on a low heat at the very least, will produce a sausage that is moist, sweet and succulent. Another 20 minutes and you will have the most delectable thing known to (carnivorous) man – that sticky, savoury, caramel-brown goo that builds up on the skin of a slowly cooked, old-fashioned butcher's sausage.

SWEET POTATOES

Grilled Sweet Potatoes with Green Peppercorn Butter

1 medium-sized sweet potato
2 teaspoons bottled green peppercorns
75g/3oz butter, softened

Scrub the potato and slice it into rounds approximately 6mm/¼in thick. Place the rounds in the grill pan. Mash the peppercorns with the butter and season lightly with salt. Smear each slice of sweet potato with butter and place under a heated grill, about 15cm/6in from the flame if possible, and cook until the surface turns bright orange and tender. Spoon or brush the melted butter over from time to time, turning the slices once till the other side is cooked too. They should be done in about 10–15 minutes, maybe less.

Serve them hot with cold roast meat, with any of the spiced butter that remains in the pan.
Serves 2

I am the first person to give something a second chance. Especially something edible. 'Tried it once and didn't like it' is a line I reserve only for tripe and jellied eels and Horlicks – and a couple of other things I had best not mention. Had I not persevered, I should have been oblivious for ever to the joy of rice pudding, chillies, gherkins, olives, anchovies, liver, gooseberries and kidneys. It would have been the same with the sweet potato.

I only recently learned that the knobbly, orange-fleshed sweet potato was the first potato we would have known in Europe, coming over, as it did, from Haiti with Columbus. It was almost 100 years later, in the late 1580s, that the white-fleshed potato hit Britain. The fact that this became our favourite vegetable rather than the sweet potato may well be more a matter of fertility than flavour. The common potato, hailing from the Andes, is more suited to growing in our cool climate than its golden-fleshed namesake.

The sweet potato is aptly named. It has a sweetness more akin to a carrot than a spud, so much so that it is often made into pies and tarts as if it were a pumpkin. I cannot say I have found these to my taste. Sweet-potato pie smacks of a desperate attempt to use up a glut of the things. But sweet they are, and it may well be this generous dose of sugar that put me off at first. We don't really expect vegetables to come as sweet as this.

This potato bakes to a glorious, fluffy mass. Its flesh is rich, deep gold in colour and temptingly moist. There is no crisp skin, unless you know a trick that I don't, but baked to tenderness in a hot oven this potato offers the bonus of exuding a sweet juice that turns a deep caramel brown in the heat. This sticky brown goo is something of a delicacy to those who like their sweet potatoes. Left too long in the oven, though, and that juice will bubble up into a crisp black cloud. Always bake your sweet potatoes on a baking sheet. Unless, of course, you actually enjoy cleaning your oven.

But the sweet potato has more to offer than just a change for baked-potato fanciers. You can grill and sauté them too. Scrubbed, sliced as thick as your little finger and brushed generously and often with butter, the sweet potato grills delectably and is a surprisingly fine accompaniment to cold roast beef and pork. Crisp, savoury roast pork crackling and hot, melting sweet potato is a pleasant enough mixture to have on your fork.

I have been disappointed occasionally by this unpromising-looking vegetable. Some varieties are white rather than orange-fleshed and have, to my taste, a coarse flavour. Their flesh is firm and fudgy like that of a tinned chestnut, rather than melting and sticky like their golden sisters. Far be it from me to encourage such things, but the only way you can tell one from the other is to scrape away some of the skin with your thumbnail while the greengrocer's back is turned. Pale pinky orange and you're in luck. Creamy white and you may be disappointed.

To many Americans, the sweet potato is as much an essential ingredient of the Thanksgiving feast as the turkey itself. A sweet feast it may be, especially with a dose of sugar-laden cranberry sauce on the side, but there is something about roast turkey, gravy and sweet potatoes that appeals. Good though it is this way, I find it at its best when partnered with something deeply savoury rather than bland. Try pan-fried sweet

Baked Sweet Potatoes with Chilli and Coriander Butter

for each sweet potato
1 medium-sized, mild red chilli pepper
50g/2oz butter, softened but not melted
a scant tablespoon of coriander leaves, chopped

Scrub the sweet potatoes, 1 medium-sized potato per person as a side dish, a large one if this is to be a light lunch, and spear through from end to end with a metal skewer. Set them in the oven, 200°C/400°F/Gas Mark 6, for 40–60 minutes, maybe less, until tender right through.

Meanwhile, make the chilli butter. Chop the chilli very finely with the coriander leaf until you have a fine red and green sludge. Mash it into the softened butter and season it with just a little salt. As you split the potato, slide a blob of butter into the middle.

If there is any butter left over it will keep in the fridge and is pretty good on just about anything, but especially green vegetables or noodles.
Serves 1

Sweet Potato Mash with Yoghurt and Ginger

A change from the usual mashed potato, this sweet and mildly spiced version works well with roast pork or beef.

2 medium-sized sweet potatoes
vegetable stock
a large knob of butter
2.5cm/1in piece of ginger root
4 heaped tablespoons thick yoghurt
nutmeg

Peel the potatoes and cut them into chunks. Put them in a saucepan with enough vegetable stock to cover. Simmer for 10–20 minutes till they are tender, but test them regularly so that they do not overcook to a slush.

Meanwhile, melt the butter in a small pan. Add the ginger, peeled and cut into shreds. Cook for 2 or 3 minutes over a moderate heat until the ginger is tender and starting to colour. Add a light grating of nutmeg.

Drain the potatoes and mash them with a fork. Stir in the yoghurt, then transfer to a warm dish. Pour the hot ginger butter over the mash and serve while hot.
Serves 2

Fried Sweet Potatoes

Slice the potatoes about 1cm/½in thick – any thinner and they will collapse as you turn them. Melt enough butter in the bottom of a frying pan to just cover it. Add the potato slices, brush with more butter and cook them until they have browned evenly on both sides, turning them from time to time as they cook.

When you have turned them for the last time, sprinkle with a little ground paprika, salt and, if you like, curry powder (a good commercial brand will do). Spoon over a little more butter and serve when hot and fragrant.

An especially suitable accompaniment to cold cuts, allow 1 potato per person.

potato with smoked bacon, liver or baked garlic mushrooms.

For those keen to try them for the first time, and others who might be tempted to give them a second chance, the sweet potato is in plentiful supply. Most decent greengrocers will stock a few, while the supermarkets all seem to have them now. A warning, though: the real whoppers, as big as an aubergine and hard as a brick, may take an age to cook – even speared by a skewer. Early in the spring, they are a more manageable size and we can expect them to take about an hour to soften.

The sweet potato does not like water. No doubt this will cause much consternation to British cooks, whose first option is always to boil something. *Ipomoea batatas* is, in fact, at its best when cooked in the direct heat of the oven or grill. Butter, rather than oil, is the fat you want here, but not as much as with the starchier common potato. A spiced butter, made with chopped chillies and coriander leaves, is a successful lubricant, as is one made with crushed green peppercorns. For once I would recommend the use of salted rather than unsalted butter too.

Tempting though its purple skin and honeyed, orange flesh are, however, the sweet potato lacks the versatility of our home-grown friends. No one will convince me that a creamy, garlic-scented *Dauphinoise* can be made with the sweet potato, and I am not sure I fancy sweet chips either. Perfect in the right place, its mega-dose of sugar can also be its own worst enemy. Basically, don't believe everything you read about sweet potato mousses and flans. My suspicion is that someone is just trying to bulk out the sweet potato chapter of their book.

Then again, perhaps I am being unadventurous and small-minded. I did say I reckon everything is worth a second chance. Well, almost everything.

TARTE TATIN

Fond as I am of the English apple pie, with its pale golden pastry and fluffy apple filling, it is the French upside-down *tarte Tatin* that gets my vote. Richer and more rustic than its neatly arranged Parisian sister, the *tarte aux pommes*, and stickier than its transatlantic cousin, the American apple pie, *tarte Tatin* is, for my money, the most successful of all the apple and pastry confections; it is as sexy as food can get.

Its charm lies not just in the fact that it is served upside down, or that its shape is interesting rather than symmetrical, or even that it comes with a fruity, caramel sauce. It is the marriage of that sweet caramel with scorched, slightly tart apples and crumbly, buttery pastry that lifts it way above the others. Yes, it has a robustness that may offend the lover of the pâtissier's art, and a home-made look to it that would embarrass the student of *haute cuisine*, but I can think of no finer way to use a pound of apples, a little butter and some flour.

Though well documented, I think its history is worth repeating. The name comes from two sisters, Caroline and Stéphanie (known to her friends as Fanny), whose eponymous hotel opposite the railway terminus at Lamotte-Beuvron, the wooded area of the Sologne, became famous for the ingenious way in which its apple tarts were baked. Legend has it that the demoiselles Tatin's oven, a blue and white wood-burning stove, had no baking oven under its burners – quite usual at the time, the latter half of the last century – as most home-baking was taken to the local baker, for cooking

Tarte Tatin

You will need a metal tin of some sort, about 23cm/9in in diameter. You can buy a special tin from kitchenware shops or use a shallow sided cake tin. I use a sauté pan, though the handle gets in the way when I come to turn it out. A frying pan with high sides (7.5cm/3in) is as suitable as anything.

for the pastry
100g/4oz cold butter, cut into chunks
175g/6oz plain flour
2 egg yolks
3 tablespoons caster sugar
for the filling
75g/3oz butter
6 tablespoons caster sugar
7 large Cox's Orange Pippins, peeled and cored

Preheat the oven to 220°C/425°F/Gas Mark 7. To make the pastry, rub the butter into the flour in a large bowl. Add the egg yolks, sugar and 2–3 tablespoons of cold water and stir until the mixture forms a ball. Wrap in greaseproof paper and leave to rest for 15 minutes.

For the filling, melt the butter and sugar in the tin (see above) over a medium heat. When syrupy and deep golden brown, remove and leave to cool. Peel, core and cut the apples into large pieces, about 6 or 8 to the apple, then add them to the caramel. Move them around in the sauce till they are roughly level (by all means arrange them neatly if you wish, but I think you may lose the joy of the dish).

Roll out the pastry to form a circle that will fit inside the tin. Lay the pastry over the apples and pat it down gently. Bake the tart in the preheated oven for 40 minutes, or until the pastry is light brown and the juice is bubbling. Leave to cool for a few minutes before running a knife around the edge and turning out on to a flat plate. I think it worth mentioning that the juice is very hot and apt to run out as you turn the tin over. Serve with thick cream or, better still, crème fraîche.

Serves 6

Pru Leith's Chicory *Tatin*

I recently read the highly enjoyable *Leith's Contemporary Cooking*, by Pru Leith, Caroline Yates and Alison Cavaliero (Bloomsbury), without realising it is actually a vegetarian cookbook. There is no preaching, no ranting, no guilt-tripping; simply a collection of delicious recipes that just happen not to contain any meat. The sort of book that gives vegetarian cooking a good name.

for the pastry
170g/6oz plain flour
55g/2oz ground rice
salt and freshly ground black pepper
140g/5oz butter, chopped
grated zest of 1 orange
1 egg beaten
for the filling
6–8 heads of chicory
110g/4oz butter
1 tablespoon honey
1 tablespoon orange juice
½ teaspoon ground coriander
½ teaspoon ground cinnamon

Preheat the oven to 200°C/400°F/Gas Mark 6. Make the pastry: sift the flour, ground rice and seasoning into a large bowl. Rub in the butter until the mixture looks like

after his bread was done. The sisters devised a way of baking the tart on top of the burners using a grid to protect the tin from the flames and a covering of a metal dome. By putting the apples on the bottom, the fruit caramelised in the direct heat while the pastry, which would otherwise have burned, cooked at a more leisurely pace above.

The fruit need not be confined to apples. Pears make a fine alternative, having something of the same texture. I should dearly like to try one with quinces, fragrant, knobbly, difficult to locate fruit that they are. There has been something of a rage for using mangoes, though I find their sweetness a little cloying when caramelised.

Vegetables work too, especially those which caramelise sweetly such as leeks or onions. Pru Leith has a typically innovative and successful recipe using chicory, contrasting the vegetable's natural bitterness with honey. I have also enjoyed a version with onions and sun-dried tomatoes, though my attempt at using root vegetables, parsnips and beetroot, lacked the stickiness that is to me the point of the dish.

Writers dither over the pastry. Some say *pâte brisée*, the rich French short pastry, others use puff pastry for a lighter result more suited to the end of a meal, yet La Confrérie de Tarte Tatin, which one could translate as the apple tart club, insists that the tradition should be upheld with France's sugar and-egg-rich *pâte sucrée*. Others still, notably in Normandy, add a spoonful of crème fraîche, making the pastry rich and crumbly in the extreme. Others prefer their crème fraîche on the side.

La Confrérie, incidentally, insists that the fruit should not be caramelised before it is baked in the oven. Easy to say when armed with ancient wood burning stoves, but modern gas and electric cookers fail to give the desired result (most are too cool, allowing a surfeit of juice to form). To my mind

coarse breadcrumbs. Stir in the orange zest. Add the egg and bind the dough together.

Alternatively put all the ingredients in a food processor and mix to bind. Chill in the refrigerator.

Make the filling: trim the chicory and remove any bruised leaves. Cut in half lengthways. Melt the butter in a 25cm/10in frying pan with a metal handle. Add the honey and orange juice. Take off the heat and arrange the halved chicory heads, cut side down, to cover the bottom of the pan, fanning out from the middle.

Place the frying pan over a moderately high heat until the butter and honey start to caramelise. It may take 10–15 minutes, but it is essential that the chicory starts to brown. Remove from the heat and scatter the spices evenly over the chicory. Roll the pastry into a 6mm/¼in-thick circle, to fit the top of the pan. Lay the pastry on top of the chicory and press down lightly. Put the frying pan on the middle shelf of the oven. Bake for 25–30 minutes or until the pastry is golden brown.

Allow to cool slightly, then turn on to a plate. Serve warm.

Serves 6–8

they also give too even and dependable a result. The joy of *tarte Tatin* is its hit-and-miss rusticity, hard to achieve in a modern-day circotherm.

Tarte Tatin, whether of traditional apple or heretical chicory, is not the easiest of pastries to

Tarte Tatin of Caramelised Pink Onions

A recipe from Richard Cawley's *Green Feasts* (Conran Octopus), which typifies his imaginative approach to cooking. Pairing the sweetness of the slow-cooked onions with the bold flavour of sun-dried tomatoes is a brilliant idea.

30g/1oz butter
900g/2lb even-sized pink onions, cut across into
  2cm/¾in slices
2 tablespoons sugar
olive oil, for greasing
55g/2oz sun-dried tomatoes in oil, drained and
  coarsely chopped
225g/8oz frozen puff pastry, defrosted
salad leaves to garnish

Preheat the oven to 220°C/425°F/Gas Mark 7. Melt the butter in a frying pan or sauté pan large enough to hold the onion slices snugly in 1 layer. Sprinkle half the sugar over the onions and season them with salt and pepper, then pour in enough cold water barely to cover the onions. Bring to the boil and simmer undisturbed for about 30 minutes, or until the onions are tender and all the liquid has been evaporated to leave a sticky glaze. Keep a careful eye on the pan towards the end of the cooking time, as the onions could easily burn.

Liberally oil the bottom of a large shallow tin about 23cm/9in in diameter, and evenly sprinkle it with the remaining sugar. Scatter the pieces of sun-dried tomato on top of that. Carefully arrange the onion slices in the prepared pan and season with salt and pepper. Roll out the pastry thinly and cut a circle just a little larger than the size of the pan. Arrange this over the onions, tucking in the edges.

Bake for 20–30 minutes, or until the pastry is crisp and golden. Turn out on to a warmed serving plate and serve hot, cut in wedges, with a few salad leaves as a garnish.
Serves 6

make. In theory it involves nothing more than browning the topping in butter and sugar and slapping a pastry crust on top, yet the whole dish stands or falls by its details. The crux of the matter is the caramelisation of the fruit or vegetables. This is essential, and is what would have made our demoiselles' *tartes* so delectable as to have the gastronome Curnonsky take the train from Paris and Monet's family drive from Giverny simply to taste them. Though it is worth noting that such *tartes renversées* were popular throughout the region long before the sisters set up their hotel.

In the famed apple version, the apples are lightly cooked in a loose caramel made from butter and sugar. Modern cooks will agree this can be done on the cooker, to a stage where the two ingredients amalgamate and colour. It does not matter if the caramel turns dark brown: its colour and sweetness will be diluted by the juice of the fruit. I declare the tart a bit of a failure if the sauce is not dark enough when it is turned out. Though, of course, it is still good to eat.

What distances the *tarte Tatin* from other apple tarts is the sublime contrast of sticky, caramelised fruit and buttery pastry. The apples should be tart. The pastry crumbly. The juice sticky. Use a metal dish, one suited to both hob and oven, and avoid the temptation to cut the apples too neatly. They should be in bold chunks, otherwise the dish becomes unsuitably elegant. The thing comes near to perfection when both pastry and fruit are slightly charred. This is not something that will please neat, prim cooks. The whole point of the dish is its wobbly, rustic charm. Burned edges and all.

WINTER PUDDINGS

The kitchen is all fugged up. There are little rivulets of water running down the windows and there is a continuous rattle coming from a saucepan on the cooker, a rattle that reassures rather than annoys. In about an hour my overdraught, cough and temperamental central heating system will pale into insignificance as I tuck into the sweet and sticky comfort food that has been steaming since five o'clock. I wonder if there is anything in the world that can so instantly put everything to rights as surely as steamed treacle pudding.

Comfort food, particularly the sort that includes butter, flour, sugar and eggs, has been enjoying something of a renaissance since the early 1980s. The supermarkets are full of ready-made versions, and good they are too. Home-made are even better. Sticky toffee pudding, steamed ginger sponge and fruity cabinet pudding are more popular than ever before. It strikes me that the more our security is undermined, from the decline of the National Health Service to the threatened demise of the doorstep pinta, the more popular such comforting puddings become. The Tory party must have done wonders for the sale of Marks and Sparks' jam roly-poly – the one we used to call dead man's leg.

The last 10 years or so have seen an enormous rise in popularity of the sort of puddings nanny supposedly made. Bakewell Pudding, Queen of Puddings, with its layers of custard, jam and meringue, and Blackcap Pudding, with its sauce of blackcurrant jam, have returned after years in exile.

Steamed Treacle Pudding

4 tablespoons golden syrup
150g/5oz butter
150g/5oz caster sugar
2 eggs
2 tablespoons milk
150g/5oz self-raising flour
extra golden syrup, warmed, for serving

Butter a 1.2l/2 pint pudding basin, then pour in the golden syrup. Cream the butter and sugar until light and fluffy. Break the eggs into a small basin and mix with a fork, then add gradually to the sugar and butter mixture. Add the milk and flour, folding it gently into the mixture with a metal spoon.

Spoon the mixture into the pudding basin, on top of the golden syrup. Cover with a piece of pleated and buttered greaseproof paper. Tie with string and cover with foil or muslin, securing with string. Place the basin on a trivet in a large saucepan of simmering water. Cover with a lid and steam for 1½ hours, topping up from time to time with more boiling water.

Carefully remove from the saucepan, allow to cool for 5 minutes and then remove the foil and paper. Turn out on to a serving dish and serve with extra warmed syrup, and cream if you wish.

Serves 4

Sussex Pond Pudding

So called because of the pool of lemon and butter syrup which flows from the centre as the pudding is cut. The sharpness of the lemon inside contrasts remarkably with the suet pastry outside. The traditional recipe usually instructs you to fill the pudding with a whole lemon. I often put in some chunks of lemon as well to give the pudding a little more shape when it is turned out – although it will collapse when you cut it. Make sure everyone gets a piece of the softened lemon.

100g/4oz shredded suet
225g/8oz self-raising flour
100g/4oz butter
100g/4oz demerara sugar
2 medium lemons or 1 lemon and a handful of
    dried fruits

In a large mixing bowl mix the suet and the flour to a soft, rollable dough with a little milk or water. Roll the pastry to a large circle, then cut out a quarter of it; this will be the lid. Butter a 1.5l/2½ pint pudding basin, then line it with the pastry, pushing the cut sides together to seal.

Cut the butter into small chunks and place a little of it, with some of the sugar, in the bottom of the basin. Place one of the lemons in the middle then fill the space around it with the remaining butter and sugar and either the remaining lemon, cut into pieces, or a handful of dried fruit. The pudding should be tightly packed with lemons, sugar and butter. Roll the remaining piece of pastry into a circle and press it down on the top, sealing the edge with a little water.

Cover tightly with a piece of greaseproof paper, folding a pleat down the centre (to allow the pudding to expand without tearing the paper). Cover with a sheet of muslin or foil, securing both tightly with string. Place on a trivet in a deep pan, with enough boiling water to come half-way up the sides of the basin. Cover and steam for 3

Most gratifying of all is the recent interest in Bread and Butter Pudding. Though I do wish chefs would stop poncing about with it – adding apricot purée or layers of caramel to the recipe. I have yet to find a man in a tall white hat who can make a better pudding than a woman in an apron.

The quintessential British pudding involves a crust or sponge made from suet or butter, sugar, flour and eggs. This bland lily is then gilded with generous quantities of jam, treacle, golden syrup, chocolate sauce, marmalade or lemon curd. The sight of an upturned treacle sponge, its layer of golden syrup oozing slowly down the side, must be one of the glories of British cooking. Only the most mean-spirited of cooks could fail to offer their loved ones such an indulgence at least once in the icy depths of winter.

Many of the best of these old-fashioned puddings, by which perhaps I mean the most comforting, are in danger of being forsaken by the home cook because they contain suet – quite the most unfashionable ingredient imaginable. But the ready-shredded stuff is not so bad, and to my mind gives a lighter result than fresh. Suet tends to be used in steamed puddings such as Apple Hat, where a strong crust is needed to hold the pudding in shape, or Sussex Pond Pudding, where a suet crust holds back an avalanche of lemon-flavoured syrup.

Breadcrumbs are sometimes used in lieu of flour, most notably in marmalade or toffee puddings. Dried fruits – currants, raisins and figs – are often found speckled in varying degrees among the sponge, the most extravagant example, of course, being Christmas pudding. The roll-call of these essentially British puddings might be both solid and aristocratic – Empress, Cabinet, Snowdon, Duchess, Queen, Royal, Washington, Wellington, Seven Cup and Gentlemen's – but generally their appeal is wider than their names would imply.

These classic puddings, with their generous helpings of butter and sugar, treacle and jam, will not appeal to everyone. Such treats are no doubt anathema to those for whom so-called healthy eating takes precedence over pleasure. The low-fat 'lite' versions of our much-loved sticky puddings sound to me about as much fun as being read a politically correct bedtime story. Such things as sticky, doughy, roly-poly pudding should be kept safe from the misguided meddling of those who choose to police our diet. But there can be few who would not at least venture a spoonful of syrup sponge. And no one is suggesting we should eat such things every day.

Although it is heartening to see our wealth of famous winter puddings on the menus of smart restaurants, it would be sad to think they have been left solely in the hands of chefs and supermarkets. Such fare is really very simple to produce at home, which, of course, is where it started, and first-timers will find it easier to make a steamed pudding than they might imagine. All that can go wrong is that water seeps inside the pudding while it is steaming, making it soggy, and that can be prevented by making sure that the greaseproof or foil top that protects the pudding is sealed tightly. To stop the cover splitting as the pudding rises, it is a good idea to fold a pleat into it.

However much jam or treacle you put in the pudding basin, it is inclined to soak into the sponge. A sponge pudding soaked through with golden syrup is manna from heaven for the addict of sugar and stodge, but it is probably best to offer something creamy alongside as well. Try clotted cream, crème fraîche or soft clouds of whipped cream, or custard, or even a mixture of them both. And if you want, a jug of warm jam, warm syrup or hot chocolate sauce too – but only for those in serious need of comfort.

hours, topping up with boiling water from the kettle from time to time. It must not be allowed to boil dry.

Remove the pudding carefully from the water. Leave for 5 minutes to settle, then remove the greaseproof and muslin or foil. Run a knife round the edge of the dish to loosen the pudding. Turn out the pudding and serve immediately, giving everyone some of the suet crust, the lemon sauce and a piece of the fruit.

Serves 4

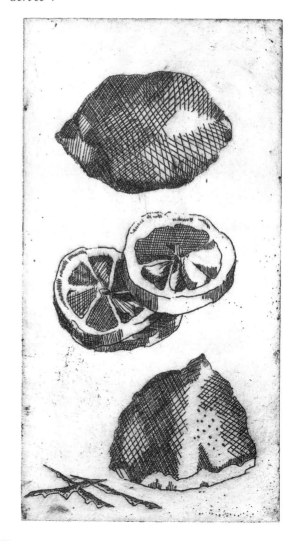

Steamed Fig Pudding

450g/1lb dried figs
150ml/5fl oz port
1 cinnamon stick
1 bay leaf
2 tablespoons honey
for the sponge
100g/4oz butter
100g/4oz white or soft brown sugar
2 eggs
50g/2oz fresh breadcrumbs
100g/4oz self-raising flour
½ teaspoon each ginger and cinnamon

Cut all but 6 of the figs into quarters, then place them all in a small heavy pan with the port, cinnamon stick, bay leaf and honey. Bring to the boil then turn down the heat and simmer for about 10 minutes. Lift the figs out with a draining spoon and then reduce the syrup to about 5 tablespoons, by boiling rapidly over the heat.

Butter a 900ml/1½ pint pudding basin. Place the whole figs (only) and syrup in the bottom. Beat the butter and sugar till pale and fluffy with an electric whisk. This will take a little longer with soft brown sugar. Add the eggs singly and beat in. If the mixture curdles, and it probably will, it will come to no harm; just fold in the breadcrumbs, chopped figs and the sifted flour and spices.

Spoon the mixture into the basin, on top of the figs and syrup. Smooth the surface flat. Place a piece of greaseproof paper over the top, folding a pleat down the centre as you do so, and secure with string. Cover with a muslin cloth or tin foil, and secure that also. Place the basin on a trivet in a deep pan, with enough boiling water to come two-thirds up the side of the basin. Steam for 1 hour, topping up the water from time to time.

Carefully remove the pudding from the water, leave for a few minutes, then remove the covers and turn out. Serve with cold cream or custard.
Serves 4

INDEX